CARPACCIO

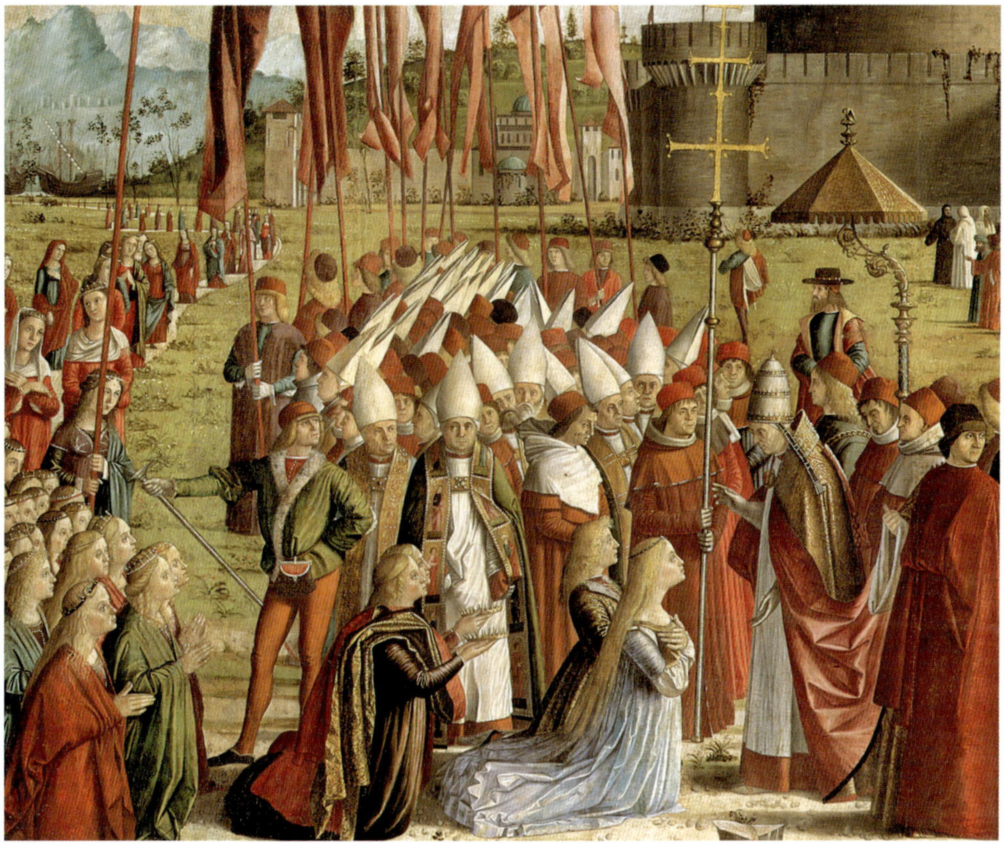

PUBLISHED BY CHAUCER PRESS
20 BLOOMSBURY STREET, LONDON WC1B 3JH

ISBN 1904449 336

A COPY OF THE CIP DATA IS AVAILABLE FROM THE
BRITISH LIBRARY UPON REQUEST

DESIGNED BY POINTING DESIGN CONSULTANCY

REPROGRAPHICS BY GA GRAPHICS

PRINTED IN CHINA BY SUN FUNG OFFSET BINDING CO. LTD.

TYPESETTING BY ROWLAND TYPESETTING

THIS BOOK, WHICH IS BASED ON A MANUSCRIPT FIRST WRITTEN IN 1979, HAS BEEN
REVISED AND UPDATED BY CHRISTOPHER WRIGHT.

PICTURE RESEARCH: VENETA BULLEN AND EMMANUELLE PERI

HALF TITLE DETAIL FROM 'ST URSULA GREETED BY THE POPE IN ROME',
VENICE, ACCADEMIA

CARPACCIO

PETER HUMFREY

CHAUCER PRESS
LONDON

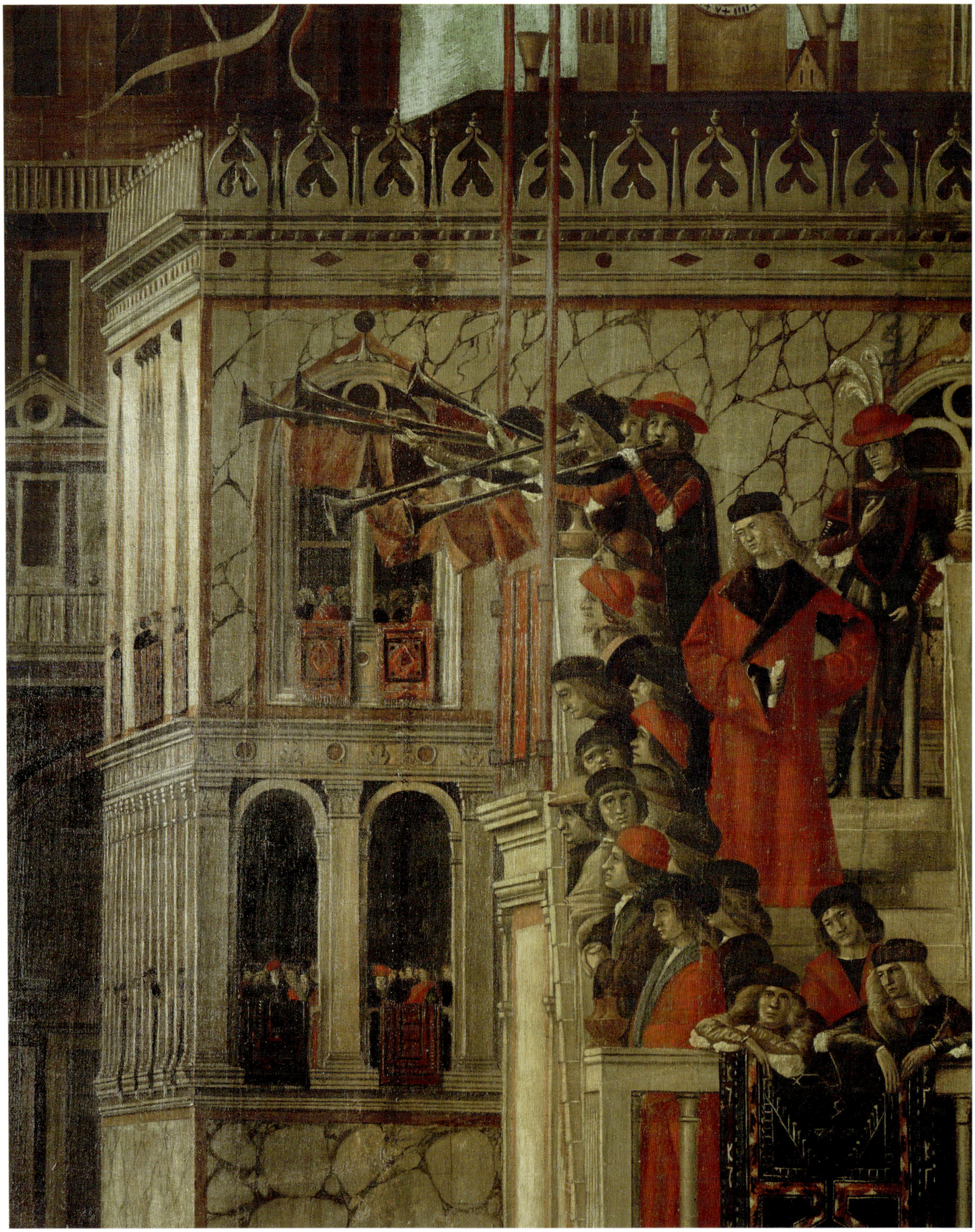

CARPACCIO

In the last decades of the fifteenth century, when Venetian maritime power stood at its peak, Venice was one of the richest and visually most splendid cities in the whole of Europe. 'It is impossible to tell or write fully of the beauty, the magnificence or the wealth of the city of Venice', wrote Canon Pietro Casola, who visited it in 1494 on the way to the Holy Land; and his enthusiasm was shared by another foreign visitor, Philippe de Commynes, who arrived in Venice in the following year on an embassy from the King of France. In his memoirs, Commynes describes how he was ferried down the Brenta Canal from Padua in a barge decked out with tapestries and carpets, and was met by twenty-five gentlemen elegantly attired in scarlet silk. He tells of how he 'marvelled greatly to see the placement of the city and to see so many church towers and monasteries and such large buildings, and all in the water', and he goes on to say that the palaces 'all have a façade of white marble, and they also have many large slabs of porphyry and serpentine on the front'. It is difficult to read these words without thinking immediately of the paintings of Vittore Carpaccio, whose famous cycle of the life of St Ursula seems more perfectly to evoke the glamour of early Renaissance Venice than any other visual image that has come down to us. *The Departure of St Ursula* (plate 10), the largest canvas of the cycle and painted in the very year of Commynes' visit, presents us with a vivid impression of the sights he would have seen: the marble-encrusted palaces rising from the water; the floating domes and campanili; the ships at anchor, with their fluttering pennants; the festive

Detail of pl. 10.

processions; the rich fabrics; the shimmering reflections. Of course, the magical city evoked by Carpaccio does not entirely correspond to the reality: although at the peak of her glory, Venice had recently suffered several serious naval defeats by the Turks, in the eastern Mediterannean, and she was soon also to be at war in the west with Commynes' master, the King of France. Nor would one guess from Carpaccio's painting that many Venetians habitually dressed in sombre black, nor that the Venetian climate is frequently misty, dank and dull. But Carpaccio's vision of opulence and pageantry does correspond to how Venice wished to present herself, both to her own citizens and to the outside world; and his painting may be seen as a sort of permanent counterpart to the numerous festivals celebrated every year in the city, staged with spectacular pomp and ceremony, and designed to glorify the Venetian Church and State.

The series of paintings to which *The Departure of St Ursula* belongs is probably the most famous example of the type of work for which Carpaccio is best known: that of the large-scale narrative cycle. The St Ursula series, which consists of eight canvases about nine feet high and of varying widths, is actually one of the earliest of such cycles to survive in Venetian painting – but it belongs to an old tradition of mural decoration in Venice, going back ultimately to the mosaics in the basilica of St Mark's. A more immediate prototype would have been the extensive decorations in the Hall of the Great Council of the Doge's Palace, which depicted a selection of momentous events drawn from Venetian history. These had been begun in the latter part of the fourteenth century, and had received particularly important contributions in the early years of the fifteenth century by Gentile da Fabriano and Pisanello; and from the 1470s onwards the work of this earlier campaign was updated and extended by the two Bellini brothers, Gentile and Giovanni. In 1508, when Carpaccio was also employed to contribute to the cycle, Giovanni Bellini was still overseer of the decoration, and he seems to have supplied Carpaccio with a design for his composition. Very little is known of the appearance of the ensemble, since it was entirely destroyed by fire in 1577; but from the fragmentary descriptions we do possess, it is easy to imagine that the canvases were painted in a spirit very close to that of *The Departure of St Ursula*, with crowds of small-scale figures deployed against a backdrop of architecture or seascape. Canon Casola's remark that the scenes in the Doge's Palace were 'represented with such richness and naturalness that I think very little could be added' seems to reinforce the impression that the wealth of incident with which Carpaccio tells his story was traditional for this kind of painting. As well as in the Doge's Palace, large-scale cyclical murals were also frequently to be found in the premises of the Venetian *scuole*, or lay confraternities. We know, for instance, that a room in the Scuola Grande di S. Giovanni Evangelista was decorated with a cycle of the life of the Virgin, painted about the middle of the century by Jacopo Bellini, father of Gentile and Giovanni. This too is lost, but Jacopo's many surviving drawings exhibit a tendency to compose in a comparable way, with small figures set against an elaborate architectural stage set, and a considerable amount of incident introduced for richness and variety of effect. Jacopo Bellini was a pupil of Gentile da Fabriano, and although conversant with Florentine innovations such as geometric perspective, he inherited an International Gothic taste for stately processions and sumptuous costume, and for picturesque accessories like birds, plants and animals – all contributing to a general aura of fairy-tale magnificence. It is symptomatic of the survival of this taste among the governors of the confraternities that when the Bellini brothers were employed from the 1490s onwards to decorate another *Scuola Grande*, that of S. Marco, their contracts specifically required them to show 'fantasia' in their designs, and to populate their narratives with 'buildings, figures and animals'.

It was Gentile Bellini, rather than his younger brother Giovanni, who seems to have been generally regarded as the leading exponent of narrative painting in the generation preceding

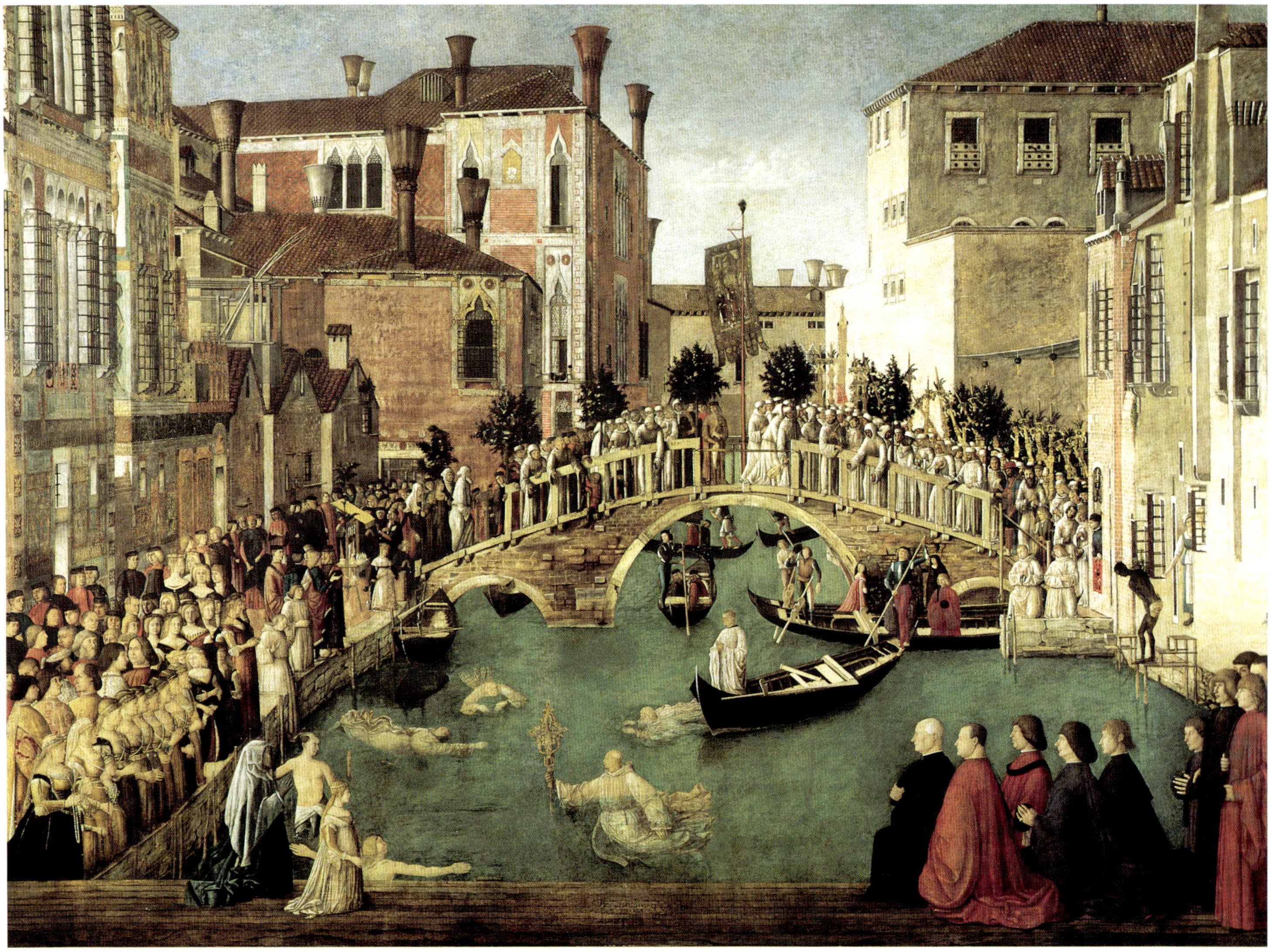

A. Gentile Bellini,
A Miracle of the Relic of the True Cross,
Venice, Accademia. Canvas, 323 x 430 cm.

Painted in 1500 as part of a cycle of canvases for the Scuola Grande di S. Giovanni Evangelista, one of the five major lay confraternities in Venice. Carpaccio's contribution to the same cycle was painted some years earlier.

that of Carpaccio. Whereas Giovanni does not appear have executed very much work of this type before the 1490s, Gentile was employed in the Doge's Palace from as early as 1474; and it seems reasonable therefore to assume that even if he was not Carpaccio's actual master, his decorations there played a major role in the formation of Carpaccio's art. The question of Carpaccio's training is a controversial one, and many widely differing theories have been proposed. The main difficulty in too easily assuming that he was a pupil of Gentile is that no large-scale works by Gentile survive from the late 1470s or early 1480s, the period when Carpaccio would have been an apprentice; while those that do survive, date from several years after Carpaccio's first canvases of the St Ursula cycle. Nevertheless, a comparison between *The Departure of St Ursula* and a painting by Gentile such as *A Miracle of the Relic of the True Cross* dated 1500 (Fig. A), does show a fundamental similarity of approach. As well as containing the same compositional ingredients – the crowds of ceremonially-dressed figures, the Venetian architecture, the stretches of water – both paintings are conceived in essentially decorative terms, with figures and objects alike appearing as flat coloured shapes evenly distributed across the picture surface. Although the architectural forms of both paintings are plausibly three-dimensional, their effect is much more of a flimsy stage-set than of solid blocks of masonry, and their compositional function is less to define deep space than to articulate the picture surface with a network of stable verticals and horizontals.

Neither painting has a strongly emphasised focal centre, and the eye tends to read both compositions like a book, moving from one incident to another. This frieze-like rather than centripetal effect gives the impression that the canvases could be infinitely extended at the sides to include still more festive architecture, and more processing figures. Even closer to Gentile's painting is Carpaccio's own *Miracle of a Relic of the True Cross*, which was painted for the Scuola

Grande di S. Giovanni Evangelista in 1494 as part of the same cycle. But as well as these similarities between Carpaccio and Gentile, there are also important differences. Carpaccio belonged to a younger generation, and was more readily able to assimilate the innovations introduced into Venetian painting during his formative years. Of particular significance was the visit in 1475–6 of the Sicilian painter, Antonello da Messina, whose major work in Venice, an altarpiece for the church of S. Cassiano (Fig. B), displayed to the Venetians a new feeling both for the construction of volumetric forms in a lucid space, and for optical verisimilitude in the treatment of surface textures. No-one was more responsive to Antonello's visit than Giovanni Bellini, who in such works as the S. Giobbe altarpiece (Fig. C), transmitted the essentials of Antonello's lessons to his younger contemporaries. Despite the decorative effect of Carpaccio's use of colour, the figures in the foreground of *The Departure of St Ursula* have more in common with those of the S. Giobbe altar, with their smoothly rounded volumes, than with the hard, linear and flat figures of Gentile. Wholly absent from the art of Gentile is Carpaccio's ability to imitate the specific properties of textures like silk, glass or marble; and similarly, the general effect of luminosity in his painting, with the play of sunlight on the palace fronts and the shimmering translucency of the water, is profoundly indebted to the example of Giovanni Bellini. It is true that Carpaccio cannot rival the prodigious sensitivity of Giovanni in his handling of paint: beside the infinite subtlety of Giovanni's gradations of light and shade, achieved by means of an elaborate build-up of transparent glazes, Carpaccio's brushwork often appears rough, dry and thin; and yet, his characteristic use of sparkling highlights, making jewels seem to flash and metals glitter, does endow the surfaces of his canvases with an effect of animation that is completely lacking in the more opaque surfaces of Gentile.

The richly decorative qualities of *The Departure of St Ursula*, so closely tied up with Venetian tradition, are particularly apparent when the canvas is seen together with the other canvases of

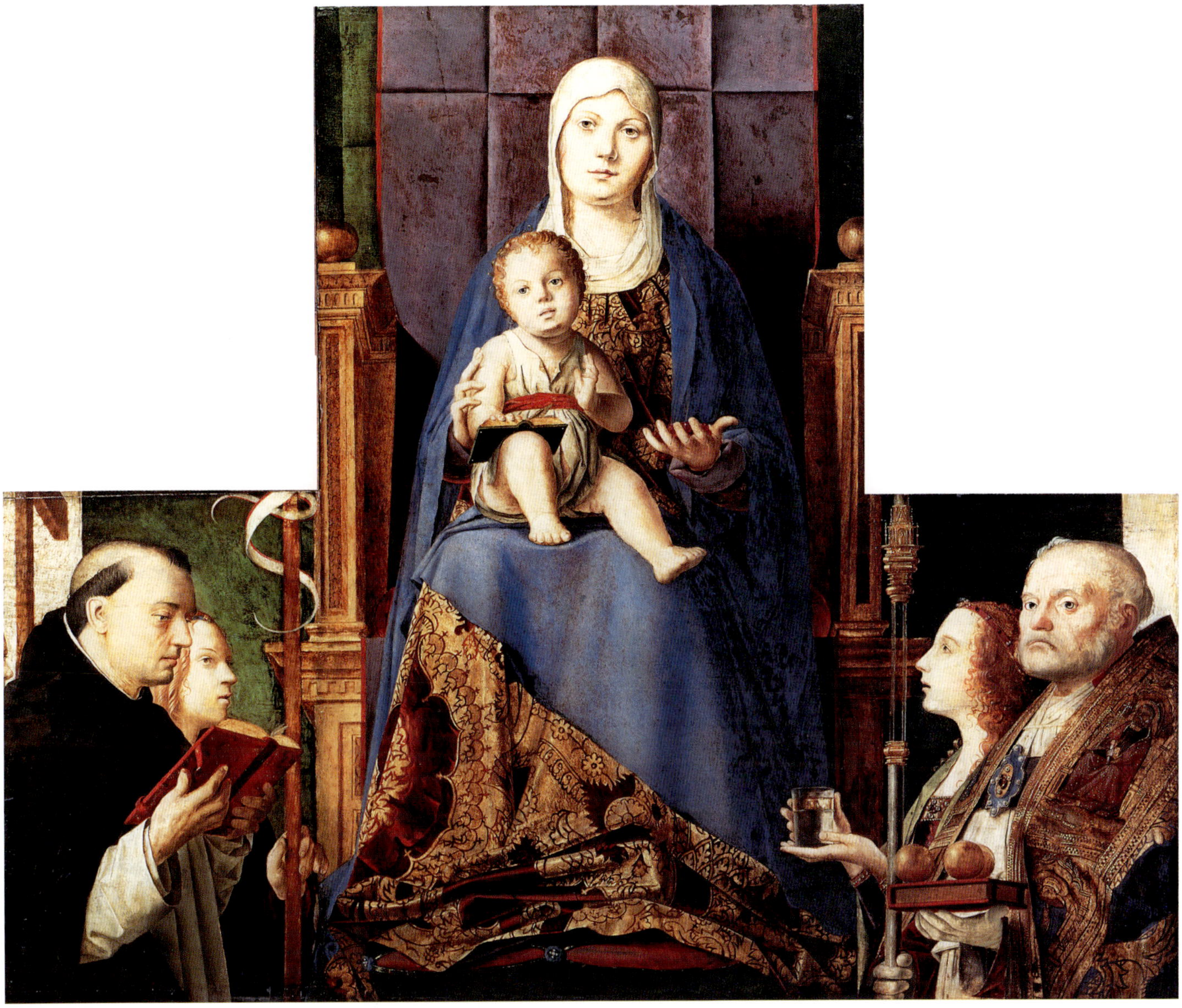

B. Antonello da Messina, *Madonna and Child Enthroned with Saints*, Vienna, Kunsthistorisches Museum. Panel, 115 x 65 cm.

The only surviving fragment of the famous altarpiece painted by Antonello in 1475 for the church of S. Cassiano in Venice. There is no record of the original appearance of the whole painting, but its composition probably resembled that of Giovanni Bellini's S. Giobbe altar (Fig. C). The art of Antonello exerted an important formative influence on Carpaccio, as well as on most other Venetian painters of his generation.

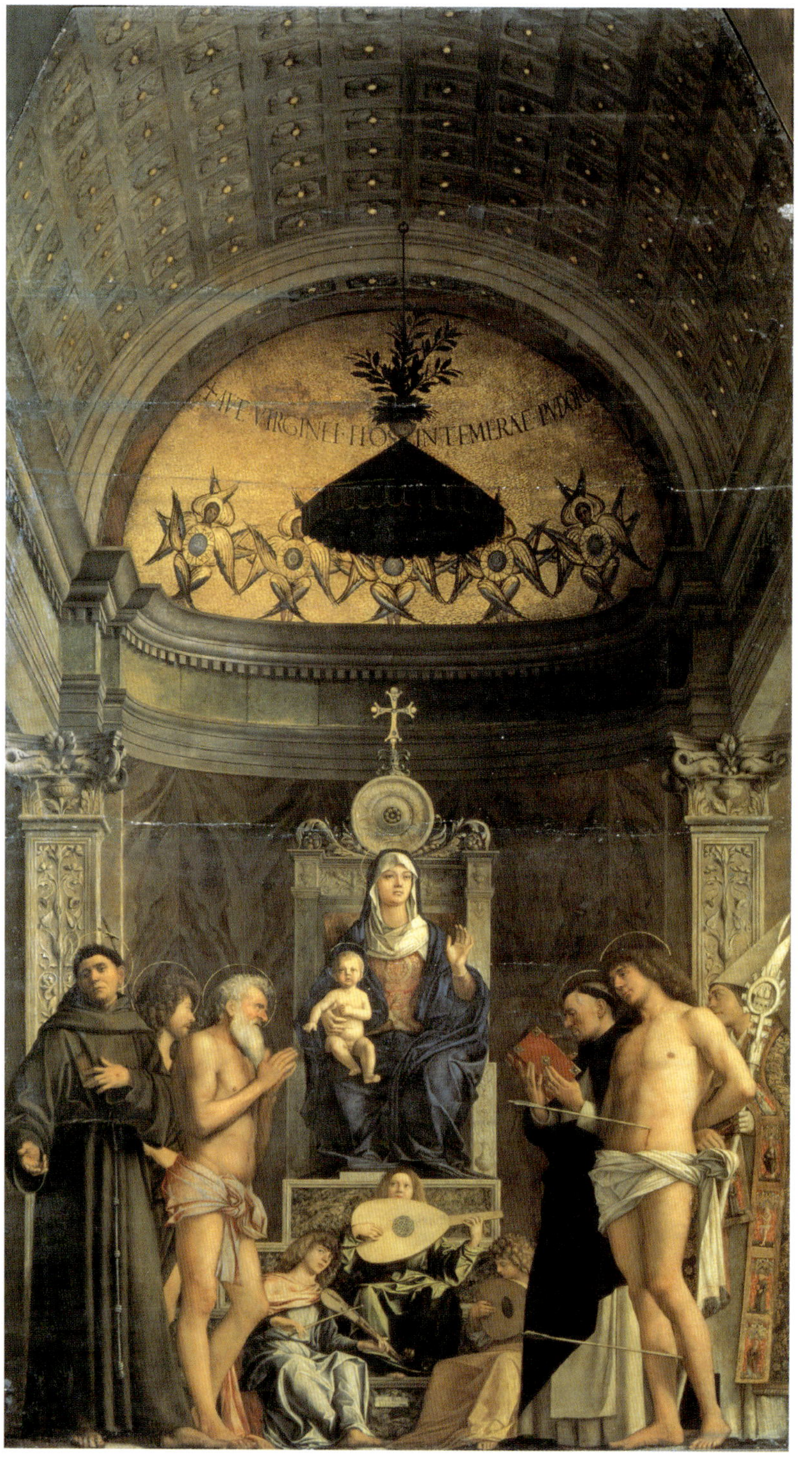

C. Giovanni Bellini,
Madonna and Child Enthroned with Saints, Venice, Accademia. Panel, 471 x 258 cm.

Painted for a side altar in the church of S. Giobbe in Venice, probably in the early 1480s. Carpaccio's *Presentation in the Temple* was painted in 1510 to hang beside it.

the series. The way in which they are displayed in the museum, extending round three walls of a single large room to create a continuous frieze of narrative, reinforces the general effect of a rich tapestry of shapes and colours, and it also corresponds closely to their original arrangement in the Scuola di S. Orsola. This confraternity, which according to its foundation statute of the year 1300, was dedicated to 'the glory and honour of Our Lord and of the Virgin', and which stood 'under the protection of saints Dominic, Peter Martyr and Ursula', was one of more than two hundred *scuole piccole* existing in late fifteenth century Venice. Their function was partly social, partly economic and partly devotional, and the wealthier confraternities usually possessed premises of their own, where they could meet, discuss business, and worship. The building of the Scuola di S. Orsola, although in fact still standing, has unfortunately during the course of the centuries been transformed almost beyond recognition; but an approximate idea of the original appearance of its interior can be gained from a scholarly reconstruction (Fig. D), showing Carpaccio's canvases arranged round the walls. The motives of the governors of the confraternity in commissioning the cycle were probably in the first place prompted by a desire to decorate the interior of their building with an appropriate magnificence, stimulated perhaps by an urge to compete with other confraternities. But Carpaccio's paintings were probably also intended to serve a more strictly religious function by providing the members of the confraternity with a constant reminder of the virtuous life of their principal patron saint, and encouraging them to follow her example. This didactic function could best be served by involving the spectator as closely as possible in the narrative, and on several occasions Carpaccio resorts to pictorial devices which implicitly close the gap between painting and reality. In *The Reception of the Ambassadors* for example (plate 6), the picture space seems to project outwards into real space; or in *The Funeral of St Ursula*, the portrait-like figure of the woman kneeling in prayer in the right foreground seems to belong half to the historical event represented in the painting, and half to the real world of the

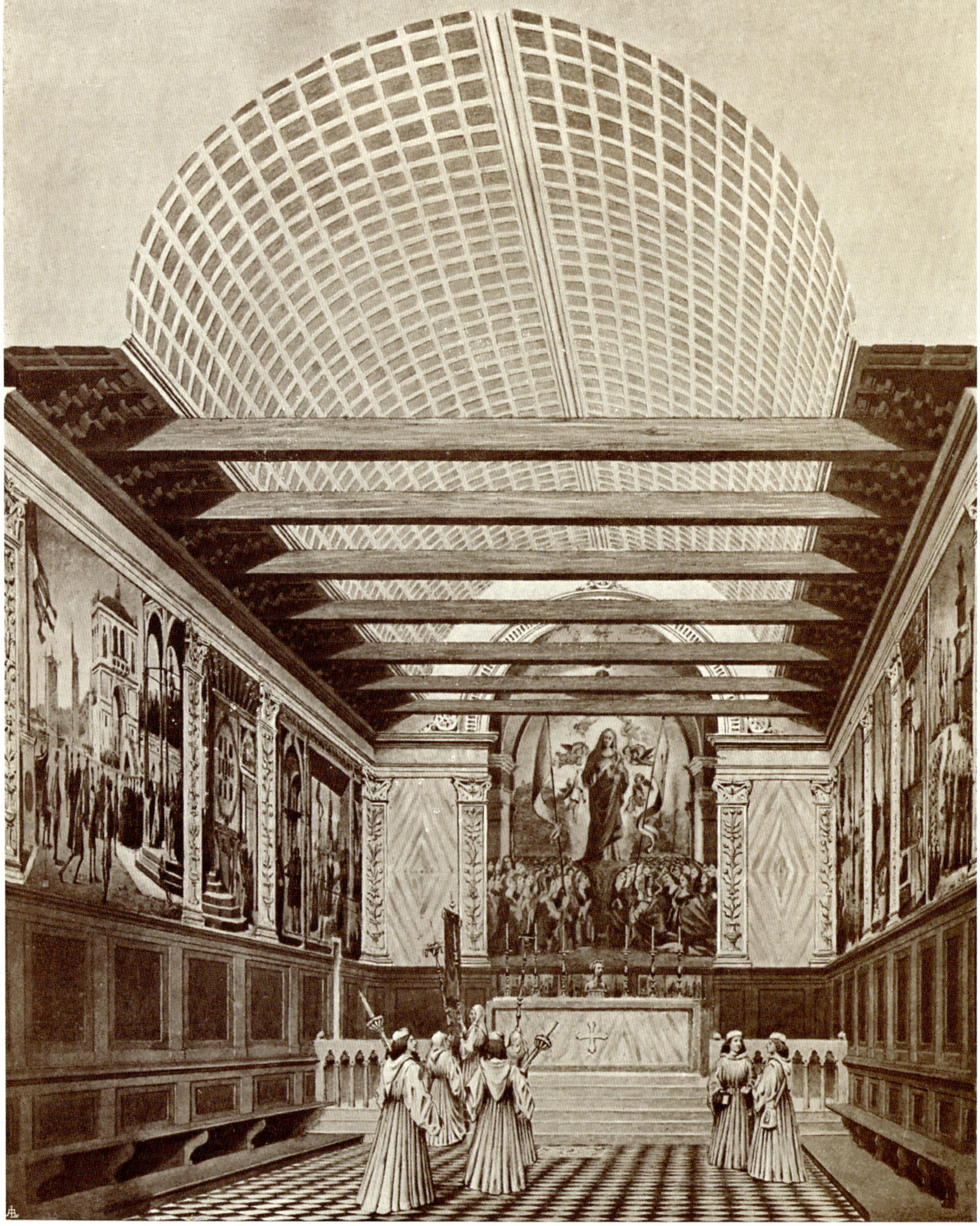

confraternity interior. A direct testimony to the purely religious effectiveness of Carpaccio's imagery is provided by the eighteenth century connoisseur and critic, Anton Maria Zanetti, who in the section on Carpaccio in his history of Venetian painting, records how he would often stand unobserved in the corner of the scuola, and watch the people who came in to pray raise their eyes to the paintings on the wall, as if to seek spiritual inspiration. Zanetti goes on to remark that one of Carpaccio's most praiseworthy characteristics as an artist is precisely this ability to stir the hearts and minds of persons with no particular knowledge or understanding of art.

Carpaccio was fortunate in that the story he was required to depict at the Scuola di S. Orsola was ideally suited to his talents. It was taken from the famous late mediaeval compilation of the lives of the saints, *The Golden Legend*, and tells of how the beautiful and virtuous princess of Brittany, St Ursula, was wooed by the prince of England, undertook a pilgrimage to Rome, and how finally she was martyred, together with her eleven thousand virgin companions, outside the gates of Cologne in about the year 452. Such a story clearly provided plenty of scope for the introduction of sights and events with which Carpaccio would have been perfectly familiar: the flurries of diplomatic activity in the opening scenes, of the kind in which Philippe de Commynes would have been involved during his mission of 1495; the embarkations, the sea voyages, the disembarkations, the public ceremony surrounding high-ranking personages. As has already been suggested, these paintings tell us much about the Venice in which Carpaccio lived and worked. The palaces, with their coloured marble inlays, their biforate windows and

D. Reconstruction by Molmenti and Ludwig of the Scuola di S. Orsola as it might have been in 1500.

It has now been proved that this reconstruction drawing, made at the end of the nineteenth century, is in many respects inaccurate: we know for instance that the narrative sequence ran clockwise, not anti-clockwise as shown here; and the elaborately vaulted ceiling is pure fantasy. But the drawing does usefully give an idea of the scale of the canvases, and of the way they were originally related to each other and to their surroundings. Above the altar is Carpaccio's *Glorification of St Ursula*.

their crenellated skylines strongly recall the palaces of Pietro Lombardo and Mauro Coducci, which were under construction during these very years. The bedroom interior in *The Dream of St Ursula*, with its happy combination of tasteful elegance and domestic comfort, gives a vivid impression of how these palaces might have been furnished, and it accords very well with the description by Commynes of 'gilded ceilings, rich mantlepieces of cut marble, gilded bedsteads, painted and gilded screens, and very fine furniture' in the various houses he was invited to visit.

Carpaccio's actors frequently wear clothes in the most up-to-date fashion: the young dandy shown in profile in the left foreground of *The Reception of the Ambassadors* has sleeves that are slashed the whole length of his arm to reveal the fine white linen under-shirt, and he has discarded the normal over-tunic, so that his tight-fitting doublet and hose show off his shapely figure to the best possible advantage. On the far right of the same canvas, St Ursula herself is seen wearing sleeves of a specifically Venetian type, divided into two sections with the lower half similarly slashed to show her white linen under-dress. The King's counsellors and the crowds of non-participating bystanders are generally clothed in the more staid robes of respectable Venetian citizens and noblemen, and although individuals are only rarely identifiable with certainty, it is likely that many of the figures are portraits of confraternity members. The many ships that appear in the background remind us that the sea was the principal source of the power and wealth of Venice, and that her Arsenal was the largest shipyard in the world. Both of the main types of ship that Carpaccio shows, the high-round-backed carrack and the long narrow galley, are completely up-to-date with the most recent designs of warship and cargo vessel developed by the Venetians in their maritime struggle against the Turks. To the modern eye, the strongly local and topical flavour of the setting may appear rather incongruous as applied to events that were supposed to have taken place in northern Europe during the fifth century – but Carpaccio's contemporaries probably experienced these events in a way that was all the more relevant and vivid for seeming to belong to a world they recognised. Furthermore, Carpaccio was by no means completely careless in the surroundings he devised for the various episodes of the legend. In *St Ursula greeted by the Pope* for instance, the looming fortress of the Castel Sant Angelo, probably borrowed from an image on a papal coin, unambiguously identifies the setting as Rome. The Hunnish soldiers in the foreground of *The Arrival in Cologne* wear suits of armour which would have been recognised as distinctly transalpine in style. Most telling of all is the way Carpaccio differentiates between a Christian kingdom in *The Reception of the Ambassadors* and a pagan one in *The Return of the Ambassadors*: in the centre background of the former, there is a church with a Byzantine dome, in shape much like the cupolas of St Mark's; in the background of the latter, there is a large palace faced with marble reliefs *all'antica*. The same contrasts are to be found in the two halves of *The Departure of St Ursula*: on the right, a Christian dome and bell-tower; on the left, several towers resembling minarets, and – on a tiny scale – a ruined triumphal arch beside an idol on a column. Although the minarets seem slightly strange perhaps in a townscape representing England in the last days of the Roman Empire, they do clearly establish the non-Christian character of the setting.

Despite the fact that the world in which the legend of St Ursula unfolds is full of reminiscences of fifteenth century Venice, it is also to a large extent one of Carpaccio's imagination. The palaces, churches and loggias that he depicts are built up from motifs derived from his experience of Venetian architecture, but none of them are portraits of any real, existing structure. The palace in the background of *The Return of the Ambassadors*, for instance, would simply not make sense in functional terms; and although the complete revetment of its exterior with coloured marbles may correspond to a contemporary architectural ideal, such luxury was never in practice realisable on so large a scale. The costumes too are frequently more gorgeous than would actually have been worn: although Venice's rather strict sumptuary laws may often have been infringed, not even the wealthiest and most powerful families would have been permitted to trim the hems of their garments with the quantity of jewellery and gold thread flaunted by some of the younger courtiers in the *Reception* and the *Return*, and in the *Departure of St Ursula*. It is also hard to believe that any soldier would have gone into battle in an outfit such as that worn by the archer who puts St Ursula to death. The landscape in the left half of the *Departure* is improbably fantastic, with a perilously overhanging cliff seen between the two large towers, and a hermitage perched on the summit of a near-vertical rock to the right. But all these liberties taken with reality only serve to enhance the fabulous quality of the narrative, and they endow it with an aura of enchantment entirely appropriate to the legendary character of the subject-matter. The raw material of historical Venice is poetically transformed into something higher and more beautiful; and yet because of its basis in the real and familiar, it retains a powerful and compelling immediacy.

Carpaccio's other principal masterpiece in the genre of the narrative cycle is the series painted for another lay confraternity, the Scuola di S. Giorgio degli Schiavoni. As its name indicates, this confraternity comprised members of the rather large Dalmatian, or Slavonic, community in Venice, and was dedicated to three saints with eastern associations, St George, St Jerome and St Tryphonius. Unlike the St Ursula cycle – or indeed, any other Venetian narrative cycle painted before the mid-sixteenth century – the S. Giorgio cycle is still to be seen *in situ*, in the scuola building for which it was intended. Although the series was in fact moved in 1551 from the upstairs room where it was originally placed to a room on the ground floor, the present-day appearance of the interior still gives us a very good idea of how such cycles were intended to be seen, with the canvases arranged round the room in a continuous frieze above a wooden dado, and converging on a small altar placed opposite the main entrance. In Carpaccio's time, the altar was decorated with a triptych in the Gothic style, with images of the three patron saints of the confraternity, and enshrined within the altar table was a precious relic of its titular saint, St George.

The nine canvases of the S. Giorgio cycle, painted between 1502 and about 1507, show three scenes each from the lives of saints George and Jerome, one from the life of St Tryphonius, and two from the life of Christ. A fourth scene from the life of St George, showing the saint's martyrdom, is now lost. As compared with the St Ursula cycle of about a decade earlier, the S. Giorgio series is smaller in scale, rather simpler in presentation, and more intimate in mood. This intimacy is especially marked in the St Jerome triad, where the humble surroundings of the two monastic scenes contrast strongly with the courtly splendour that surrounds the life of the Breton princess. The buildings in the background, while still based on Carpaccio's Venice, recall not so much the stately edifices on the Grand Canal and in the Plazza S. Marco, as the more shabby and rustic buildings in Cannaregio and Castello, on the outer fringes of the city, with washing hanging out of windows and roofs picturesquely overgrown with vegetation. Unlike the scene of St Ursula's funeral, where the saint's bier is carried on the shoulders of four bishops under an embroidered canopy accompanied by a long procession of mourners, the funeral of St Jerome takes place in the tranquility and simplicity of his monastery, with the heads of the kneeling brethren bowed in prayer. Carpaccio is no less concerned than before to give the event local colour, and an indication that it took place in the Holy Land is provided by the groups of strolling orientals in the background, and the rows of palm trees stretching into the distance. Equally intimate, though in rather a different way, is the mood of the third of the St Jerome series, *The Vision of St Augustine*, where Jerome appears in a vision to his fellow Doctor of the Church, St Augustine, as he sits working in his study. Iconographically, this canvas derives from the Flemish tradition of representing a scholar seated in his study, usually none other than St Jerome himself, surrounded by his books. At least two examples by Jan van Eyck are known to have reached Italy during the fifteenth century, and Antonello's own *St Jerome in his Study* (National Gallery, London) which may well have been based on one of them, was recorded in a Venetian collection in the early sixteenth century. Even if Carpaccio did not know this particular work, he would certainly have known panels of a similar type, and his *St Augustine* is also clearly influenced by their meticulous technique. The large number of small-scale objects that cover the tables and shelves in the study are all rendered with minute precision, down to the tiniest detail; and equally Flemish is the artist's sensitivity to the fall of light as it floods in from the windows on the right, filling the room with a warm radiance, and giving a naturalistic gleam to the surfaces of metallic objects. It was especially important that these various objects were clearly legible, since many of them are charged with a symbolic significance, and allude to the harmonious reconciliation of sacred and profane learning. The bronze figure of the Risen Christ in the central niche, for instance, has its profane counterpart in the bronze statuette of a female nude, probably a Venus, placed on the shelf on the far left; the liturgical furniture in the cupboard under the altar is matched by the astrolabe next to the right-hand window, symbolic of scientific enquiry; and the musical scores prominently displayed in the right foreground have been identified as a sacred hymn and as a secular folk-song. These symbols are perfectly appropriate for St Augustine, who in his life combined an acute sensitivity to the pleasures of the senses with a rigorous dedication to the more elevated joys of the spirit; but they also typify the intellectual aspirations of late fifteenth century humanist learning in Venice, and particularly those of its leading exponent, Ermolao Barbaro. In keeping with this interpretation is the identification of the head of the saint as an idealised portrait of Cardinal Bessarion, the learned prelate who bequeathed his magnificent collection of Greek and Latin codices to the Venetian Republic in 1468, and who earned this place of honour in the Scuola di S. Giorgio by having granted it certain extraordinary privileges in 1464. Carpaccio commemorates these privileges by representing the episcopal seal of Bessarion in the foreground of the painting, directly below the figure of the saint.

The three scenes from the life of St George (plates 26, 27 and 28) take us back to the atmosphere of romantic chivalry that pervaded the St Ursula cycle. This time however, the

North African setting of the legend provided Carpaccio with an excuse to indulge to the full his taste for exotic effects. This is particularly true of his use of costume – the crowds of beturbaned bystanders in the second two scenes are quite obviously intended as orientals – but the background buildings, too, have a strongly Saracen flavour, perfectly consistent with the traditional associations of the confraternity's patron saint. Indeed, so convincing is the artist's use of exotic detail that at least one distinguished Carpaccio scholar has felt sure that he must have travelled at some time to the eastern Mediterranean, perhaps together with Gentile Bellini in 1479, when the elder painter was sent on a mission to Constantinople. It seems altogether more likely, however, that Carpaccio derived his oriental-looking details not from personal experience of the east, but from prints, drawings and books available to him in Venice. It is known, for instance, that three of the structures in the background of *The Triumph of St George* (plate 27) – the circular temple at the centre, and the two towers to the left – were based on woodcuts representing buildings in the Holy Land, which appeared in an account of a pilgrimage by Bernhard von Breydenbach, *Sanctarum Peregrinationum in Montem Syon, ad venerandum Christi Sepulchrum in Jersualem . . . Opusculum*, first printed in Mainz in 1486 (Fig. E). This same volume also contained woodcuts showing Moslem costumes and head-dresses, some of which Carpaccio adapted for use in the St George canvases; and he would certainly also have had access to drawings made in the east by Gentile Bellini. There was in any case no lack of information about oriental costumes available in Venice itself: the city's strong commercial links with the east were after all the prime source of her prosperity; and the constant traffic of European pilgrims to and from the Holy Land was traditionally carried by Venetian shipping.

In his attempts to provide his narratives with convincingly authentic surroundings, Carpaccio was obviously on much safer ground when the events depicted had actually taken place in Venice. His *Miracle of a Relic of the True Cross*, painted in 1494 contemporaneously with the St Ursula cycle, commemorates an event that had happened on a balcony of the Patriarch's palace at Rialto in the very same year. As with the other canvases of the same cycle, painted by several artists including Gentile Bellini (Fig. A), the topographical accuracy with which the Venetian townscape is rendered must at the time have provided a powerful confirmation of the miracle's status as a documented fact. For us, the painting is an invaluable record of how the Grand Canal at Rialto looked in the year 1494. The sight of the principal thoroughfare of Venice teeming with boats recalls the remark by Philippe de Commynes that the Venetians 'have no other form of transport except by . . . barges, of which I believe thirty thousand might be found'. Spanning the Canal – called by Commynes 'the most beautiful street in the whole world' – is the old wooden Rialto Bridge; and beyond it to the right is the old Fondaco de'Tedeschi, the large warehouse of the German merchant community, which was to go up in flames in 1505. It is interesting to notice that the Fondaco and several of the palaces opposite it on the left bank are decorated with ornamental patterns, a practice which was quite common at the time and which heightened the city's aspect of festive splendour. This concern to record the topography of Venice with complete fidelity was also apparently characteristic of the cyclical decorations in the Hall of the Great Council in the Doge's Palace. Here too, accurate topography would have had a documentary value: the cycle depicted a sequence of historical events of the highest significance for the political and religious prestige of the Venetian State, and it was important that they were portrayed as circumstantially and correctly as possible. The exact nature of Carpaccio's contribution to this cycle is unclear, but it seems that he had a hand in at least two of the scenes, one of which represented Pope Alexander III celebrating mass in St Mark's. It is probably safe to assume that his view of the interior of the ducal basilica was not only immediately identifiable, but also topographically completely accurate.

Carpaccio's *Miracle of a Relic of the True Cross* is a large work, larger than most of the St Ursula canvases – and so too presumably were his contributions to the cycle in the Doge's Palace. The last two narrative cycles he painted – the series for the Scuola degli Albanesi (plates 31–36) and

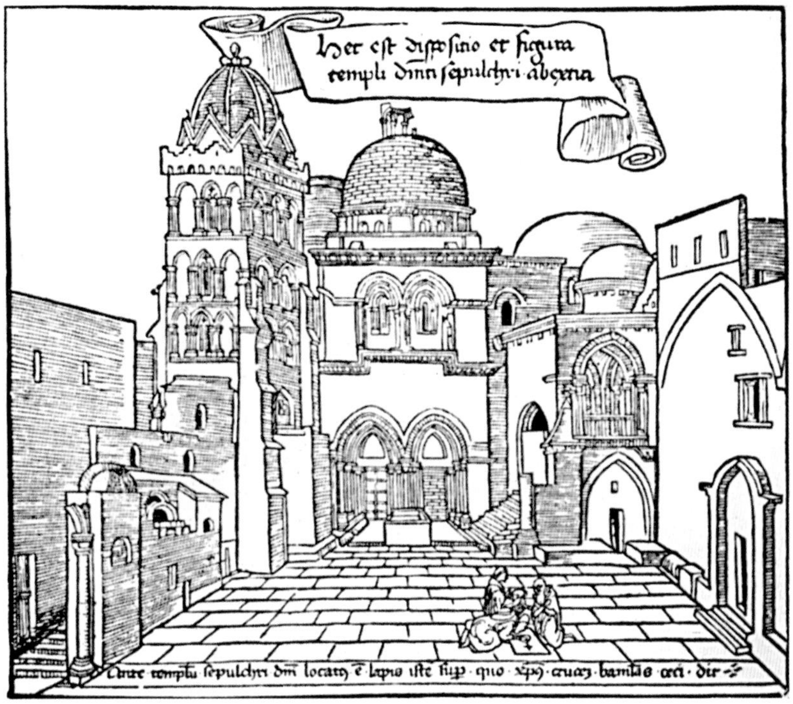

(a) The Church of the Holy Sepulchre in Jerusalem

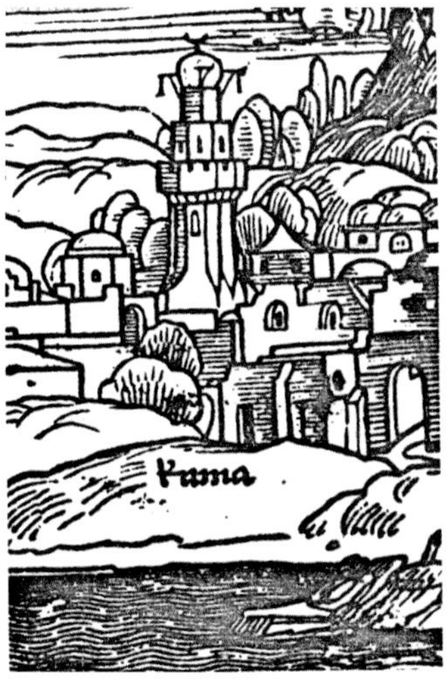

(b) The Mosque of Rama

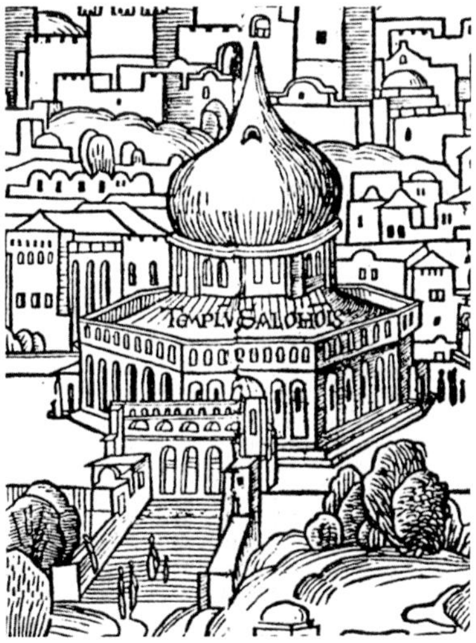

(c) The Temple of Solomon in Jerusalem

E. Woodcuts made by the Dutch draughtsman, Erhard Reuwich, to accompany an account of a pilgrimage to the Holy Land by Bernhard von Breydenbach, and adapted by Carpaccio for use in the background of his *Triumph of St George* (plate 46).

that for the Scuola di S. Stefano – are more modest in scale even than the S. Giorgio series. The six scenes from the life of the Virgin, painted for the confraternity of Albanians more or less contemporaneously with the cycle for their Dalmatian rivals, are scarcely more than four feet high, and they were originally arranged along a single wall of the Scuola chapel. They are also rather modest in quality: the draughtsmanship has become slack and mechanical, and the treatment of colour and light hard and dull; and Carpaccio is beginning to repeat himself. The female figure seated on the right in *The Birth of the Virgin,* for instance, is a direct transcription of the figure of the Virgin herself in a devotional panel now in Washington. The comparative weakness of the Albanesi cycle may in part be due to collaboration by members of the artist's workshop; but there can be no doubt that from about the middle of the first decade of the new century, Carpaccio's powers of invention and execution were beginning to fall into decline. This unfortunate development is also apparent in some of the later canvases of the S. Giorgio cycle such as *St Tryphonius exorcising the Demon*, which appears almost like a pastiche of the opening scenes of the St Ursula cycle, with the seated figure of the emperor derived directly from that of the King in *The Return of the Ambassadors*. The normal and most plausible explanation for this sudden decline in quality is that Carpaccio was suffering a loss of confidence in face of the most recent developments in Venetian painting. The works of Giorgione, Carpaccio's junior by about fifteen years, may not initially have had an impact commensurate with their revolutionary character, since they were for the most part small in scale and in the hands of private owners; but from about 1508, when the first set of frescoes by Giorgione and his young assistant Titian were completed on the newly rebuilt Fondaco de'Tedeschi, the obsolescence of Carpaccio's style must have been immediately apparent to any informed observer. The heroic, energetic and highly idealised figures painted by the leaders of the new generation would at one stroke have made those of Carpaccio, even at his best, look timid, constrained and pedestrian. It seems ironic that Carpaccio himself helped sign the death-warrant of his own art by serving on the committee that evaluated and approved the Fondaco frescoes in 1508.

The four (originally five) canvases painted between 1511 and 1520 for the Scuola di S. Stefano, depicting scenes from the life of its patron St Stephen, clearly reveal the artist's stylistic predicament during these years. In many respects, they show Carpaccio manfully struggling to come to grips with the fundamentals of the new style. Especially in *The Stoning of St Stephen* (plate 55), the figures are larger in relation to the picture field and more compactly organised into groups than in the earlier cycles; and the compositions are generally simpler, clearer and less cluttered with extraneous incident. In the *Stoning* there is also an attempt to update the treatment of the background landscape: whereas an earlier landscape such as that of *St George and the Dragon* had been constructed in essentially architectonic terms, with the straight row of palm trees receding like telegraph poles, and every detail rendered in equally sharp focus, the later one is conceived in a much more Giorgionesque manner, with loose and cursive rhythms and an atmospheric softening of edges. But Carpaccio is only moderately successful in his attempt to modernise himself: his actors still lack the mobile fluency and the heroic dimension of the High Renaissance figure style, and their draperies are still very stiff and angular. Furthermore, his art has to a large extent lost the very qualities that made the earlier cycles so appealing: the picturesque details, the vividness of anecdote, the mood of festive gaiety. The *Stoning* is not only stylistically archaic for its inscribed date of 1522 – by this time Titian had already completed his great Frari *Assunta* and his mythologies for the Duke of Ferrara – but it also compares unfavourably with Carpaccio's own work of two or three decades earlier.

All this is not to say that the S. Stefano cycle is altogether devoid of merit. The old narrative liveliness has by no means entirely disappeared, and all four canvases retain a richly decorative character. What qualities the series does possess may be ascribed to the fact that Carpaccio was still engaged on the type of work for which his talents were undeniably best suited – the narrative cycle. But from the very beginning, he was very much less successful with another type of commission equally in demand by the Venetian public – the church altarpiece. The unchallenged leader of this line of production in late fifteenth century Venice was Giovanni Bellini, who by the time of Carpaccio's artistic beginnings had already produced a series of authoritative prototypes, including the highly influential S. Giobbe altar (Fig. C). This work demonstrates how perfectly Bellini was able to match the mood and design of his painting to its function as an altarpiece: the gentle and meditative expressions of the saints and the illusionistic pull of the architecture actively encourage the pious spectator to approach with his prayers; while at the same time, an appropriate effect of distance is maintained by the hierarchical arrangement of the figures and the prevailing solemnity of their mood. Carpaccio could not ignore Bellini's example, and in the altarpiece he painted for the Scuola di S. Orsola – intended as the climax of the narrative cycle, and representing St Ursula's glorious reception into heaven – he endeavoured to emulate the grandeur of Bellini's altarpieces by giving the figures an added weight and fullness, and by imposing a rigid symmetry on the design. Equally indebted to Bellini is the use of a classicising architectural framework to enclose the scene, a device that serves to create a combined effect of monumental dignity and cubic space – all the more since originally this painted architecture would have been illusionistically joined to the architectonic form of the picture frame (see Fig. D). But a comparison between the *Glorification* and any of the narrative scenes of the cycle is highly unfavourable to the altarpiece. Beside the charm and inventiveness with which the saint's life on earth is depicted, the scene of her apotheosis seems dull and contrived, with the figures appearing artifically inflated rather than truly grandiose, and the symmetry of their grouping monotonous rather than impressively solemn. It is as if Carpaccio were aping the external characteristics of works such as Bellini's S. Giobbe altar or Antonello's S. Cassiano altar (Fig. B), without comprehending their inner spirit.

Carpaccio's altarpieces are not all as unappealing as the *Glorification*. In the *St Thomas Aquinas Enthroned* of 1507, for instance, the large volumetric figures, and the clarity and simplicity of their arrangement, do succeed in generating an appropriate mood of calm and dignity. Giovanni Bellini himself by this date had moved on to the softer and much less sculptural style of his later career, and here Carpaccio seems to have turned with profit to the example of his close contemporary Cima da Conegliano, who unlike Carpaccio specialised mainly in devotional rather than narrative pictures. Cima's St Peter Martyr altar (Fig. F), which was probably painted not more than a year before the *St Thomas Aquinas*, shows how very much more thoroughly he had absorbed the lessons of Antonello and Bellini of the 1470s and 1480s, with the smoothly rounded central figure of St Peter Martyr grandly towering upwards like a column on its base. Despite the awkwardness of the transition between the upper and lower halves of Carpaccio's composition, and the ambiguities of space and scale that prevail within the celestial region, his three saints have much in common with those in the Cima, and are similarly invested with an iconic stillness and a certain majesty. Perhaps even more successful than the *St Thomas Aquinas* is the *Presentation in the Temple*, which Carpaccio painted three years later for the altar immediately to the left of Bellini's altarpiece in the church of S. Giobbe. Although the *Presentation* is in fact a narrative scene, Carpaccio has clearly taken over from Bellini the standard compositional formula for non-narrative representations of the Madonna enthroned with saints, with its architectural backdrop, symmetrical grouping and angel musicians in the foreground. True, Carpaccio's own methods of story-telling were not so easily shaken off, and the two figure groups appear almost as the leaders of two converging processions, with the priests on the right entering the scene with a certain undignified haste. But in this case at least, the overall effect is one of a happy compromise between Carpaccio's taste for narrative charm and picturesque accessories, and the need for the quiet solemnity and elevated mood appropriate to the church altarpiece. In the great majority of his works of this

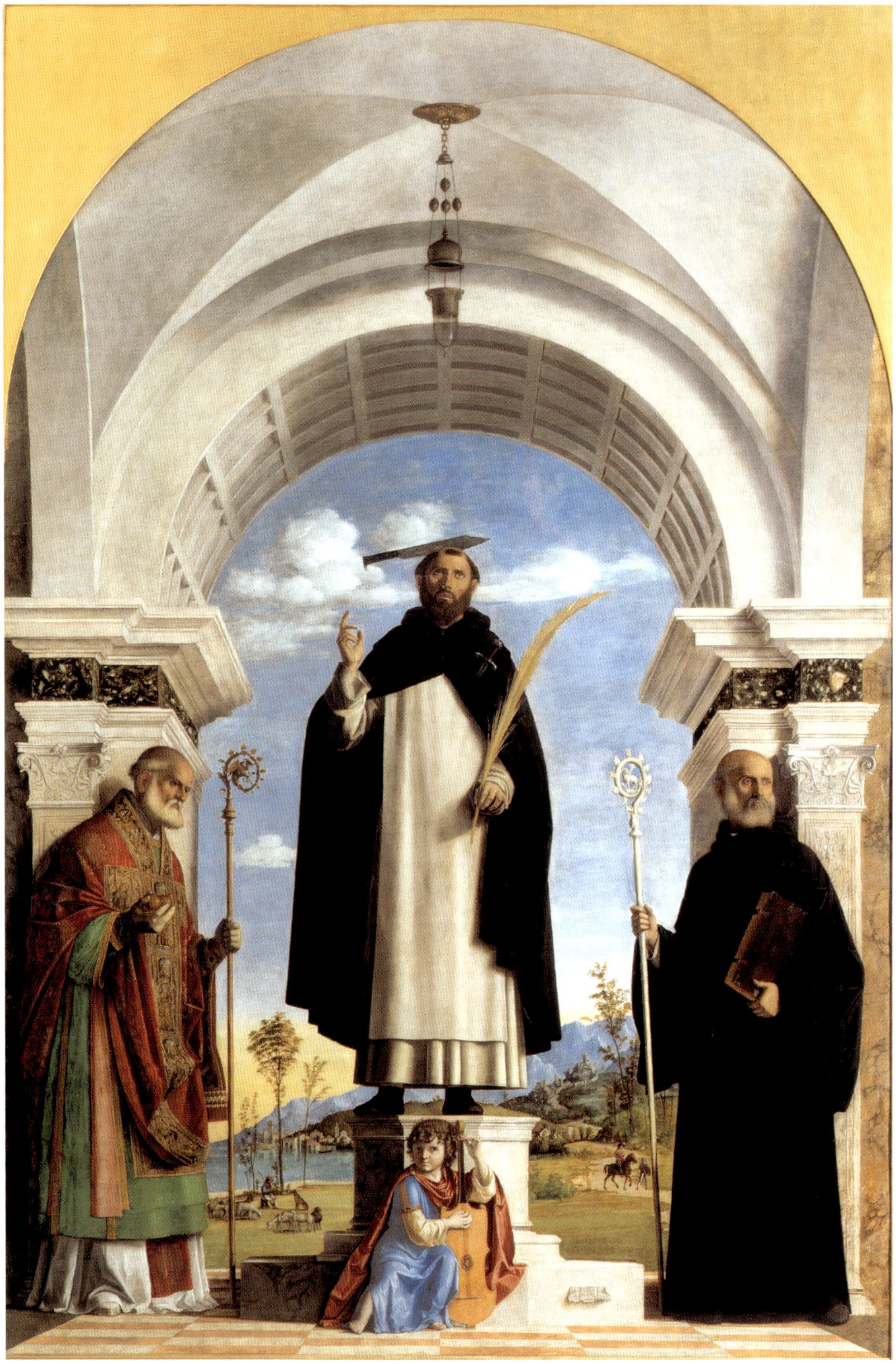

F. Cima da Conegliano, *St Peter Martyr with Saints Nicholas and Benedict*, Milan, Brera. Panel, 216 x 330 cm.

An altarpiece painted in about 1505 for the church of Corpus Domini in Venice by Carpaccio's close contemporary Cima da Conegliano.

type however, the results are far less felicitous, and it is doubly unfortunate that the number of altarpiece commissions Carpaccio received began to increase considerably after about 1510 – in other words, at the very time when his artistic powers were in any case beginning to decline. In *The Martyrdom of the Ten Thousand* of 1515, the confusion of the composition and the clutter of details may perhaps be forgiven on the grounds that the subject-matter must have been peculiarly uncongenial; but other late altarpieces, such as the *St Vitalis on Horseback* of 1514 and *The Meeting of Joachim and Anna* of 1515, with their perfunctory composition and lifeless figures, are equally lacking in inspiration and conviction. The latter work was painted not for a church in Venice itself, but for the *terra ferma* town of Treviso; and increasingly in Carpaccio's last years, he was employed by patrons from the Venetian provinces who were considerably less demanding than their metropolitan counterparts. *The Virgin and Child enthroned with Saints* of 1516, painted for the cathedral in Capodistria, reveals Carpaccio's decadence all too clearly in the laboured quality of the handling, and in the mechanical adaption of the central musician angel from the earlier *Presentation*.

As a painter of devotional subjects, Carpaccio was much more at home when working on a relatively small scale, or on pictures intended for an informally domestic rather than a solemn ecclesiastical setting. Here too, the field was dominated by the art of Giovanni Bellini, who throughout his long career produced a large number of half-length representations of the Madonna and Child, and of themes connected with Christ's Passion such as the *Pietà*. Carpaccio could not avoid Bellini's influence – a panel such as the *Dead Christ with Mourners* is obviously deeply indebted to similar compositions by Bellini – but much more than with the church altarpiece, Carpaccio was able to make his own distinctive contribution to the type. The *Virgin with the Infant Christ and St John the Baptist* in Frankfurt may be taken as characteristic of his approach: compared with a Bellini such as the '*Madonna degli Alberetti*' of 1487 (Fig. G), the mood of the Carpaccio is sweeter, more intimate and more obviously appealing. Bellini maintains the hieratic solemnity of his altarpieces, with the two figures bound together into a tight formal unity at the centre of a rigidly symmetrical composition, and the Virgin wearing an expression of a thoughtful and slightly melancholy reserve, as if to affirm her status as Queen of Heaven. Carpaccio's panel, by contrast, has much of the anecdotal charm of his narrative cycles, with the Christ Child prettily dressed up in a costume such as the child of a well-to-do Venetian family might wear, and leafing through an illuminated manuscript, while the infant Baptist points at him with a chubby finger. The casually asymmetrical composition suggests that the scene is set in the corner of an actual interior, with the curtain behind the Madonna appearing not, as in the Bellini, as a symbolical device to express regality, but as a natural item of domestic furnishing. A similar approach to the Madonna and Child theme is to be found in a drawing in the Wildenstein collection. This is probably a compositional sketch for the painting of which *The Virgin Reading* in Washington is the only surviving fragment; and here too, the fashionably dressed and domestically employed Virgin stands in the greatest possible contrast to the sorrowfully introspective Madonnas of Bellini.

This same spirit informs several larger works illustrating themes from Christ's infancy, such as the Avignon *Holy Family* (plate 41), the Mellon *Flight into Egypt* (plate 39) and the Gulbenkian *Adoration of Christ with two Donors*. Despite the fact that the figures are shown in full length, these paintings were probably also intended for a domestic rather than a liturgical setting, and the informality of Carpaccio's approach is again quite appropriate. A vestige of the stately architecture of the S. Giobbe altar is perhaps apparent in the rocky archway that spans the middle-ground of the Avignon *Holy Family*; but the high seriousness of Bellini's altarpiece is completely dissolved by the playful mood of the foreground figures and by the busy incident filling the background landscape. This kind of Holy Family group, which was to have an important progeny in the many *plein-air* settings of Palma Vecchio, Titian and Paris Bordone in

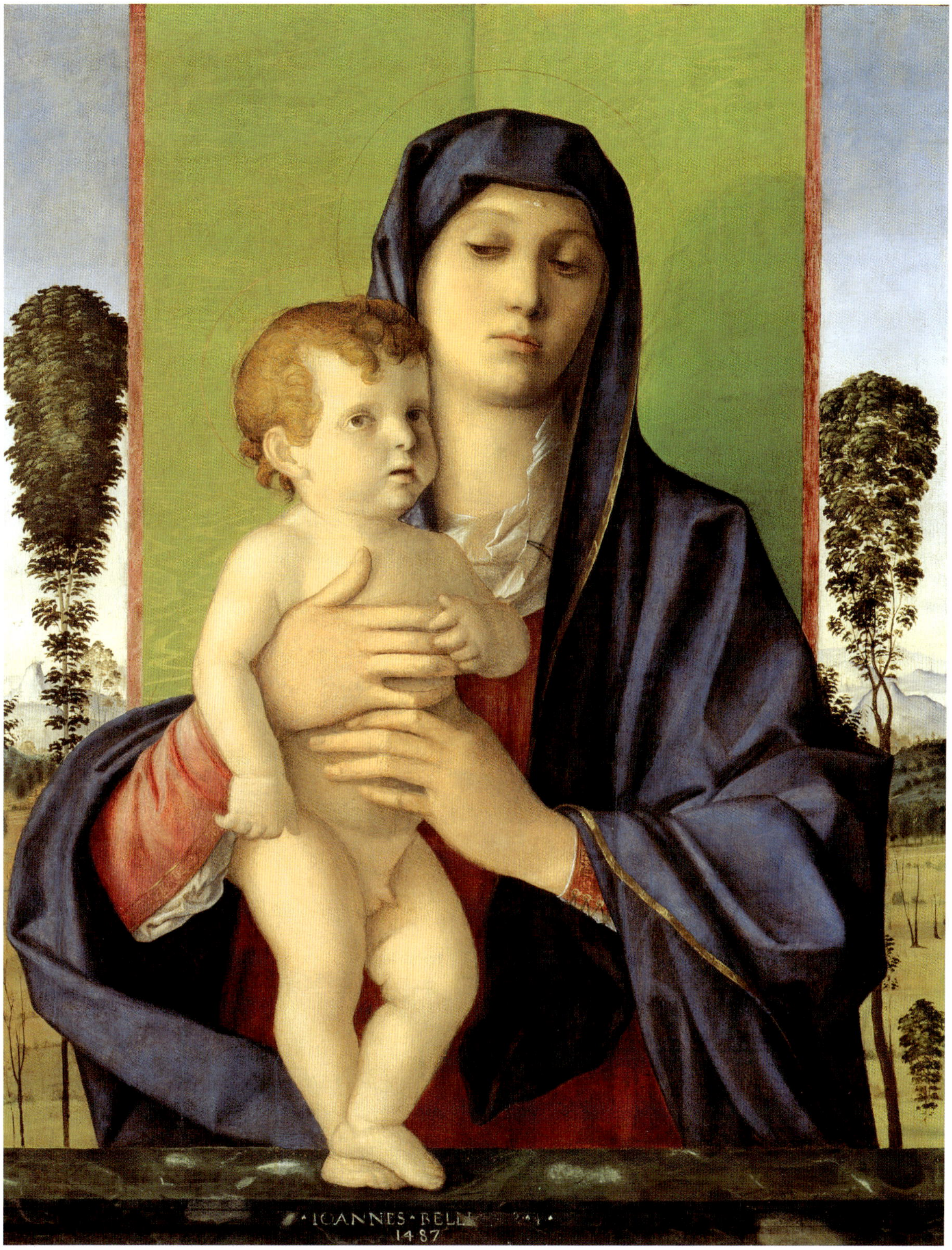

G. Giovanni Bellini, '*Madonna degli Alberetti*', Venice, Accademia. Panel, 74 x 58 cm. 1487

A characteristic and impressive example of Giovanni Bellini's rendering of the theme of the half-length Madonna and Child.

the sixteenth century, may well have been inspired by German prints such as Dürer's *Holy Family* woodcut of 1498 (Fig. H), where the figures are similarly set into natural surroundings teeming with plants and animals. The relaxed and cheerful way in which Carpaccio treats this and the various other scenes from Christ's infancy, while obviously in complete accord with the natural bent of his own temperament, probably also considerably enhanced their didactic value as pictures for the home. In a manual on the education of children written in the early fifteenth century by Cardinal Dominici – a Dominician who had spent some years in the Venetian monastery of S.S. Giovanni e Paolo – the author speaks, among many other things, of the beneficial effects of holy images. He recommends that children be brought up surrounded by religious representations of a kind with which they can closely identify; and he suggests as suitable subjects the Christ Child shown together with his Mother, holding a little bird or perhaps a pomegranate, or the Christ Child playing with the child Baptist. It is easy to imagine that the genre-like charm and intimacy of Carpaccio's Holy Family pictures would have had just the appeal in domestic circles that Dominici had in mind.

Since Carpaccio's treatment of devotional subject-matter tends on the whole to be sweet rather than profound, lacking the emotional austerity of Giovanni Bellini, it comes rather as a surprise to find a new depth and seriousness in two religious works closely related in theme, and probably also in date: *The Meditation on the Dead Christ* now in New York and *The Entombment of Christ* in Berlin. In both paintings, the Passion of Christ is treated in terms of mystical contemplation rather than of historical narrative; and their pictorial handling is much harsher than is usual in Carpaccio, with their arid and stony landscapes more reminiscent of Mantegna than of any Venetian painter. The use of recondite symbolism and the mood of intense piety suggests that they were not intended primarily for domestic enjoyment, but rather as practical aids to meditation on the inner significance of Christ's self-sacrifice and Resurrection. It has been suggested that the flavour of their spirituality reflects that of a particular circle of

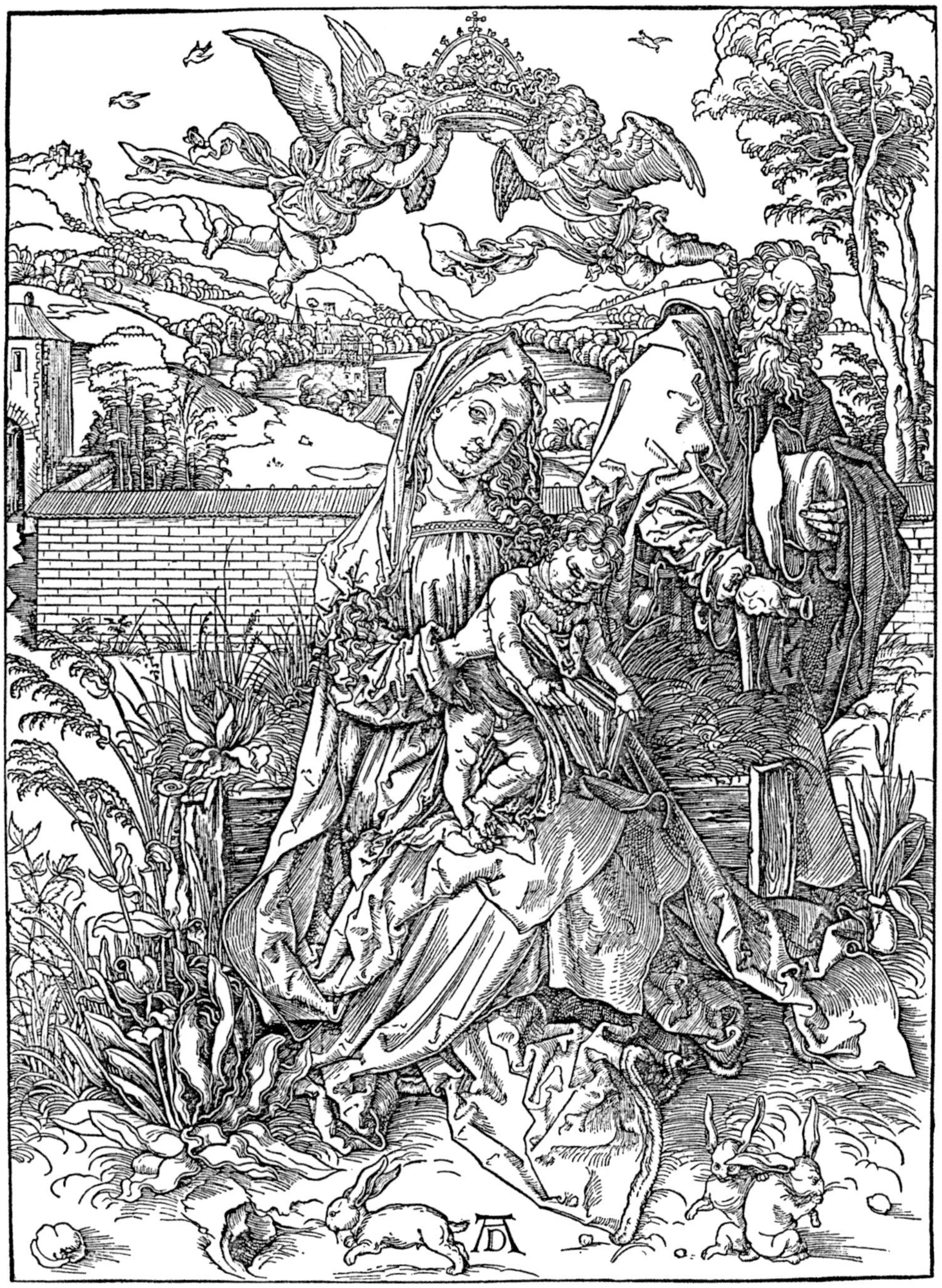

H. Albrecht Dürer, *Holy Family with Three Hares*, Woodcut, ca. 1498 (Kurth 104).

reforming clerics in Venice, centring around the personality of Paolo Giustinian. From his earliest years, this ascetically devout Venetian nobleman had reacted violently against the wordly pomps and pleasures of Renaissance Venice, and after a career dedicated to the pursuit of poverty, solitude and penance, he finally retired to the remote Camaldolese hermitage of Monte Corona in 1520, to spend the rest of his days as far away as possible from the noise and bustle of Rialto. His influence on contemporary religious thought in Venice was considerable, and although there is no certain evidence that Carpaccio had any direct contact with Giustinian or his immediate circle, it does seem likely that whoever commissioned these two works was in close sympathy with their ideals, and had a religious outlook rather different from that of Carpaccio's customary employers.

In his lifetime, Carpaccio seems to have enjoyed a high reputation as a portrait painter. There is documentary evidence that he executed the portraits of at least three eminent contemporary men of letters, and in the mid-sixteenth century Giorgio Vasari speaks of 'numerous portraits from the life' painted by Carpaccio, which were 'generally held in great esteem'. Although very few independent portraits by Carpaccio appear to have survived, this information is scarcely surprising: the canvases of his narrative cycles are packed with individually characterised faces, many of which would have been instantly recognisable to contemporary spectators. A drawing such as the *Head of a Middle-aged Man* in the British Museum (plate 9), where the features have been sketched rapidly and vividly with a combination of black chalk and the tip of a brush, probably gives an accurate idea of the kind of preliminary study Carpaccio would have made for all the portrait heads included in his narrative cycles. Portrait-painting was in fact one of the principal activities of Carpaccio's putative master, Gentile Bellini, whose series of official portraits of the doges of Venice was destroyed in the fire that gutted the Hall of the Great Council in 1577. But whereas most of Gentile's portraits were profiles, the preferred formula of Carpaccio was the three-quarter view, as for instance in his *Portrait of a Woman* now in

Denver. This type of arrangement, with the sitter portrayed in bust length and three-quarter profile against a neutral ground, with one hand holding an identifying attribute just appearing above the bottom edge of the picture, was Flemish in origin, and was probably received by Carpaccio through the intermediary of Antonello. A quite different arrangement is that of the *Portrait of a Young Knight* in the Thyssen Collection, Madrid (plate 47), where the figure is seen in full-length against a richly detailed landscape background. Carpaccio deserves credit here for producing one of the very first independent full-length portraits in Italian painting, a type that was later to be developed by Titian. The Düreresque style of the work suggests that Carpaccio may have derived the formula from German painting, where full-length portraits were not unknown; but it is also worth pointing out that the *Portrait of a Young Knight* – with the sitter portrayed as a chivalrous man of action set against a romantic and picturesque backdrop – represents the logical outcome of Carpaccio's lifelong activity as a painter of comparable figures in his narrative cycles.

More drawings survive by Carpaccio than by any other Venetian painter before the later sixteenth century. The reason for this is not necessarily that he drew more than his contemporaries: although Giorgione and Titian may often have depended entirely on the roughest of under-drawings sketched straight on to the canvas, it is likely that all the artists of the previous generation made numerous preliminary drawings before starting to paint. If only a tiny proportion of drawings by the Bellini brothers or by Cima have survived, it is because they were conceived simply as a means to an end, and were discarded after use. In the case of Carpaccio too, the drawings that survive must represent a mere fragment of his total output as a draughtsman, but their relative quantity is probably at least in part due to the fact that many of them were deliberately preserved by his son Benedetto, who inherited the family workshop after his father's death. Benedetto Carpaccio was an artist almost entirely devoid of original talent, and his father's stock of drawings provided him with an invaluable storehouse of ideas which he continued to repeat until his own death in the 1540s. Carpaccio's surviving drawings tend to fall into two main groups, corresponding to their functions in the preparatory process: compositional sketches and studies of details. Particularly fine examples of the first group are the sketches for *The Dream of St Ursula* or for *The Funeral of St Jerome*. In both these drawings, the spatial settings are clearly and fully worked out, while the figures and details are indicated only very lightly and hazily. It has been observed that even at this early stage Carpaccio is conscious of the effects of light and atmosphere that are to play so important a part in establishing the poetic mood of the finished painting. In certain other compositional sketches, such as *The English Prince Taking Leave of his Father*, the artist concentrates rather on the figures, studying their gestures and formal inter-relationships. Instead of blurring and softening the details with an ink wash, as in the *Dream*, he draws in the forms boldly and vigorously, with quick strokes of the pen, expressive of the animation and bustle of the scene. Characteristic examples of the second group of drawings, studies of details, are the *Head of a Woman*, and *Standing Figure*. Instead of being jotted down from the imagination, these are carefully drawn from life, using gradations of tone and a white heightening to model the forms in three dimensions. It is interesting to notice that here too, by making frequent use of coloured papers for such studies, Carpaccio is able to suggest the pictorial effect of the end product. Drawings of this kind were clearly susceptible to re-use in different contexts: the *Head of a Woman* was made in connexion with *The Glorification of St Ursula*, perhaps as early as ca. 1490, but it was later pressed into service again for the *Presentation in the Temple*, of 1510. The repetitiveness of Carpaccio's later works was in fact the direct result of an excessive dependence on pre-existing detail studies by the master and his shop, Benedetto being an even worse culprit than his father.

A comparison between Carpaccio's drawings and the paintings for which they were made can often be instructive about his priorities as an artist. The compositional sketch for the *Vision of St Augustine* shows how completely he had mastered the Central Italian art of constructing three-dimensional space through geometric perspective. The relative size and position of every object in the saint's study is immediately comprehensible, and the spatial coherence is further clarified by the fall of light. In the painting however, although there is no loss in perspective logic, the spatial effect is considerably modified by Carpaccio's characteristically Venetian use of colour. The contrasts of red and green that dominate the colour composition are not affected in their intensity by relative nearness or distance. The green of the immediate right foreground, for example, is precisely equivalent to the greens on the right hand wall, and to the green seen through the doorway on the left. Furthermore, local colour is only to a limited extent subject to effects of light and shade. Whereas the white triangle in the right foreground of the drawing is immediately understood as a splash of light on a horizontal surface, the corresponding patch in the painting appears rather as an abstract shape, placed vertically against the neighbouring area of green. The total effect of the painting is of a series of broad planes of colour, evenly spread across the surface of the picture, and creating a powerful effect of flat pattern. In his respect for the integrity of the picture plane, and his sense of the decorative and expressive value of pure colour, Carpaccio proves himself heir to an old Venetian tradition stretching back to the mosaics of St Mark's.

Although Carpaccio is one of the most Venetian of painters, both in his compositional technique and in the raw material of his subject-matter, his place in the history of Venetian painting is not easy to assess. John Ruskin, in Letter 71 of his *Fors Clavigera*, declared Carpaccio's message to be 'the sweetest, because the truest, of all that Venice was born to utter'; and in another letter, written from Venice in October 1876, Ruskin named Carpaccio in the same breath as Hesiod, Plato and Dante, as one of the small band of select who understood the truths necessary to human life. But Ruskin was not always the most objective of critics, and in his zeal to communicate a new-found enthusiasm, he certainly exaggerated Carpaccio's artistic stature. Even at his best, Carpaccio never quite reaches the quality of his great contemporary

Giovanni Bellini, and at his worst, he is scarcely better than the most mediocre of Bellini's followers. Nor can Carpaccio compare with Bellini as an influence on the future development of Venetian painting: although certain aspects of his art were to be followed up in the eighteenth century, in the townscapes of Canaletto for instance, or in the genre paintings of Pietro Longhi, his importance for his immediate successors in the sixteenth century was slight. Yet the charm that Ruskin found so irresistible, and the qualities that put Carpaccio high in the esteem of his contemporaries, are not so easily dismissed. The Carpaccio room in the Accademia in Venice, where the St Ursula canvases now hang, is probably the most popular room in the gallery, with the seemingly endless variety of figures, objects and views providing the visitor with an inexhaustible source of fascination. Not the least part of this fascination consists in the fact that even today, it is difficult to walk the streets of Venice without constantly catching glimpses of Carpaccio in its palaces, churches, canals, roof-gardens and chimney-pots. In other words, Carpaccio's own personal vision of the city of the lagoons has stamped itself so vividly on the imagination of posterity that it has become difficult to disentangle the reality from its poetic transformation. This achievement, which makes the unfavourable comparison with Giovanni Bellini seem almost irrelevant, perhaps constitutes Carpaccio's most enduring claim to our admiration and affection.

BIBLIOGRAPHICAL NOTE

The basic monograph in English on Carpaccio is J. Lauts, *Carpaccio: Paintings and Drawings*, London, 1962, with a critical catalogue and a full bibliography up to 1960. G. Ludwig and P. Molmenti, *Vittore Carpaccio*, English edition, London, 1907, although inadequate from the point of view of stylistic criticism and in many respects outdated, is still the richest source of information about Carpaccio himself, and the milieu in which he lived.

Among the more important contributions to the Carpaccio literature since 1960 are the following:

G. Perocco, *Tutta la Pittura del Carpaccio*, Milan, 1960.

R. Pallucchini, *I Teleri del Carpaccio di S. Giorgio degli Schiavoni*, Milan, 1961.

T. Pignatti, 'Rapporti fra il Cima ed il Carpaccio attorno al primo decennio del cinquecento', in *La Provincia di Treviso*, 9–11, 1962.

Reviews of Lauts' monograph by A. Martindale in *The Burlington Magazine*, CV, 331, 1963; by T. Pignatti in *Master Drawings*, 1/4, 47–54, 1963; by G. Robertson in *The Art Bulletin*, XLV, 157–8, 1963; and by E. Ruhmer in *Pantheon*, XXI, 111–2, 1963,

P. Zampetti, *Vittore Carpaccio – Catalogo della Mostra*, Venice, 1963.

Reviews of the 1963 Carpaccio Exhibition in the Doge's Palace by R. Marini in *Arte Veneta*, XVII, 228–35, 1963; by G. Robertson in *The Burlington Magazine*, CV, 385–90, 1963; and by E. Ruhmer in *Pantheon*, XXI, 375–8, 1963; A. Busiri Vici, 'Vicende di un dipinto: la "Caccia in Valle" di Vittore Carpaccio', in *Arte Antica e Moderna*, XXIV, 345–56, 1963.

R. Gallo, 'La Scuola di S. Orsola: I Teleri del Carpaccio e la Tomba di Gentile e Giovanni Bellini', in *Bolletino dei Musei Civici Veneziani*, 1963, I–II, 1 ff; and P. Zampetti, 'Per la Scuola di Sant 'Orsola', *ibid.*, III–IV, 1 ff.

F. Valcanover, *Vittore Carpaccio: Le Storie di S. Orsola*, Milan, 1963.

R. Weiss and V. Branca, 'Carpaccio e l'Iconografia del più grande Umanista veneziano (Ermolao Barbaro)', in *Arte Veneta*, XVII, 35–40, 1963.

K. Ambrozic, 'Due dipinti di Vittore Carpaccio', in *Arte Veneta*, XVIII, 162–4, 1964.

L. Magagnato, 'Il Momento architettonico di tre pittori veneti del tardo quattrocento', in *Bolletino del Centro Internazionale di Studi d'Architettura A. Palladio*, VI, 228–38, 1964.

M. Muraro, *Carpaccio*, Florence, 1966.

Reviews of Muraro's monograph by R. W. Kennedy in *Renaissance Quarterly*, XX, 471–5, 1967; and by A. Martindale in *The Burlington Magazine*, CXI, 39, 1969.

W. Pokorny, 'Carpaccio's Alcyone Cycle', in *The Burlington Magazine*, CVIII, 418–21, 1966.

P. Zampetti, *Vittore Carpaccio*, Venice, 1966; and *idem*, 'L'Oriente del Carpaccio', in ed. A. Pertusi, *Venezia e l'Oriente Fra Tardo Medioevo e Rinascimento*, Florence, 511–26, 1966.

M. Cagnoni and G. Perocco, *L'Opera Complete del Carpaccio*, Milan, 1967.

Z. Wazbinski, 'Portrait d'un Amateur d'Art de la Renaissance', in *Arte Veneta*, XXII, 21–9, 1968.

M. Muraro, 'Vittore Carpaccio o il Teatro in Pittura', in ed. M. T. Muraro, *Studi sul Teatro Veneto Fra Rinascimento ed Età Barocca*, Florence, 7–19, 1971.

G. Pochat, 'Bemerkungen zu Carpaccio und Mantegna', in *Konsthistorisk Tidskrift*, XL, 99–106, 1971.

J. Fletcher, 'Sources of Carpaccio in German Woodcuts', in *The Burlington Magazine*, CXV, 599, 1973.

M.Q. Smith, 'Carpaccio 's Hunt in the Lagoon', *Apollo*, XCIX, 240–4, 1974.

G. Perocco, *Carpaccio: Le Pitture alla Scuola di S. Giorgio degli Schiavoni* (with English translation), Treviso, 1975.

M. Serres, *Esthétiques sur Carpaccio*, Paris, 1975.

M. Muraro, *I Disegni di Vittore Carpaccio*, Florence, 1977.

F. Pesenti, Vittore Carpaccio, in *Dizionario biographico degli italiani*, Rome, XX, 568–73, 1977.

Giorgione: la Pala di Castelfranco Veneto, Milan, 1978.

Giorgione a Venezia: catalogo della Mostra, Milan, 1978.

V. Sgarbi, 'Vittore Carpaccio: poetica e committenza', in *Prospettiva*, XIV, 31–46, 1978.

S. Varzaru, 'Tre fonti letterarie riguardanti l'opera di Vittore Carpaccio', in *Revue roumaine d'Histore de l'Art* (Série Beaux-Arts), XV, 117–20, 1978.

T. Pignatti, *The Golden Age of Venetian Painting*, exhibition catalogue, Los Angeles County Museum of Art, Los Angeles, 1979.

A. Rosenbaum, *Old Master Paintings from the Collection of the Baron Thyssen-Bornemisza*, Washington, 1979.

V. Sgarbi, *Carpaccio*, Bologna, 1979.

F.R. Shapley, *Catalogue of the Italian Paintings*, National Gallery of Art, Washington. 1979.

F. Rossi, 'Pittura a Bergamo intorno al 1500: ricositituzione di un patrimonio diserso', in *Atti dell'Ateneo di Scienze, Lettere ed Arti di Bergamo*, XLI, 77–96, 1979.

D. Charmelot, *Les anges de Carpaccio, Des femmes*, 1979.

M. Daly Davis, 'Carpaccio and the Perspective of Regular Bodies', in *La Prospettiva Rinascimentale*, a cura di M. Dalai Emiliani, Florence, I, 183–200, 1980.

G. Goldner, 'A late fifteenth-century Venetian painting of a bird hunt', in *J. Paul Getty Museum Journal*, VIII, 23–5, 1980.

J. Bernasconi, 'The dating of the cycle of the Miracles of the cross from the Scula di San Giovanni Evangelista', in *Arte Veneta*, XXXV, 198–202, 1981.

Le Scuole di Venzia, a cura di T. Pignatti, Milan, 1981.

P. Reuterswärd, 'The dog in a humanist's study', in *Konsthistorisk Tidskrift*, L, 53–69, 1981.

J. Raby, *Venice, Dürer and the Oriental Mode*, London, 1982.

R. Goffen, 'Carpaccio's Portrait of a Young Knight: Identity and Meaning', in *Arte Veneta*, XXXVII, 37–48, 1983.

L. Lazzarini, 'Il colre nei pittori venezianni tra il 1480 e il 1580', in *Bollettino d'Arte*, VI serie, n. 5, Supplemento, 135–44, 1983.

M. Lucco, 'Venezia fra Quattro e Cinquecento', in *Storia dell'Arte Italiana: Dal Medioevo al Quattrocento*, V, Turin, 447–77, 1983.

A.M. Pedrocchi, 'La tavola con i Santi giovanni Evangelista, Antonio Abate, Giacomo, Domenico, lorenzo e Nicola da Bari dell'Accademia Carrara di Bergamo attribuita a Carpaccio', in *Bollettino d'Arte,* VI serie, n.5, Supplemento, 145–50, 1983.

A. Rona, 'Zur Identität von Carpaccios Ritte', in *Pantheon*, XLI, 295–303, 1983.

The Genius of Venice 1500-1600, catalogue, Royal Academy of Arts, curated by J. Martineau and C. Hope, London, 1983.

P. Fortini Brown, 'Painting and History in Renaissance Venice', in *Art History*, VII, 263–94, 1984.

D. Marshall, 'Carpaccio, St Stephen and the Topography of Jerusalem', in *The Art Bulletin*, LXVI, 610–20, 1984.

F. Bardon, 'La Peinture Narrative de Carpaccio dans le cycle de Ste Ursule', in *Atti dell'Istituto Veneto di Scenze, Lettere ed Arti (Classe di Science Morali, Lettere ed Arti*, XXXIX, fasc.4, 1985.

G. Nepi Scirè-F. Valcanover, *Gallerie dell'Accademia di Venezia*, Milan, 1985.

A. Gentili, 'Nuovi documenti e contesi per l'ultimo Carpaccio I: L'Incontro di Gioacchino e Anna per san Francesco di Treviso', in *Artibus et Historiae*, VII n. 13, 55–65. 1986.

N. Huse-W. Wolters, *Venedig: Die Kunst der Renaissance*, Munich, 1986.

P. Humfrey, 'La pittura del secondo Quattrocento a Venezia', in *La Pittura in Italia; Il Quattrocento,* a cura di F. Zeri, Milan, 184–209, 1987.

L. Zorzi, *Capaccio e la rappresentazione di Sant'Orsola*, Turin, 1987.

P. Fortini Brown, *Venetian Narrative Painting in the Age of Carpaccio*, London-New Haven, 1988.

A. Gentilli, 'Nuovi documenti e contesti per contesti per l'ultimo Carpaccio. II: I teleri per la Scuola di san Stephano in Venezia', in *Artibus et Historiae*, IX n. 18, 79–109, 1988.

P. Humfrey, 'Vittore Carpaccio', in *Gothic to Renaissance: European Painting 1300-1600*, catalogue della mostra,

Colnaghi (London and New York), curated by D. Garstang, New York, 1988.

S.M. Newton, *The Dress of the Venetians 1495-1525*, Aldershot, 1988.

T. Pignatti, 'Una scheda per "Le Cortigane", del Carpaccio, in *Arte Veneta*, XLII, 40, 1988.

C. Santore, 'The fruits of Venus: Carpaccio's "Two Courtesans"', in *Arte Veneta*, XLII, 34–9, 1988.

P. Humfrey, 'Politica e devozione; la traizione narrativa quattrocentesca', in *La Pittura nel Venteto: il Quattrocento*, a cura di M. Lucco, Milano, 295–338, 1989.

P. Humfrey, *Carpaccio; Catalogo completo*, Cantini, Florence, 1991.

Carpaccio, Bellini, Tura, Antonello: E altri restauri quattrocenteschi della Pinacoteca del Museo Correr, Electa, 1993.

V. Sgarbi, *Carpaccio,* Fabbri, 1994.

V. Sgarbi, *Carpaccio: Leben und Werk,* Hirmer, 1999.

G. Nepi, *Carpaccio: Le Storie De Sant'Orsola (Dentro la pittura)*, Scire Art Books, 2000.

S. Mason, A. Ellis (Translator), *Carpaccio: The Major Pictorial Cycles*, Skira, 2000.

BIOGRAPHICAL OUTLINE

ca. 1465	Vittore Carpaccio born in Venice, the son of a furrier.
1472	First documented mention of Carpaccio, in the will of an uncle.
1490	Carpaccio signs his earliest surviving dated work, *The Arrival of St Ursula at Cologne.*
1490-ca. 1498	Cycle for the Scuola di S. Orsola.
1496	*The Blood of the Redeemer.*
1501–2	Carpaccio executes a painting, now lost, for the Sala dei Pregadi in the Doge's Palace.
1502-ca. 1508	Cycle for the Scuola di S. Giorgio degli Schiavoni.
ca. 1500–10	Cycle for the Scuola degli Albanesi.
1505	*The Adoration of Christ with two Donors.*
1507	*St Thomas Aquinas Enthroned.*
1507	Carpaccio is called in to assist Giovanni Bellini complete the monumental decoration of the Sala del Maggior Consiglio in the Doge's Palace.
1508	Carpaccio is chosen as a member of the committee which is to evaluate the recently completed frescoes by Giorgione on the Fondaco de'Tedeschi.
1510	*The Presentation of Christ in the Temple.*
1510	*Portrait of a Young Knight.*
1511–20	Cycle for the Scuola di S. Stefano.
1511	Carpaccio writes to Francesco Gonzaga, Marquis of Mantua, in the hope of persuading him to buy a large canvas which he terms 'uno Jerusalem'.
1514	*St Vitalis on Horseback.*
1515	*The Meeting of Joachim and Anna.*
1515	*The Martyrdom of the Ten Thousand.*
1516	*Madonna and Child Enthroned with Saints.*
1519	Polyptych for Pozzale di Cadore.
1523	Carpaccio is paid for an alterpiece of the Nativity, now lost, painted for the Patriarch of Venice.
1526	Carpaccio is mentioned in a document as recently deceased.

Also useful in compiling the present survey have been the following: Jacobus de Voragine, *The Golden Legend* (English translation of the thirteenth century *Legenda Aurea* by G. Ryan and H. Ripperger), New York, 1969.

G. Dominici, *Regola del Governo di Cura Familiare*, ed. D. Salvi, Florence, 1860.

Canon Pietro Casola's Pimgrimage to Jerusalem in the Year 1494, trans. M. Newett, Manchester, 1907.

The Memoirs of Philippe de Commynes, ed. S. Kinser, trans. I. Cazeaux, 2 vols, Columbia, S. C., 1969.

Anton Maria Zanetti, *Della Pittura Veneziana*, Venice, 1771.

John Ruskin, *St Mark's Rest*, in *The Works of John Ruskin*, ed. E. T. Cook and A. Wedderburn, XXIV, London, 1906.

J. Leclercq, 'Le Bx Paul Giustiniani et les ermites de son temps', in *Problemi di Vita Religiosa in Italia nel Cinquecento*, Padua, 1960.

G. Folena, 'La Cultura Volgare e l'Umanesimo Cavalleresco nel Veneto', in ed. V. Branca, *Umanesimo Europeo e Umanesimo Veneziano*, Venice, 141–58, 1963.

H. Honour, *The Companion Guide to Venice*, London, 1965.

S. Ringbom, *Icon to Narrative: The Rise of the Dramatic Close-up in Fifteenth century devotional painting*, Åbo, 1965.

D. Chambers, *The Imperial Age of Venice*, London, 1970.

N. Huse, *Studien zu Giovanni Bellini*, Berlin, 1972.

V. Branca, 'Ermolao Barbaro and late Quattrocento Venetian Humanism', in ed. J. Hale, *Renaissance Venice*, London, 218–43, 1973.

F. Lane, Venice: *A Maritime Republic*, London, 1973.

G. Paccagnini, *Pisanello* (English edition), London, 1973.

E. Birbari, *Dress in Italian Painting 1460–1500*, London, 1975

NOTE on the illustrations:

The arrangement of the illustrations is in general intended to give an idea of the internal development of Carpaccio's style over a period of about forty years. The order is not strictly chronological, however: especially in the case of the narrative cycles, it has been thought better to illustrate them in the order of the events recounted than in the order Carpaccio painted them. In other cases, paintings not too far apart in date have been paired together on account of similarities of subject matter.

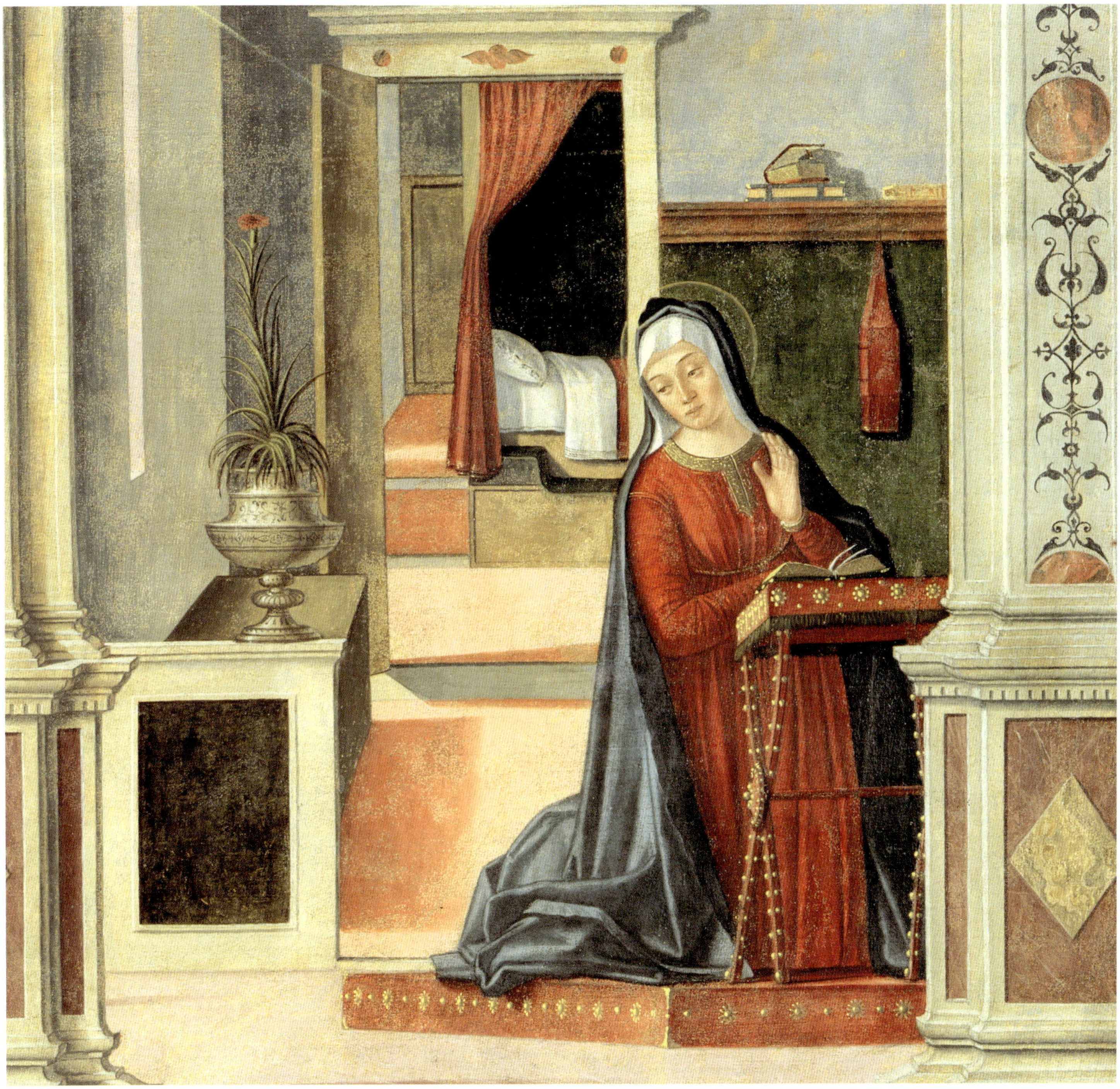

Detail of pl. 34.

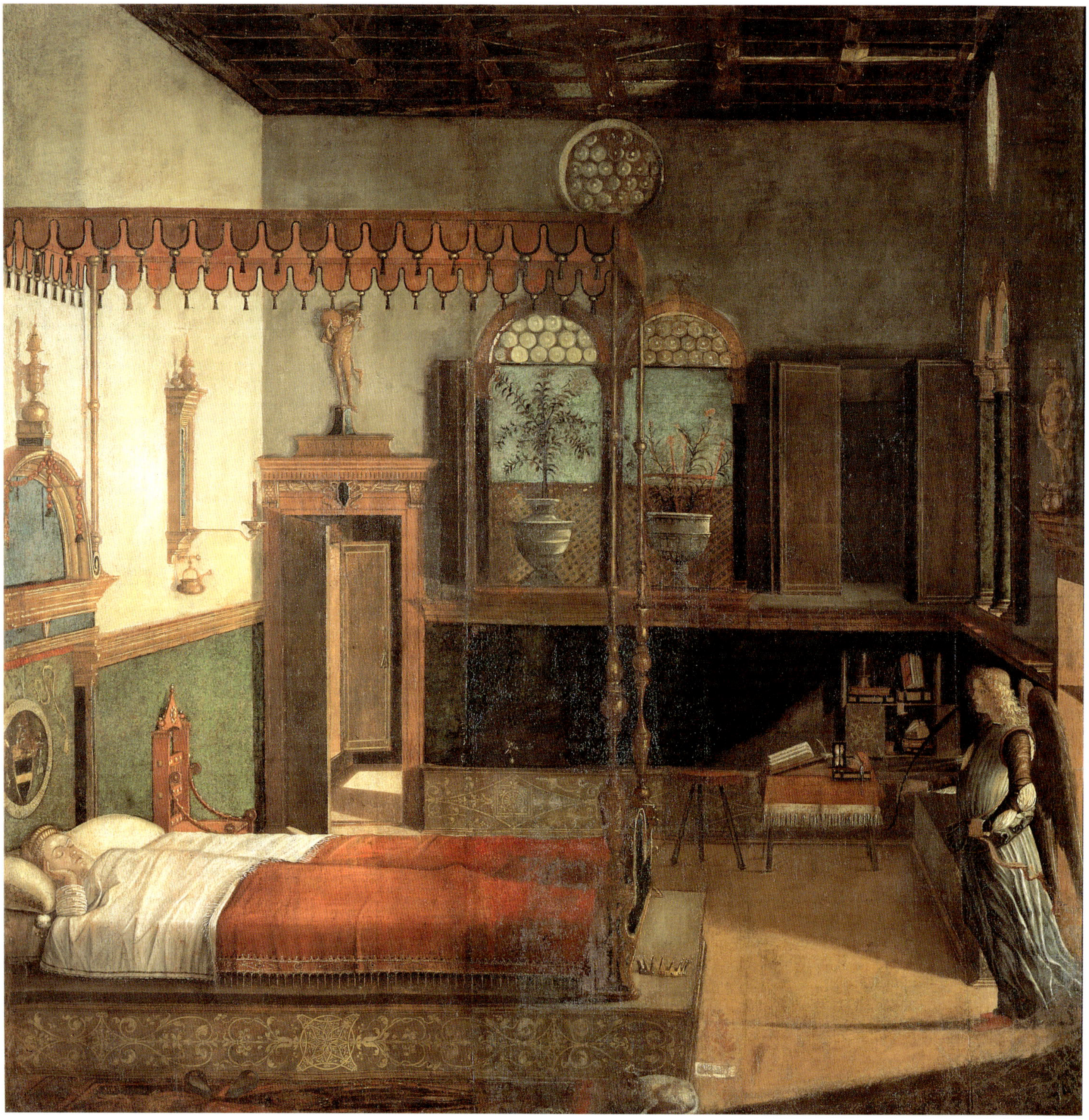

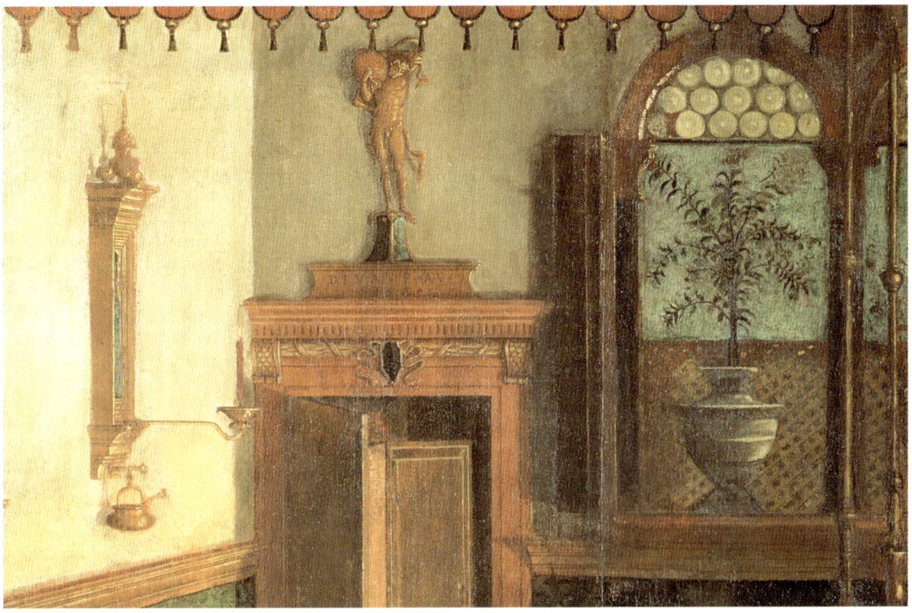

1 *THE DREAM OF ST URSULA*
Venice, Accademia
Canvas, 274 x 267 cm. Inscribed: VICTOR, CARP.F. MCCCCLXXXXV.

From the cycle of the Scuola di S. Orsola. Passing through Cologne on her way to Rome, St Ursula is warned by an angel in a dream that when she returns to Cologne, she will be martyred for her faith. The import of the angel's message is made clear for us by the palm he carries in his right hand. This view of St Ursula's bed-chamber gives a vivid impression of the interior of a Venetian private palace in the late fifteenth century: of particular interest are the statuettes above the door lintels, reflecting the contemporary taste for bronze sculpture *all'antica*, and the holy image to the left of the bed, lit by a burning taper. Carpaccio's compositional drawing for this work shows that the painting has been cut down on all four sides.

(above) Detail of pl. 1.

2 *A MIRACLE OF THE RELIC OF THE TRUE CROSS*
Venice, Accademia
Canvas, 365 x 389 cm.

One of a cycle of canvases, with contributions by Gentile Bellini (see Fig. A), Lazzaro Bastiani, Mansueti and Benedetto Diana, as well as by Carpaccio, painted to decorate the Scuola Grande di S. Giovanni Evangelista. Several of the paintings show miracles performed through the agency of a precious fragment of the True Cross, which the confraternity had in its custody. Most of the miracles had taken place in Venice within recent history: that recorded by Carpaccio happened in 1494, the very year in which the canvas seems to have been painted. In the upper floor loggia on the left, the Patriarch of Grado, Francesco Querini, is to be seen curing a man possessed of a demon by raising the reliquary above the patient's head. Witnessing the miracle is a group of confraternity members, dressed in their white ceremonial robes and carrying heavy candlesticks. They form the head of a long procession stretching down the staircase, along the quay and back across the drawbridge. The scene appears to be a topographically accurate record of the Grand Canal at Rialto, and many of the architectural features are still to be seen today – for instance, the type of Gothic window, or the characteristically Venetian chimney-pots. The liberal application of gold leaf throughout the painting – for instance, on the candlesticks, and on the architectural details of the Patriarch's palace – is common to all the paintings in the cycle, and considerably enhances their total effect of richness and decorativeness. A strip of canvas which had been cut out of the bottom left hand corner in the mid-sixteenth century was later provided with a rather crude substitution.

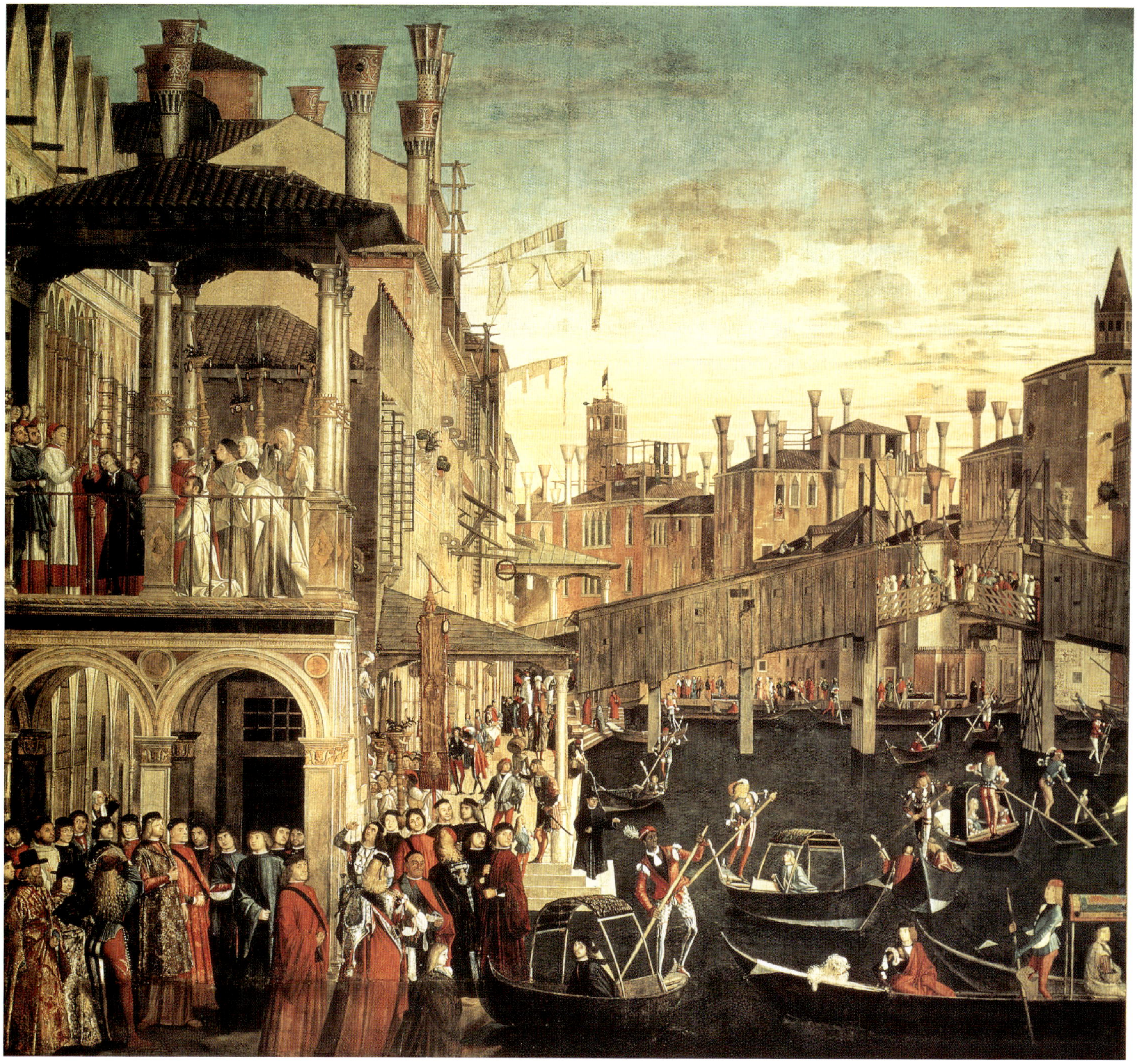

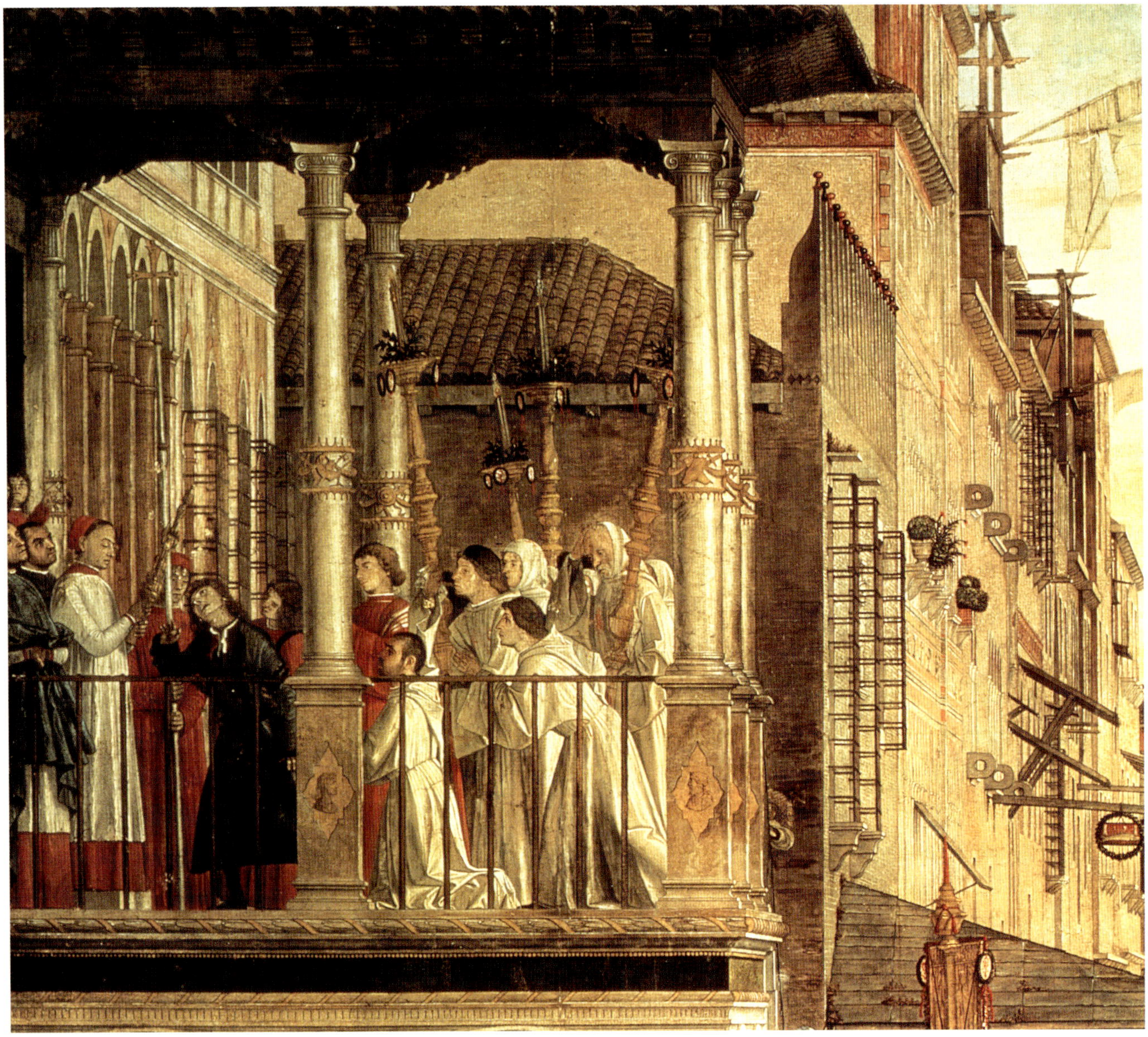

Above, detail of Healing of the man possessed of demons in the house of the Patriarch of Grado.
Right, detail of the old wooden Rialto Bridge and canal side buildings, sharply defined by Carpaccio's light.

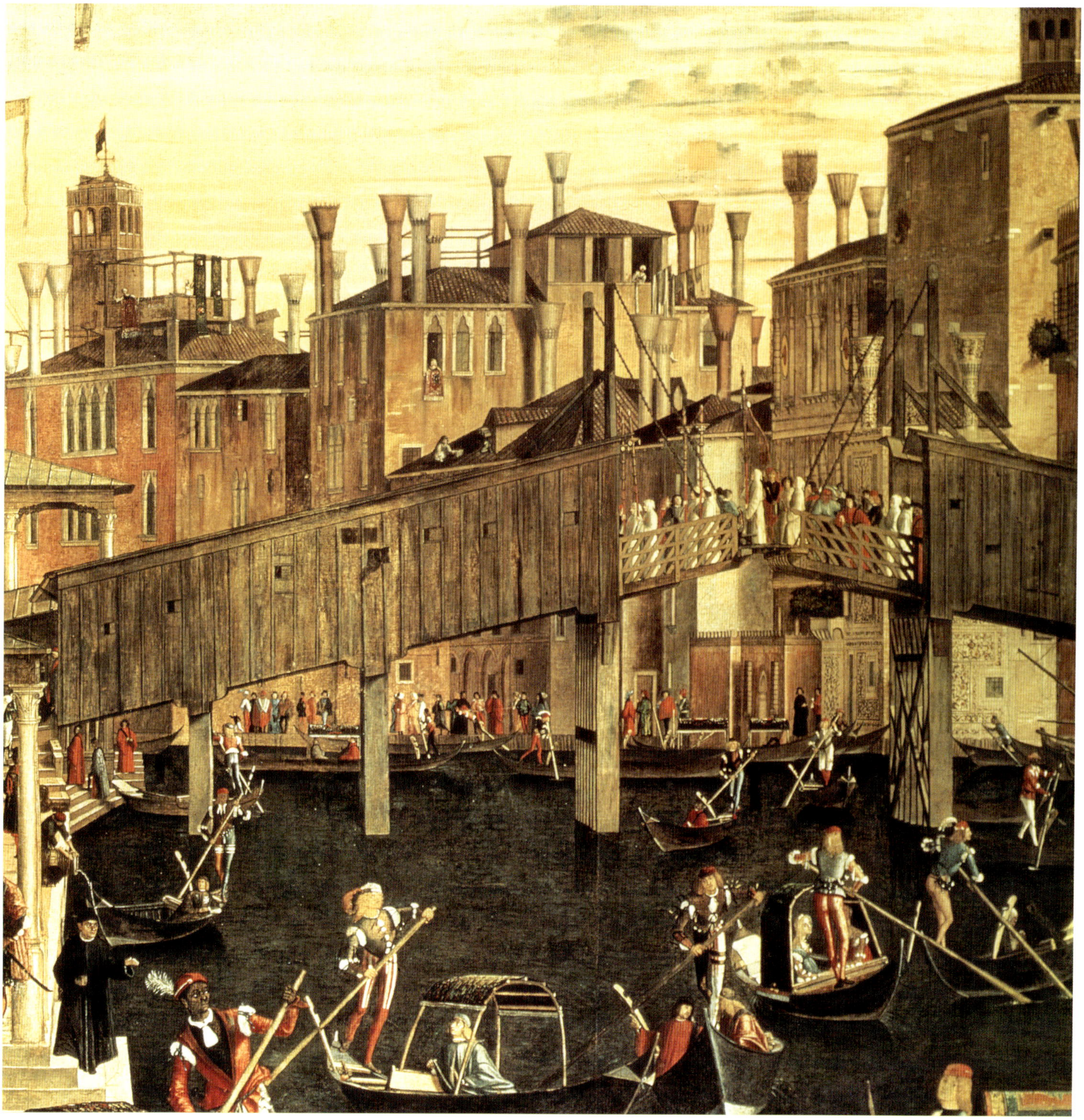

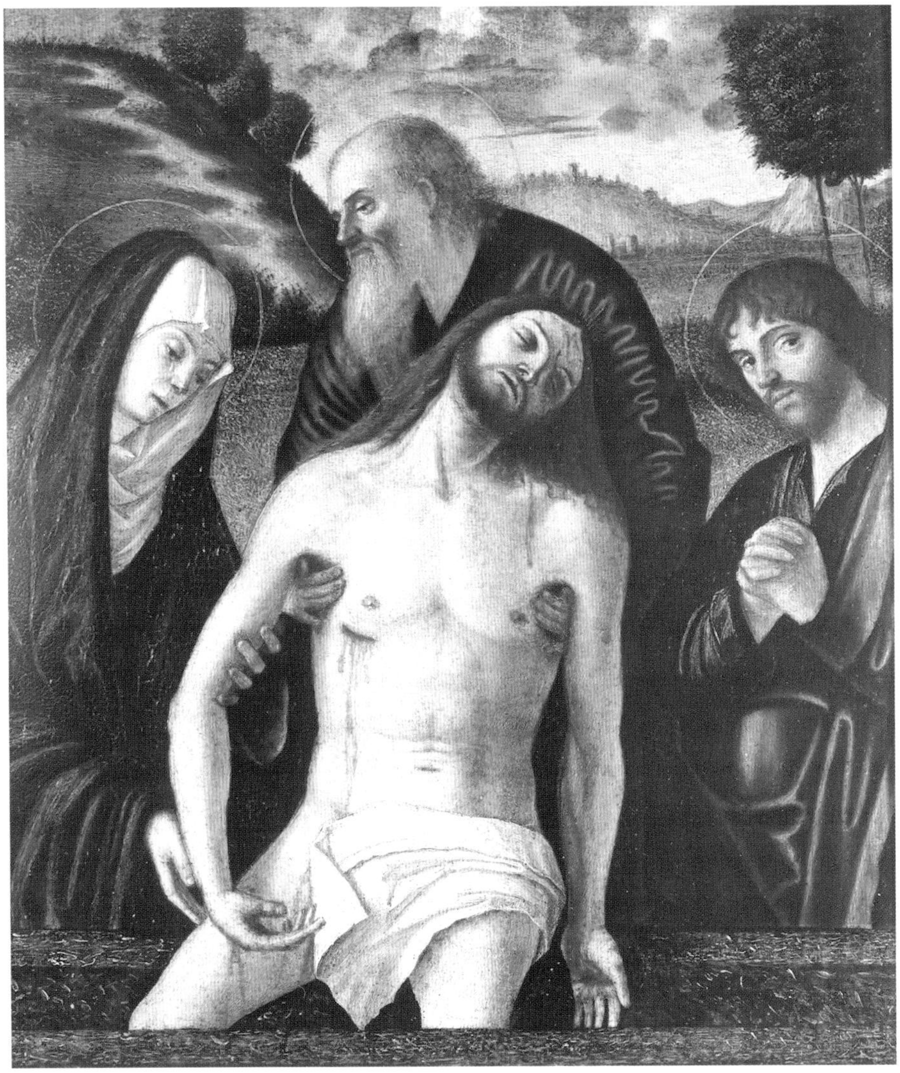

3 *THE DEAD CHRIST WITH MOURNERS*
Florence, formerly Contini-Bonacossi Collection.
Panel, 43 x 38 cm.

A small-scale panel for private devotion, with its affective sentiment calculated to make the spectator participate in the grief of the mourners. The compositional formula with the Dead Christ seated on a sarcophagus and supported by the figures of the Virgin, St Joseph of Arimathea and St John the Evangelist, is derived from a type made current by Giovanni Bellini. Probably one of Carpaccio's earliest works, dating from the late 1480s.

4 *THE VIRGIN WITH THE INFANT CHRIST AND ST JOHN THE BAPTIST*
Frankfurt, Städelsches Institut.
Panel, 69 x 54 cm. Inscribed: VICTORIS CARPATIO / VENETI OPUS

A small panel painted for devotional use in the home. It probably dates from quite early in Carpaccio's career, ca. 1490.

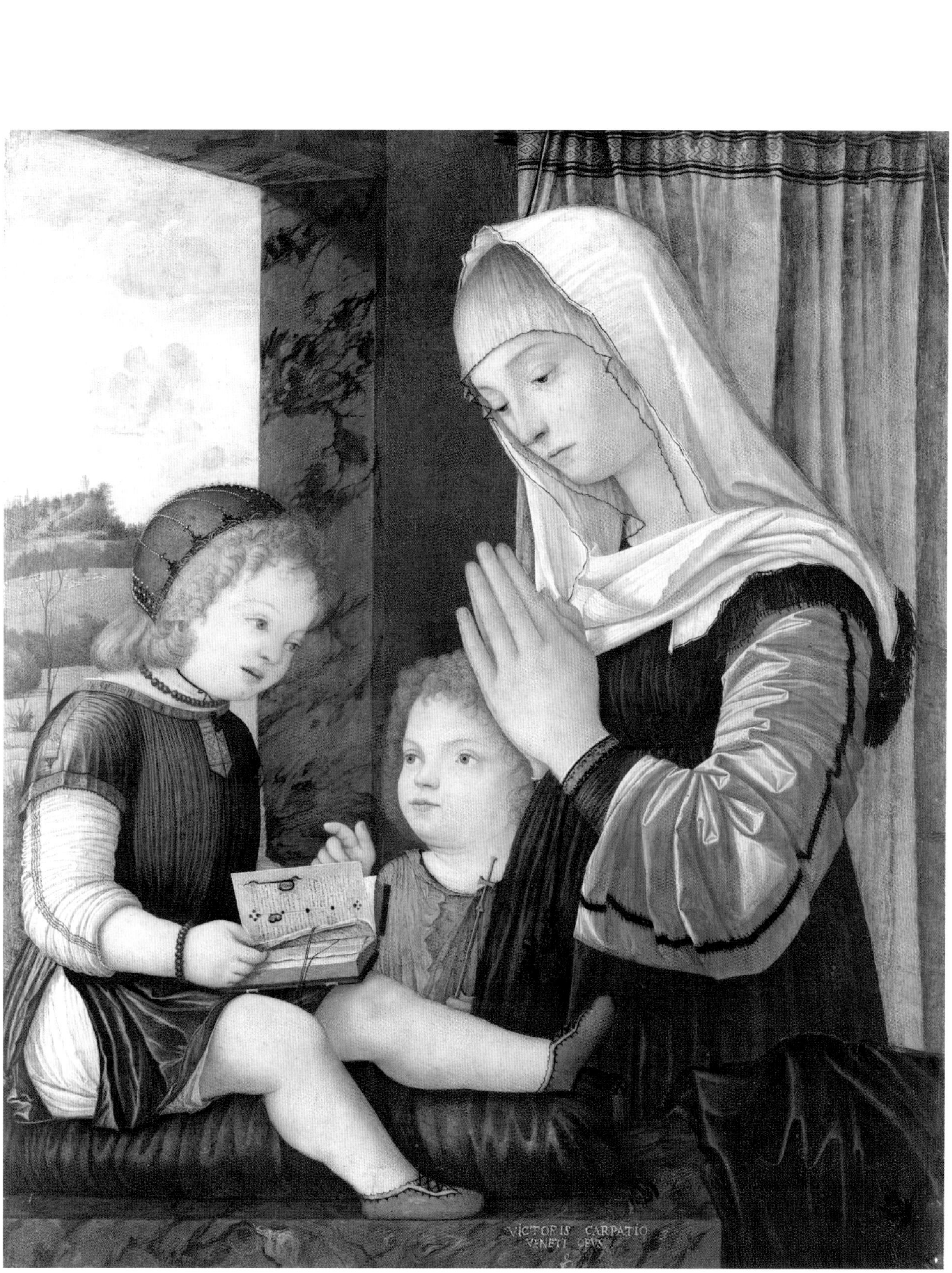
VICTORIS CARPATIO
VENETI OPVS

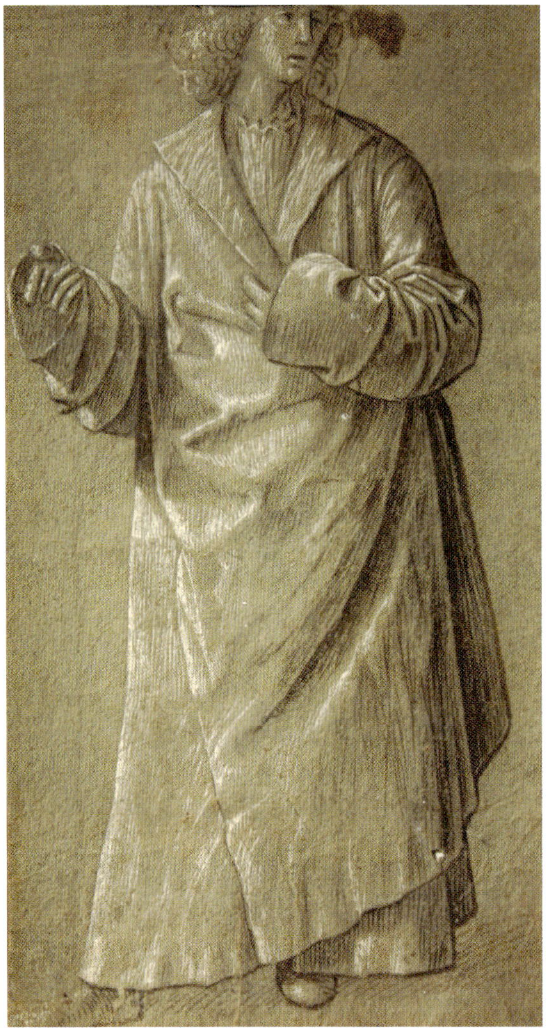

5 *STANDING FIGURE*
Valletta (Malta), National Museum.
Black chalk and pen in brown ink on blue paper, heightened with white. 215 x 114 mm.

A preliminary drawing, where no attention is paid to composition, for the figure standing immediately behind the foremost kneeling ambassador, in pl. 6. Carpaccio was evidently making use here of a studio model to study the fall of drapery. In the completed painting, the model's head was replaced by that of an older man, probably based on a separate portrait study of one of the confraternity officials.

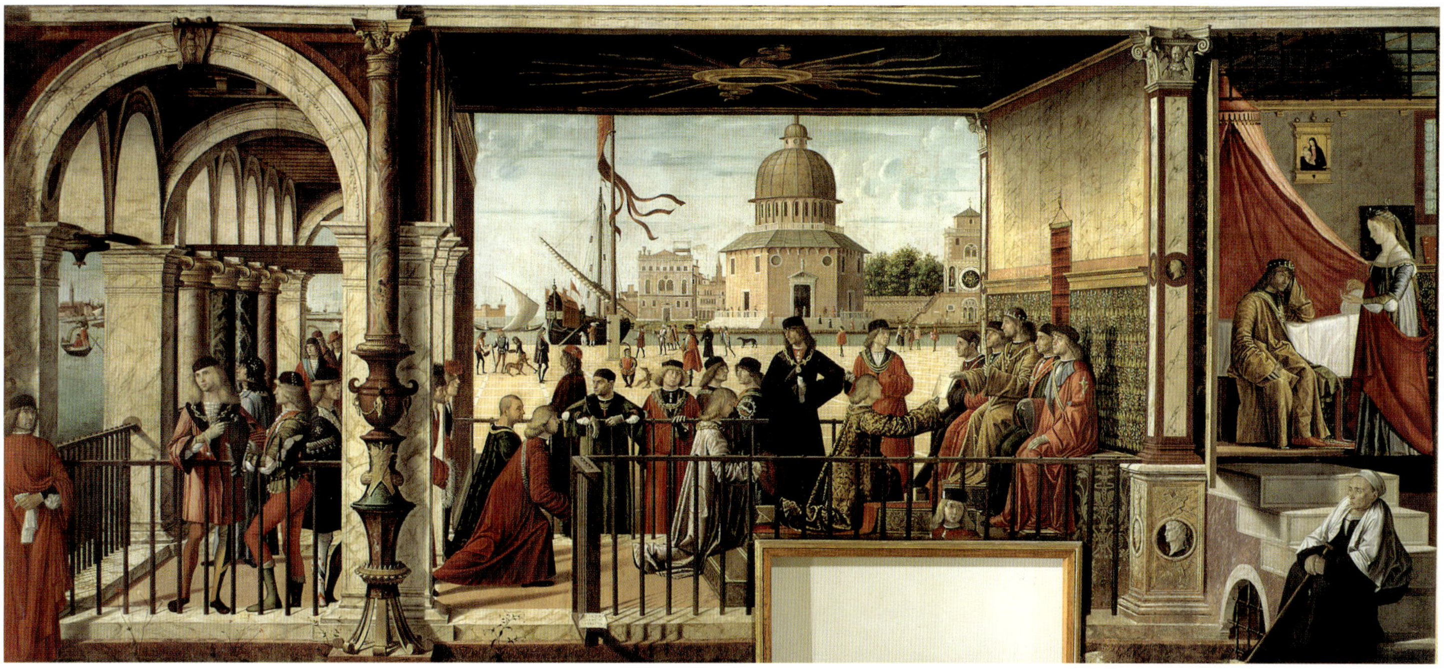

6 *THE RECEPTION OF THE AMBASSADORS*
Venice, Accademia.
Canvas, 275 x 589 cm.
Inscribed: OP. VICTORIS / CARPATIO / VENETI

The opening scene of the life cycle of St Ursula shows the reception by King Maurus of Brittany of a delegation sent by the pagan king of England. The ambassador is in the act of handing King Maurus a request that he give his daughter Ursula, renowned for her wisdom, holiness and beauty, in marriage to the son of the king of England, prince Ethereus. The king and his advisers receive the message courteously, but apprehensively: he is unwilling to wed his daughter to a pagan, and yet he very much fears the greater military power of England. In the scene on the right, which is separate in time and place from the main scene, the distraught King Maurus discusses his predicament with his daughter. The saintly princess, of a more decisive character than her father, resolves to accept the suit, provided certain conditions are met. These she enumerates on her fingers: firstly, her suitor must grant her ten virgins as companions; secondly, each of these must be accompanied by one thousand more virgins; and thirdly, prince Ethereus must be baptised in the Christian faith. He must also agree to delay the wedding for three years, allowing time for St Ursula and her eleven thousand virgin attendants to make a pilgrimage to Rome.

The inscription on the canvas does not record the date of its execution, but it is generally agreed that it must have been one of the last of the series to be painted. Particularly sophisticated is the manipulation of illusionistic space: since the front plane of the architecture coincides with that of the picture surface, various elements in the immediate foreground – the man in a gown on the far left, the marble column on its elaborate base, the plants, the sharply foreshortened iron gate, and the flight of steps with the old woman on the far right – appear to project into the real space of the spectator. The area cut out of the canvas in the bottom centre corresponds to the top part of a door in the original Scuola building.

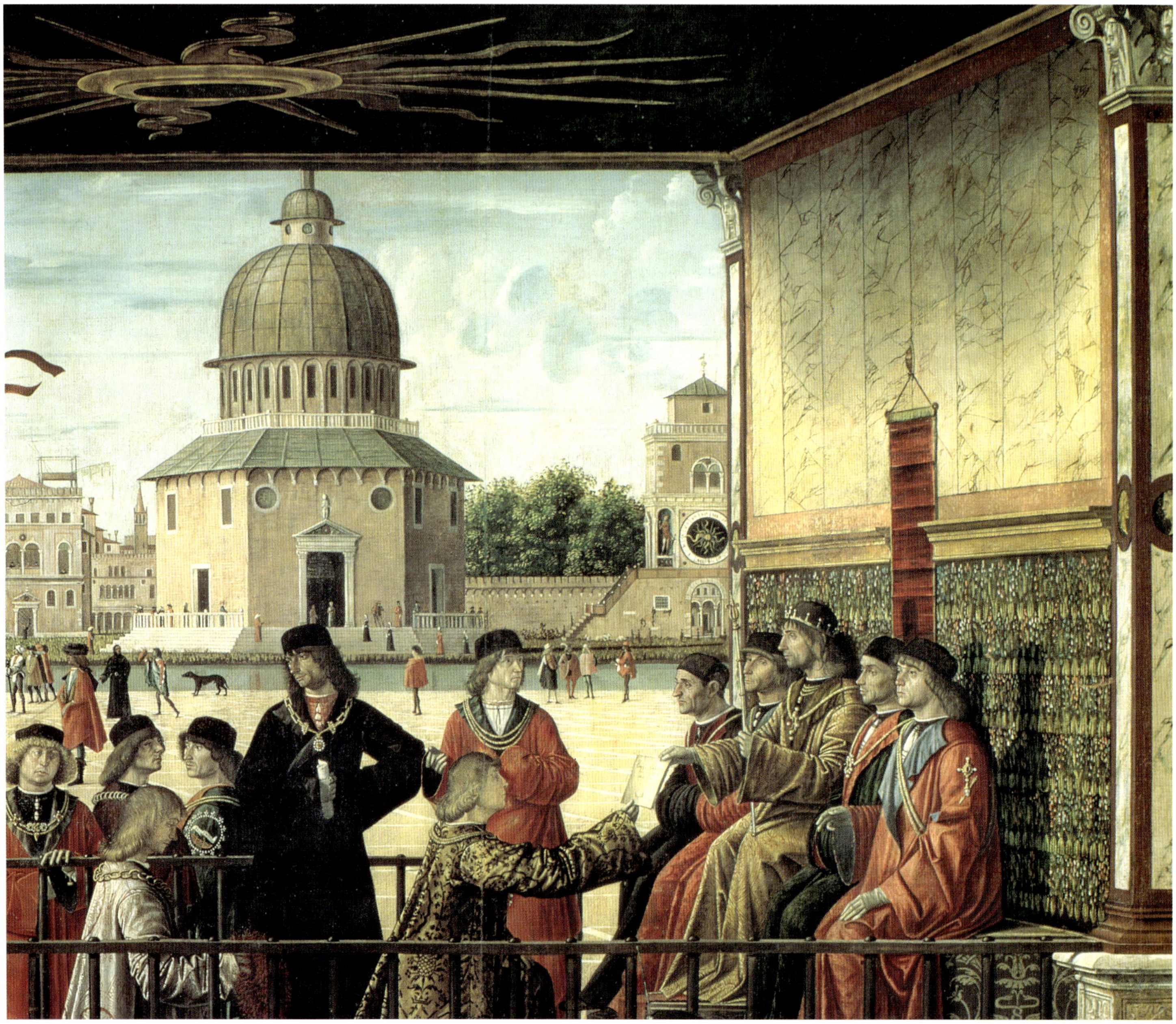

Detail of pl 6.

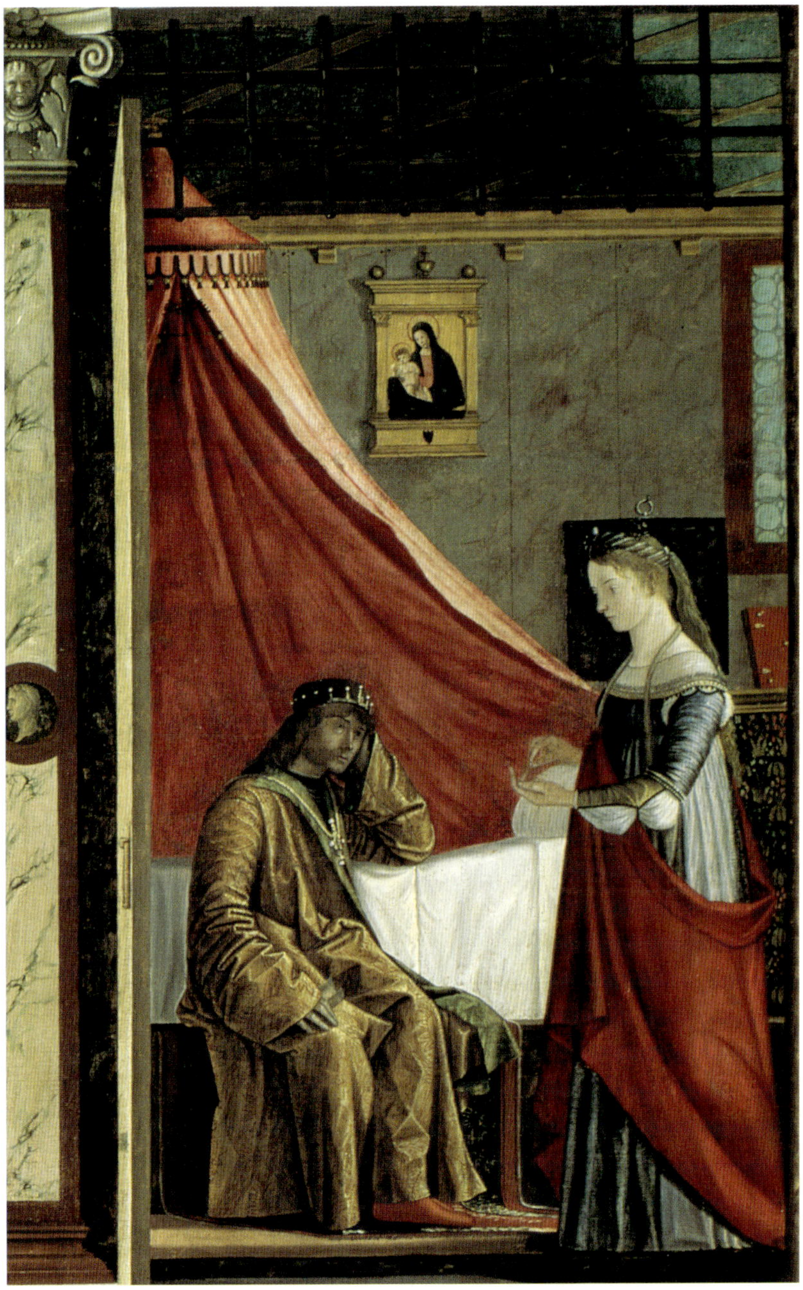

Details of pl. 6.

An intimate scene of discussion between St Ursula and her anxious father. Above the bed is a half-length painting of the Virgin and Child, a type of holy image very popular in fifteenth century Venice. The implication is presumably that the saint receives heavenly guidance in all her actions.

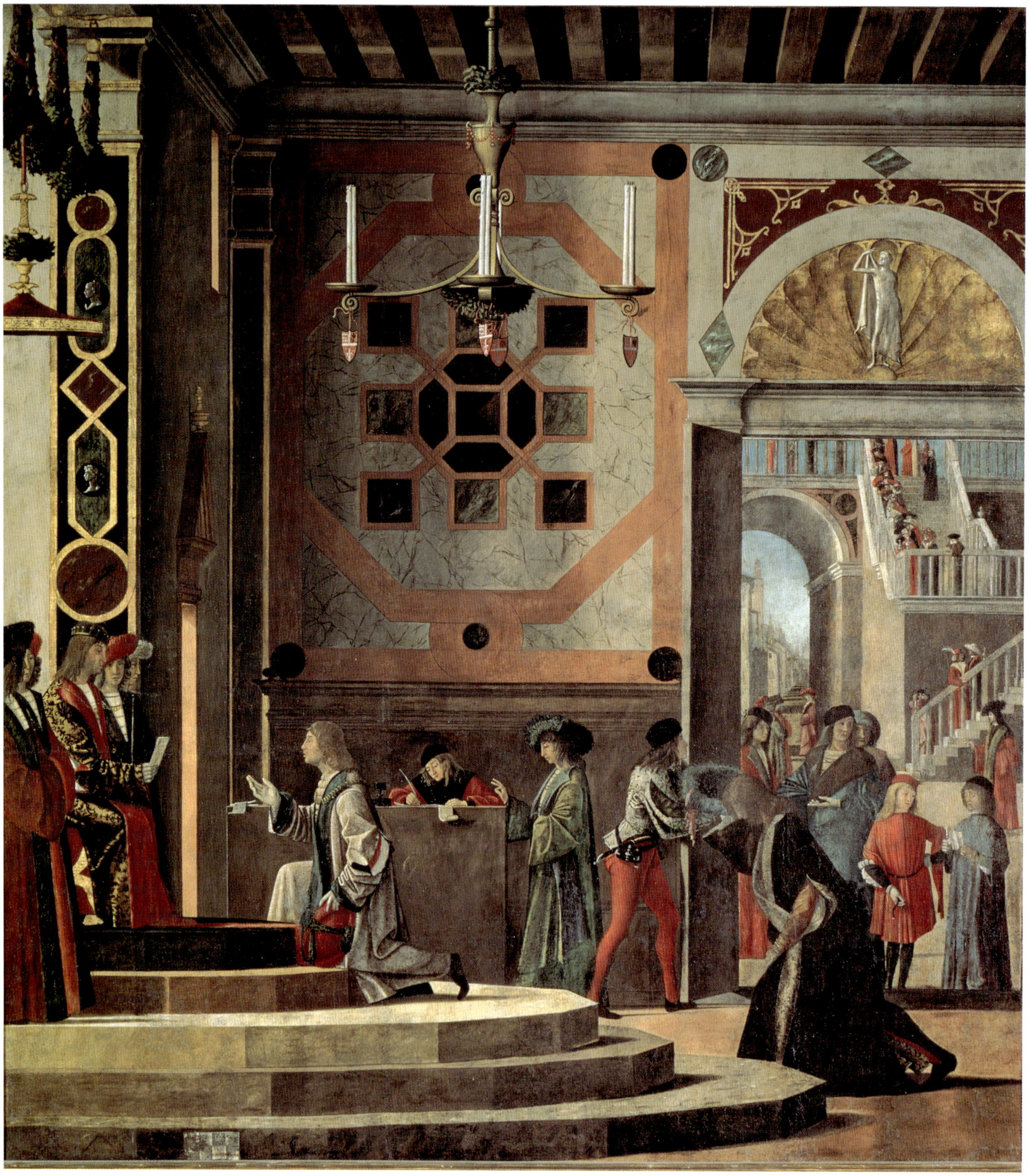

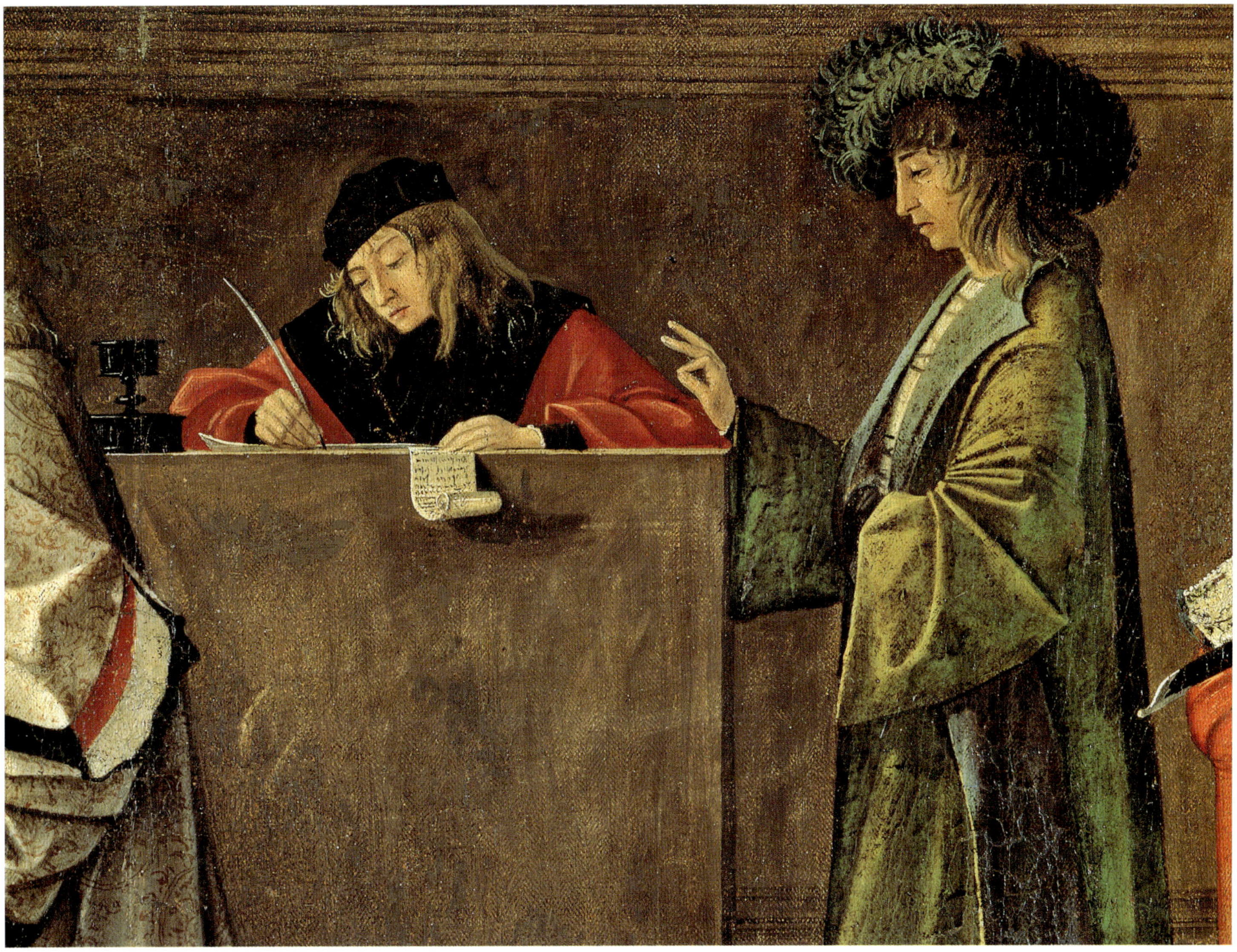

7 *THE ENGLISH AMBASSADORS TAKING THEIR LEAVE*
Venice, Accademia.
Canvas, 280 x 253 cm. Inscribed: CAR/PACIO VENETI/OPUS

In a hall within the royal palace, King Maurus makes known to the English ambassadors his daughter's conditions of acceptance, and they take their solemn leave. The splendour of the setting reflects the Venetian taste for revetting public interiors with patterned inlays of different coloured marbles, the most famous contemporary example of which is the church of S. Maria dei Miracoli. Together with the previous and succeeding scenes, datable to ca. 1496–8.

(above) Detail of pl. 7.

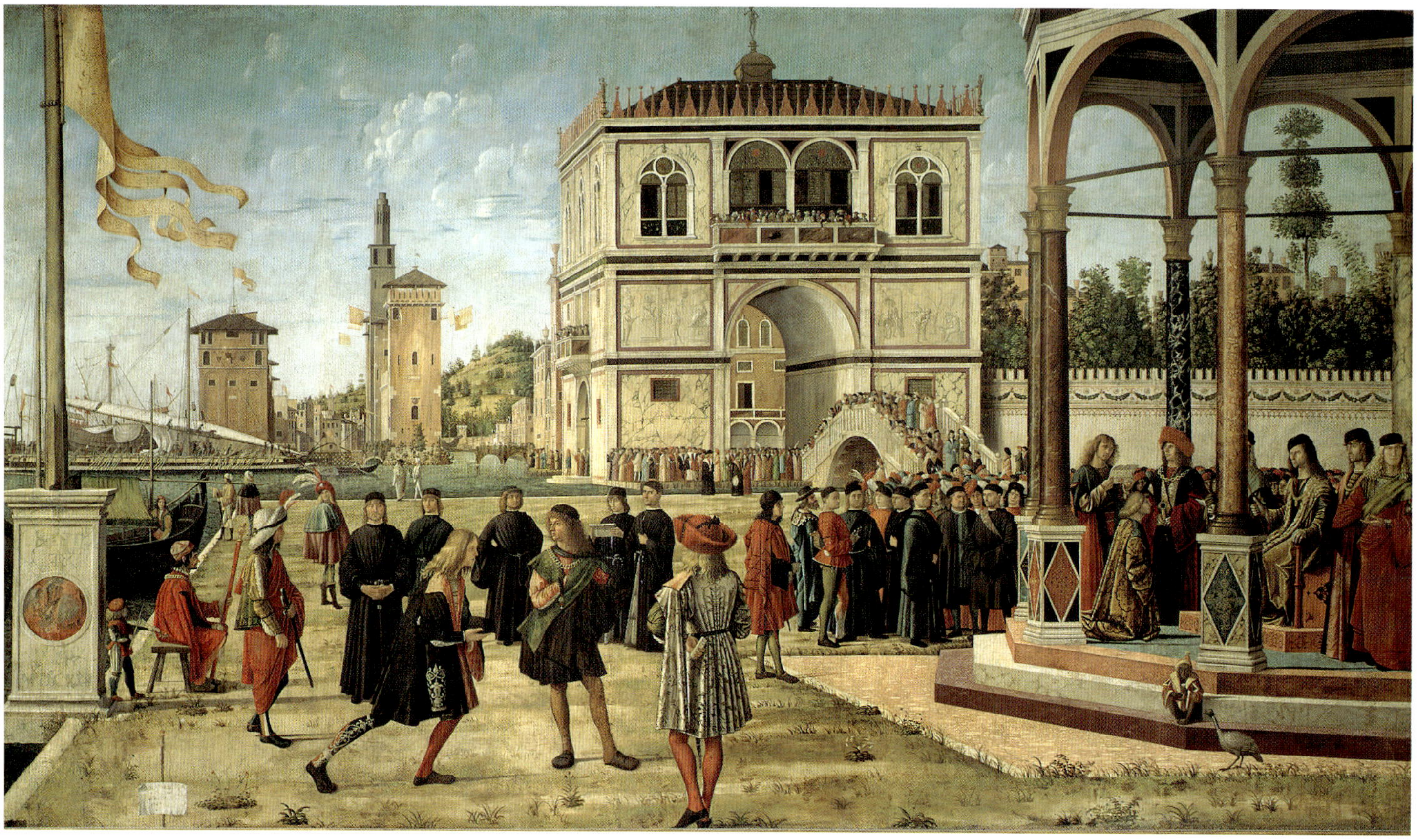

8 *THE RETURN OF THE AMBASSADORS TO ENGLAND*
Venice, Accademia.
Canvas, 297 x 527 cm. Inscribed:
VICTORIS/CARPATIO/VENETI/OPUS

The ambassadors arrive back in England, and deliver St Ursula's message to their master. The prince is so enamoured of her that he agrees to accept her conditions. The large building in the background is probably meant to represent the royal palace, and various aspects of its design – the triumphal arch at the centre, the free-standing figure on the roof, and the marble relief inlays on the walls – suggest that Carpaccio was attempting to create a specifically pagan type of architecture. The relief on the right-hand side is adapted from a bronze plaque by the Venetian sculptor Vittore Camelio, of which versions now exist in the Ca'd'Oro in Venice, and in the Victoria and Albert Museum in London. It represents two scenes from the life of Cupid: on the left, he is educated by Mercury, with Mars looking on; and on the right, he is held up by his mother Venus, while Vulcan forges him a pair of wings at an anvil. Perhaps Carpaccio intended the theme of Cupid as a commentary on the love of the English prince for St Ursula. To the right of the palace is a walled garden of a type quite common in Carpaccio's Venice.

(right) Detail of pl. 8.

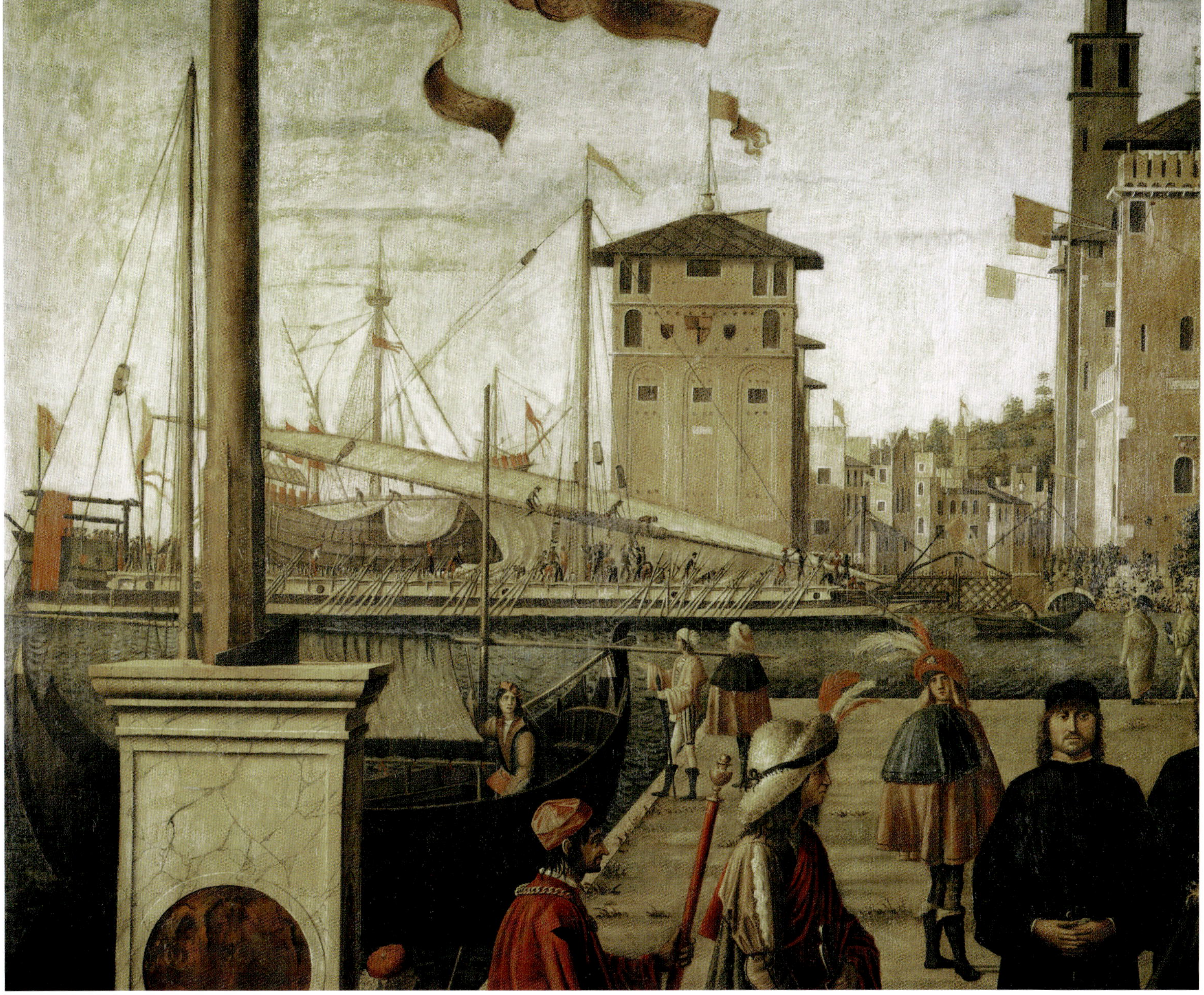

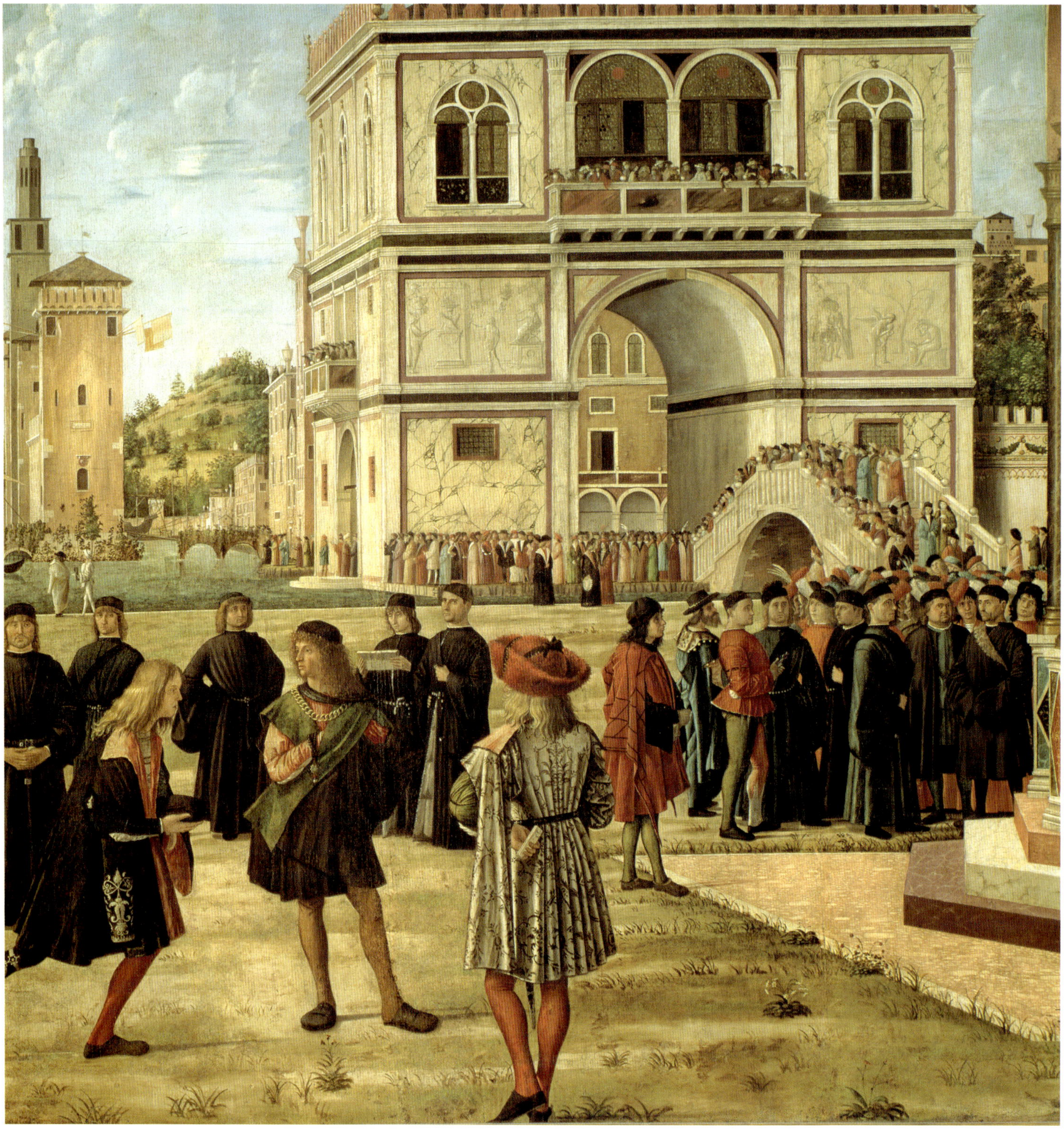

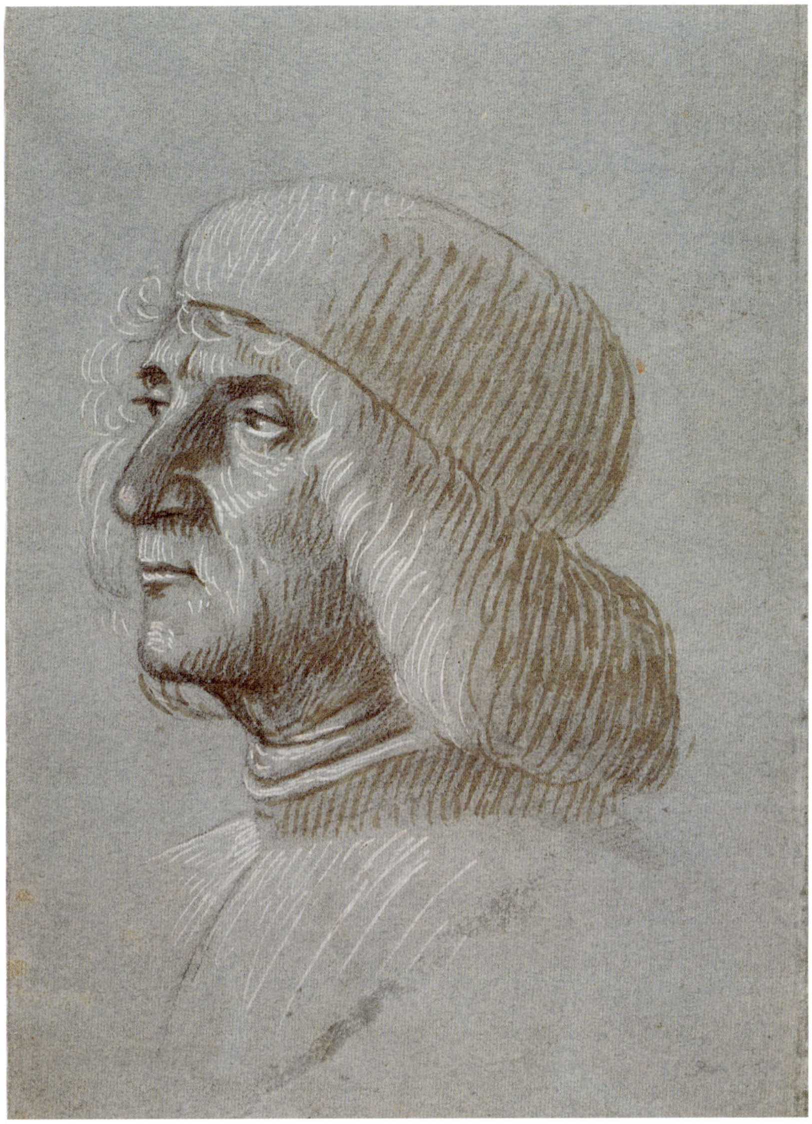

9 *HEAD OF A MIDDLE-AGED MAN*
London, British Museum.
Brush in brown, over a preliminary drawing in black chalk on blue paper, heightened with white, 267 x 187 mm.

Apparently the portrait of a specific individual, perhaps intended for inclusion in one of the crowd scenes of the St Ursula cycle. Carpaccio, like Gentile Bellini before him, probably made dozens of such portrait studies in preparation for his narrative cycles.

(left) Detail of pl. 8.

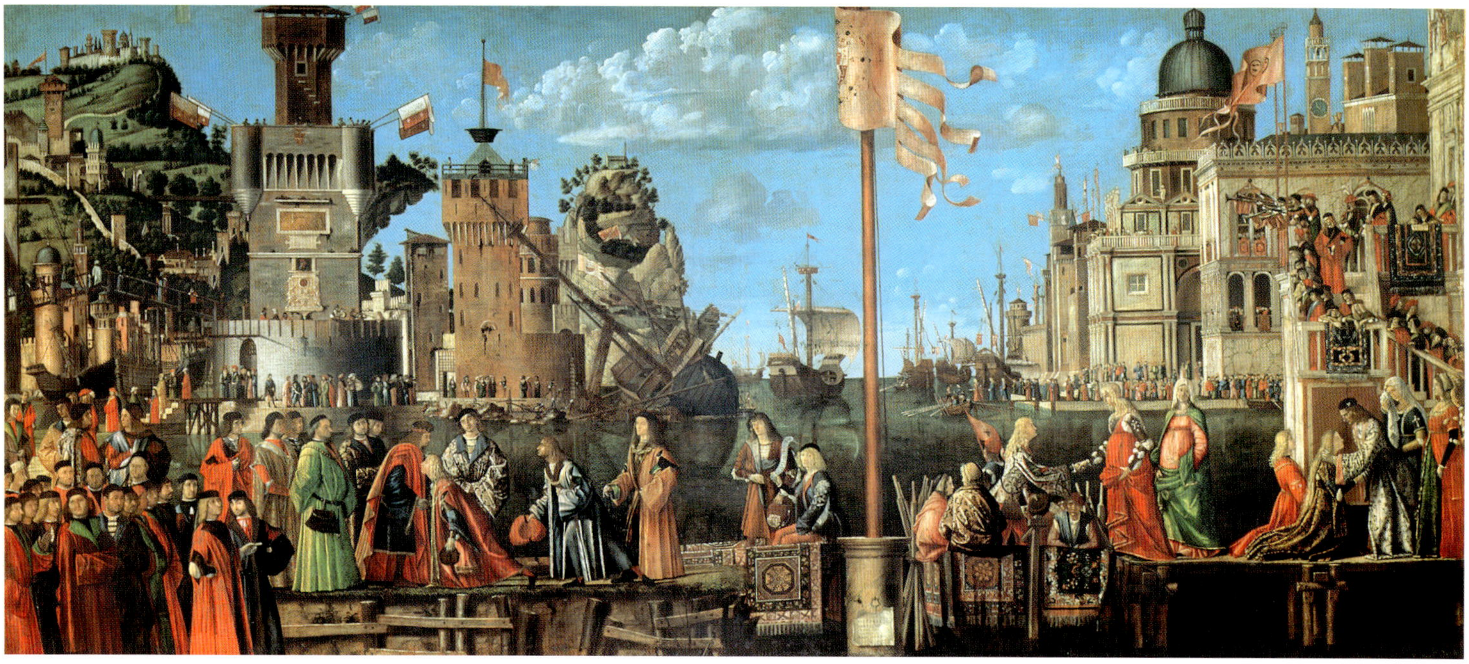

10 *THE DEPARTURE OF ST URSULA*
Venice, Accademia.
Canvas, 280 x 611 cm. Inscribed:
VICTORIS/CARPATIO/VENETI/OPUS/
MCCCCLXXXXV.

In the largest canvas of the cycle, two separate scenes are depicted on either side of the foreground flagstaff. On the left, Prince Ethereus bids farewell to his father as he sets off to join his betrothed on her pilgrimage. At the far right, the prince is seen again, kneeling with St Ursula as she embraces her own father; to the right of the flagstaff, a group of the princess's companions are helped into the rowing boat that is to ferry them to one of the galleys waiting in the harbour beyond. Further groups of virgins are to be seen embarking in the background. The scorpion visible on the base on the flagstaff immediately above the *cartellino* bearing the inscription is an astrological reference to the fact that on the Feast of St Ursula (October 21st) the sun enters the sign of Scorpio.

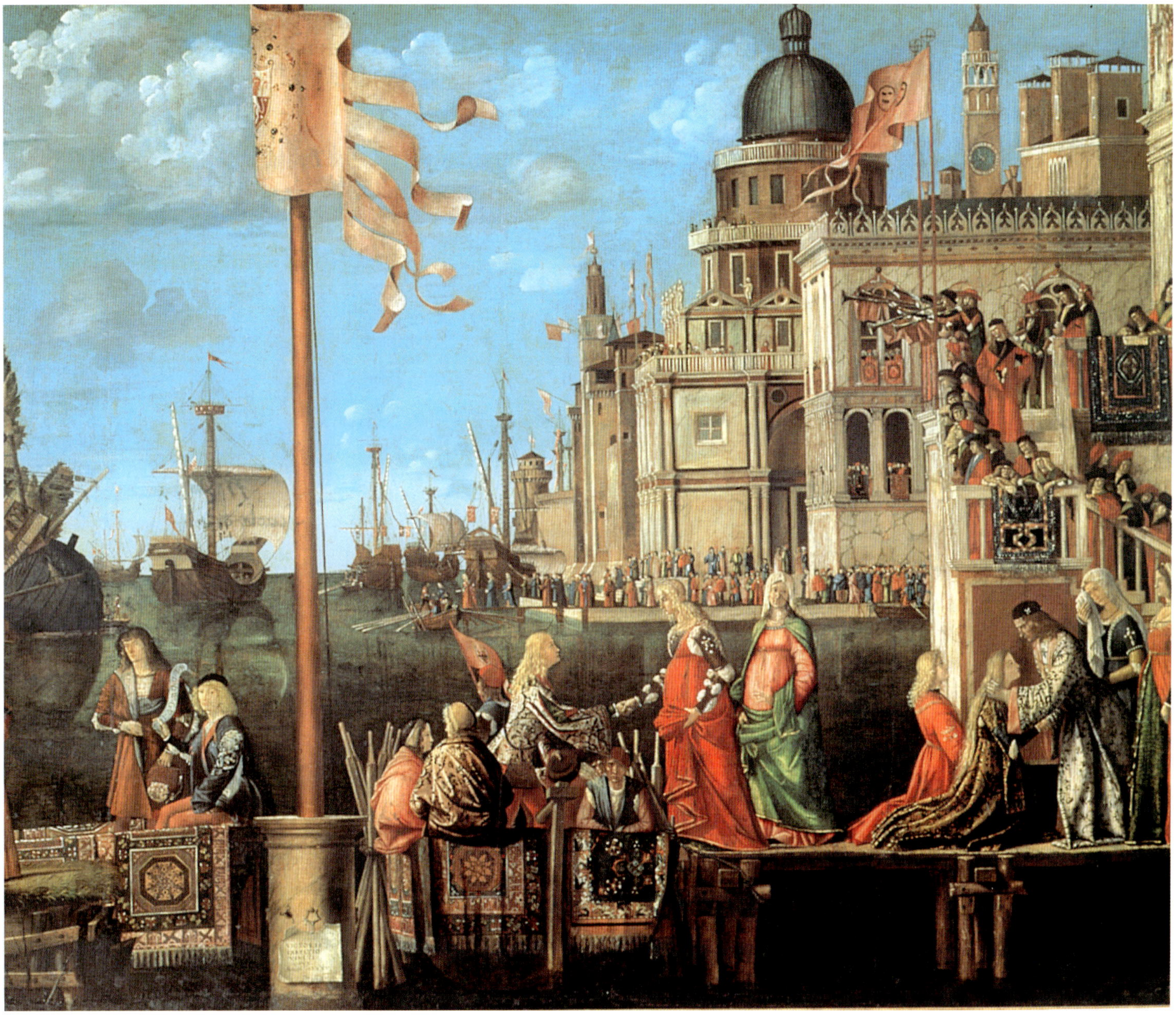

Detail of pl. 10.

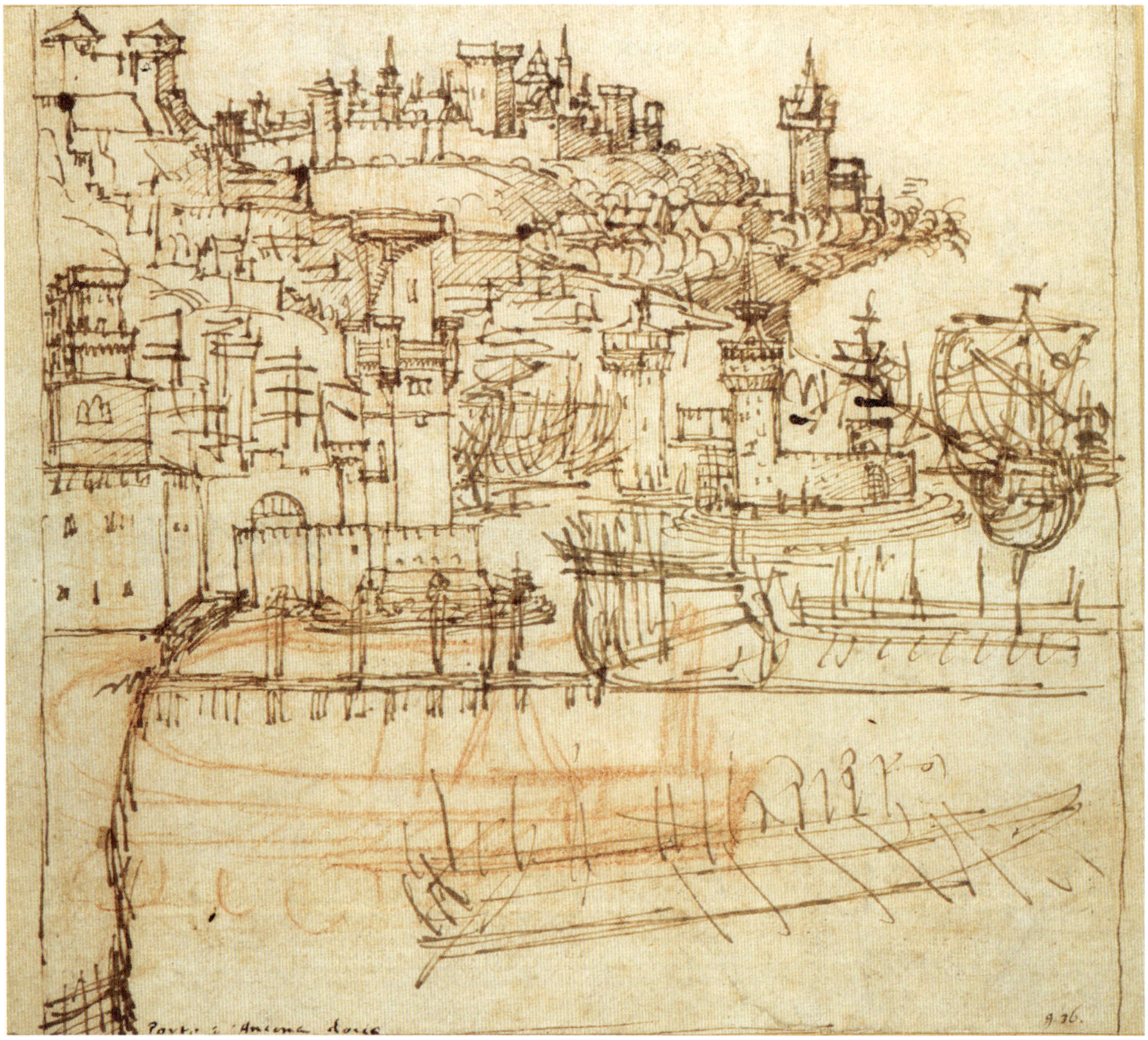

11 *FORTIFIED HARBOUR WITH SHIPS*
London, British Museum.
Pen and ink over a sketch in red chalk, 172 x 192 mm.

Usually considered to be a sketch for the left background of pl. 10 although the looseness of the relationship has also prompted the suggestion that it may have been connected rather with one of the paintings Carpaccio executed for the Doge's Palace. Two of the towers most prominently visible in the middle-ground were adapted from woodcuts made by Reuwich of the towers at Candia on Crete, and at Rhodes; their inclusion in the painting does not seem to have any particular iconographical justification, and may be ascribed purely to Carpaccio's taste for the picturesque.

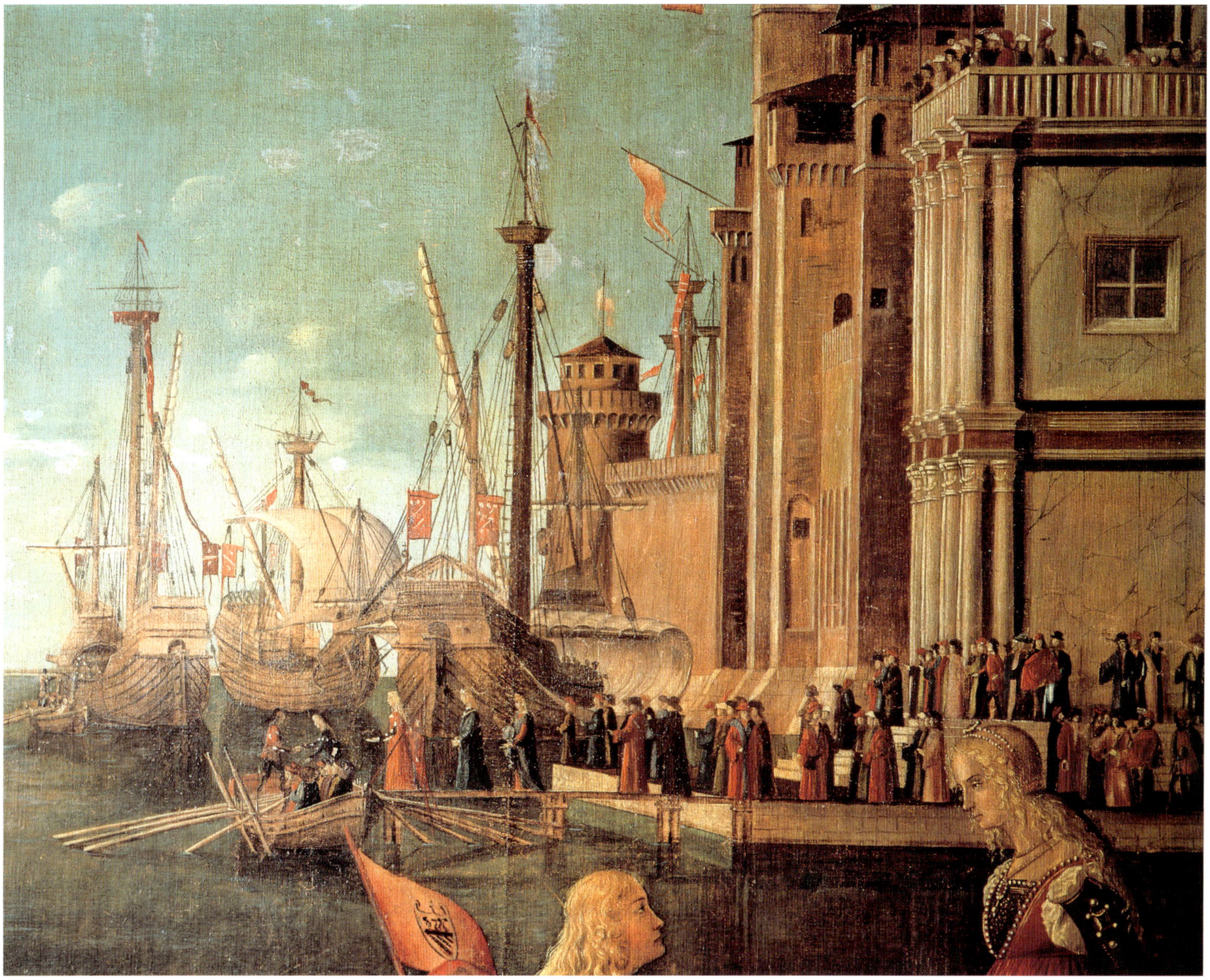

Detail of pl. 10.

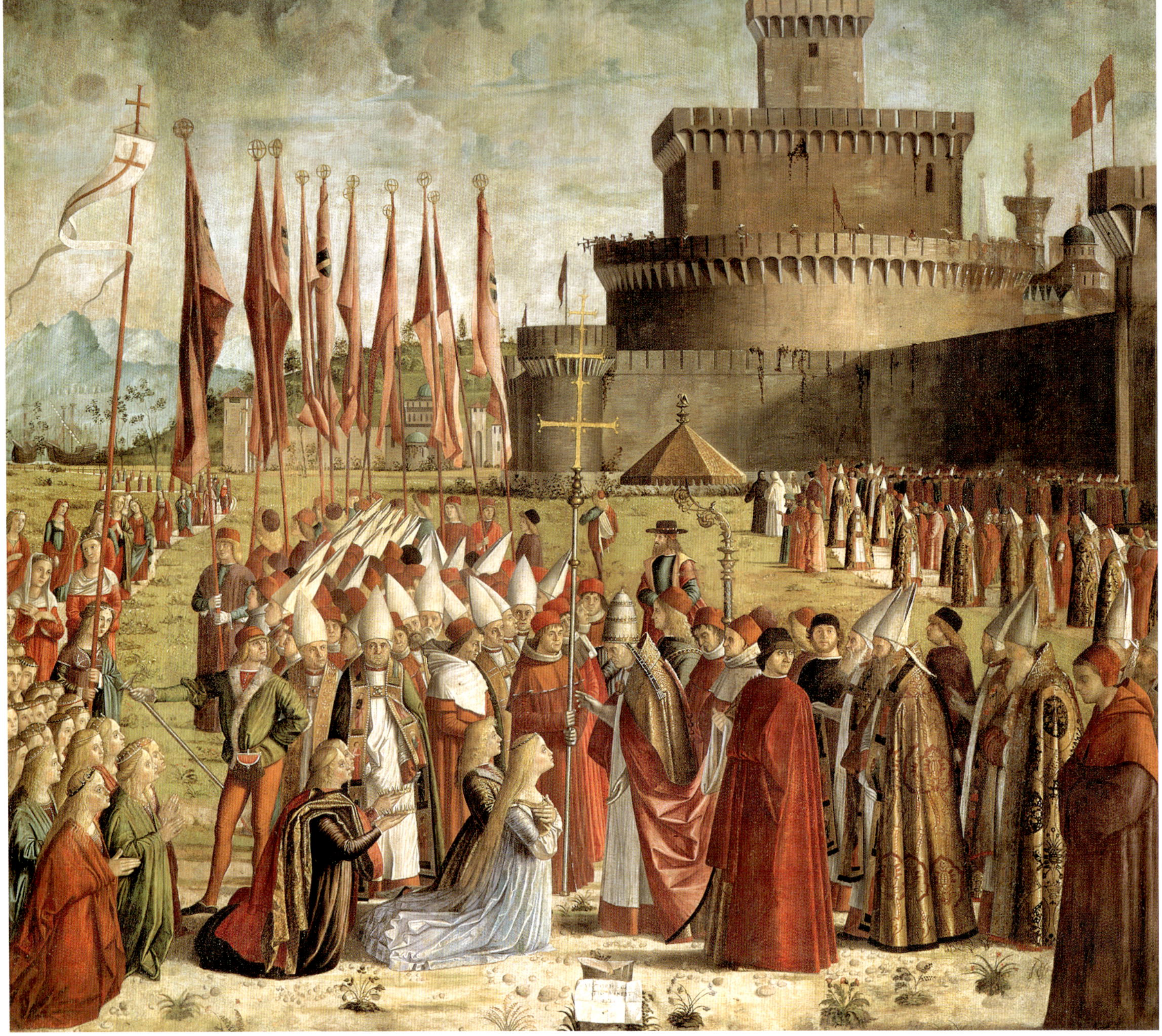

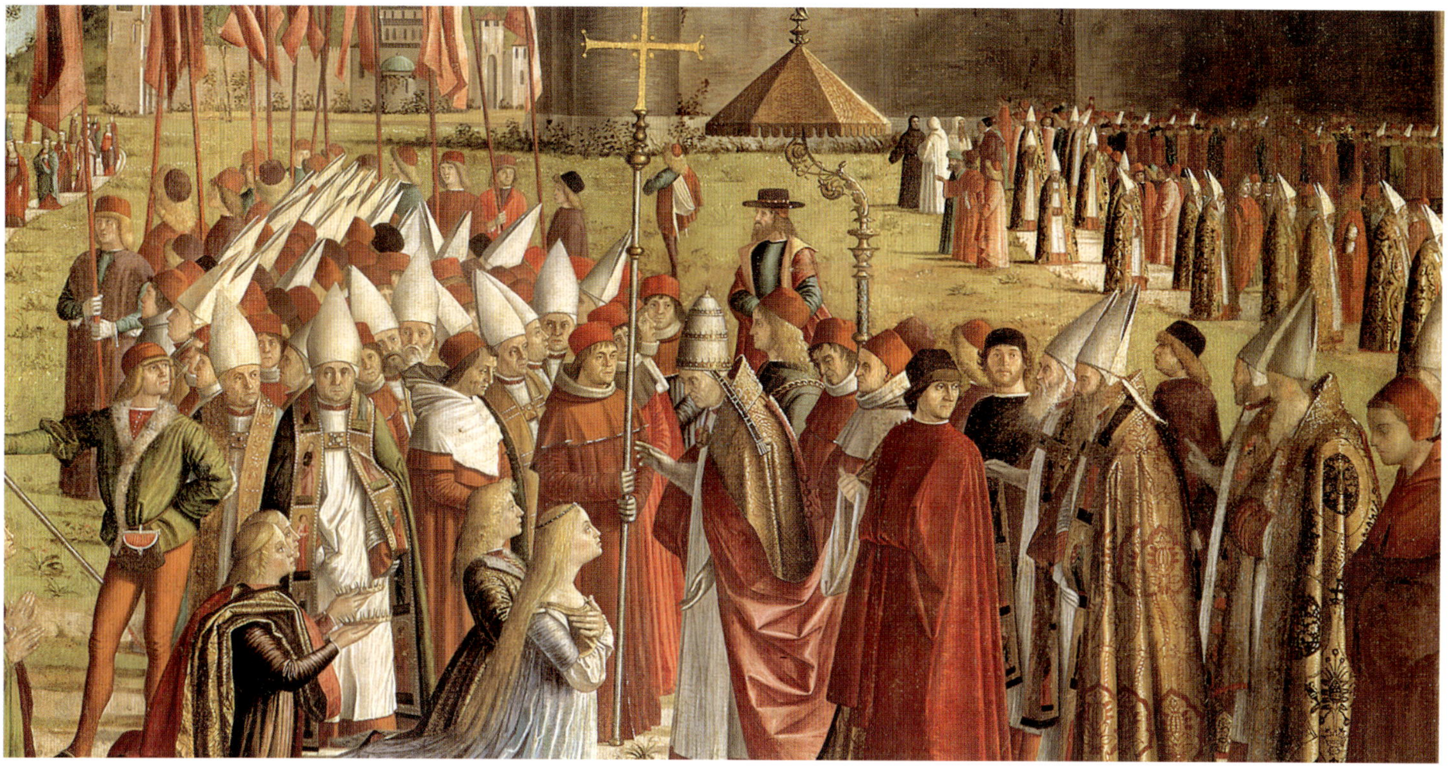

(left)
12 *ST URSULA GREETED BY THE POPE IN ROME*
Venice, Accademia.
Canvas, 281 x 307 cm. Inscribed: VICTORIS CAR/PATIO VENETI/OPUS.

Upon their arrival in Rome, the bethrothed couple are met by Pope Cyriacus and the members of his curia. To the left is the long procession of St Ursula's attendants, making their way from the harbour in the far distance. In the left background is the city of Rome, dominated by the papal fortress of the Castel Sant'Angelo.
The inscription on the canvas does not record its date, but stylistic and historical considerations suggest a dating of ca. 1493–4 (see following note).

(above) Detail of pl. 12.

The dignitary in the foreground standing to the right of the Pope, with his eyes cast backwards over his shoulder, has been convincingly identified as a portrait of Ermolao Barbaro, the distinguished humanist scholar who was exiled from Venice in 1491, following his appointment as Patriarch of Aquilea without the prior approval of the Venetian Government. Barbaro then retired to Rome, where he died in 1493. Although the fact that he is not shown in his patriarchal robes might seem to indicate that the canvas was painted before 1491, it has been pointed out that in the last years of his life Barbaro's name was held in disgrace in Venice, and hence the portrait is more probably posthumous. A date of ca. 1493–4 also seems more consistent with the painting's style. More difficult to prove, but equally attractive, is a theory identifying the head immediately to Barbaro's right, with eyes looking out at the spectator, as a portrait of Carpaccio himself. If he had made a youthful visit to Rome, as some scholars believe, he might indeed have wished to commemorate the event in this way.

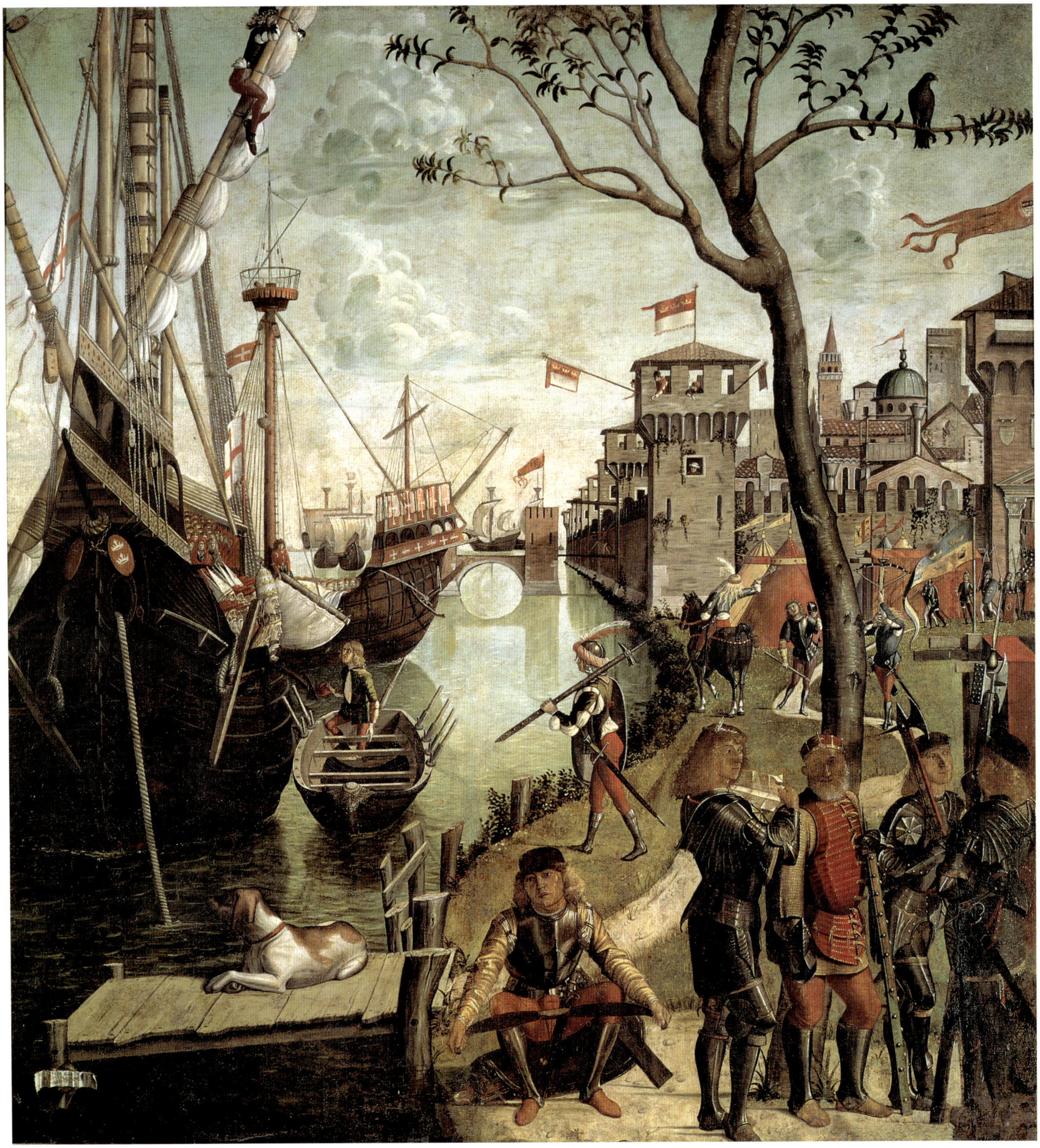

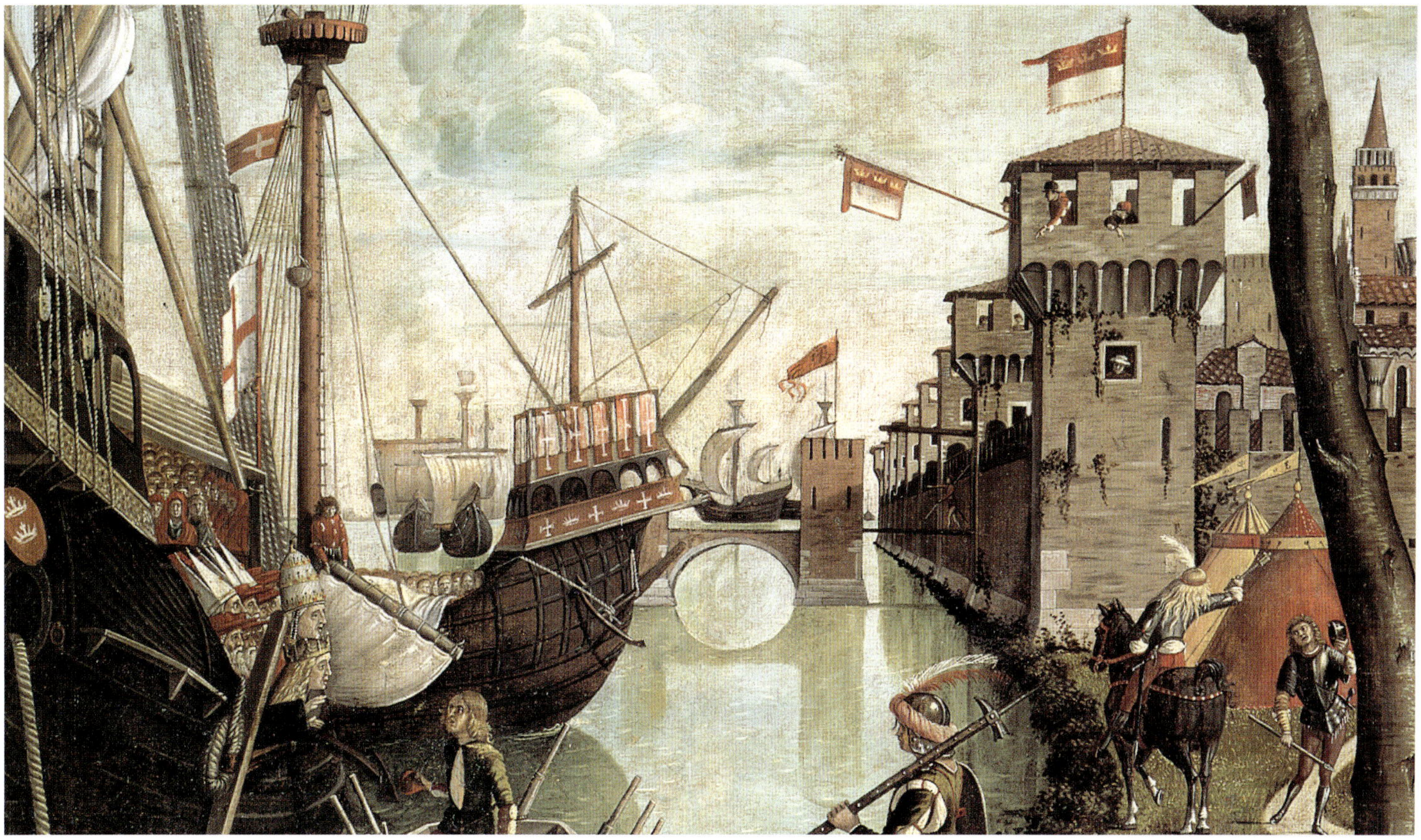

13 *THE ARRIVAL OF ST URSULA AT COLOGNE* Venice, Accademia.
Canvas, 280 x 255 cm. Inscribed: OP. VICTORIS. CHARPATIO / VENETI MCCCC LXXXX M. /SEPTEMBRIS.

On her return from Rome, St Ursula and her companions are accompanied by the Pope and a retinue of cardinals. As they sail up the Rhine to disembark at Cologne, they find the city besieged by an army of Huns. This canvas, inscribed September 1490, is Carpaccio's earliest dated work, and scholars have deduced from it the approximate date of the artist's birth: since it is evidently so much less mature than the later canvases of the cycle, it is probably the work of a master only recently matriculated, and therefore aged around twenty-five. The fortifications of the city strongly recall those still in part surviving in Venetian *terraferma* towns like Treviso and Castelfranco.

(above) Detail of pl. 13. The drawbridge is reflected in the still water. Flags and pennants are flying vigorously from corbeled towers manned by excited guardsmen.

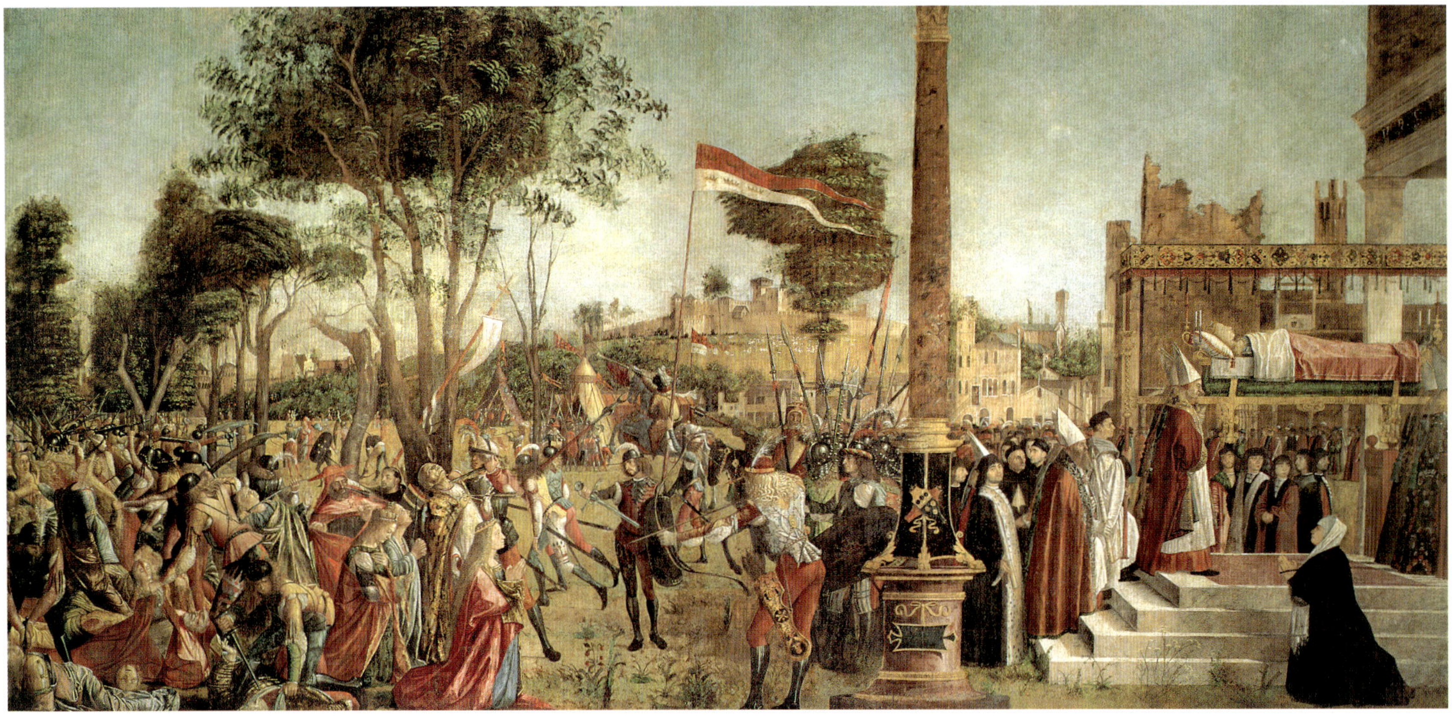

14 *THE MARTYRDOM AND FUNERAL OF ST URSULA*
Venice, Accademia.
Canvas, 271 x 561 cm. Inscribed: VICTORIS CARPATIO/VENETI. OPUS/ MCCCCLXXX/XIII

Again, two separate scenes are shown. On the left, St Ursula, the Pope and their companions are massacred by Huns, in fulfilment of the angel's prophecy; on the right, the martyred saint is carried on her funeral bier to her tomb. Conspicuously placed on the base of the dividing column is the escutcheon of the Loredan family, well-known benefactors of the confraternity of St Ursula; the pious lady kneeling in prayer on the right foreground may well be a portrait of a member of the family.

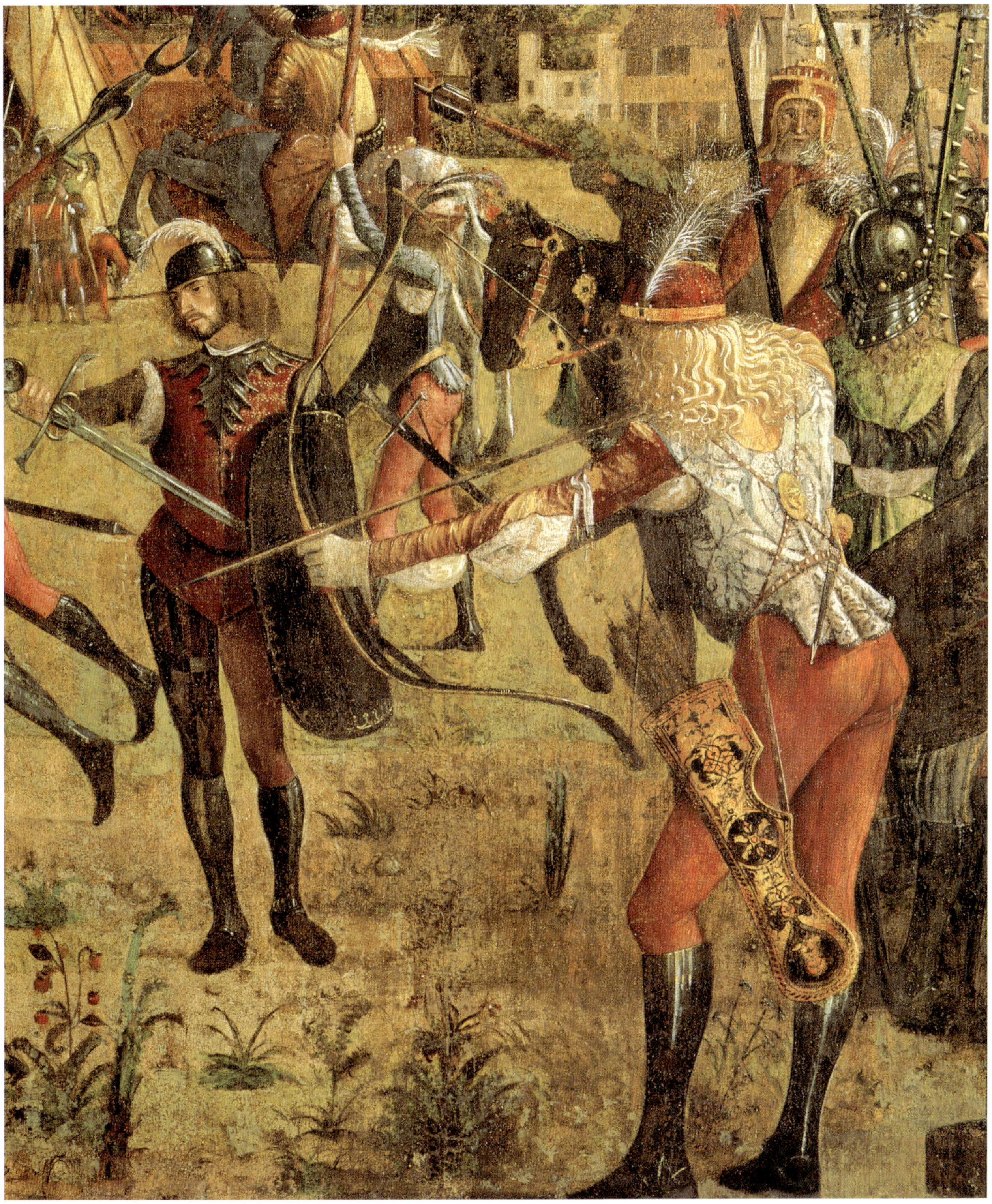

Detail of pl. 14.

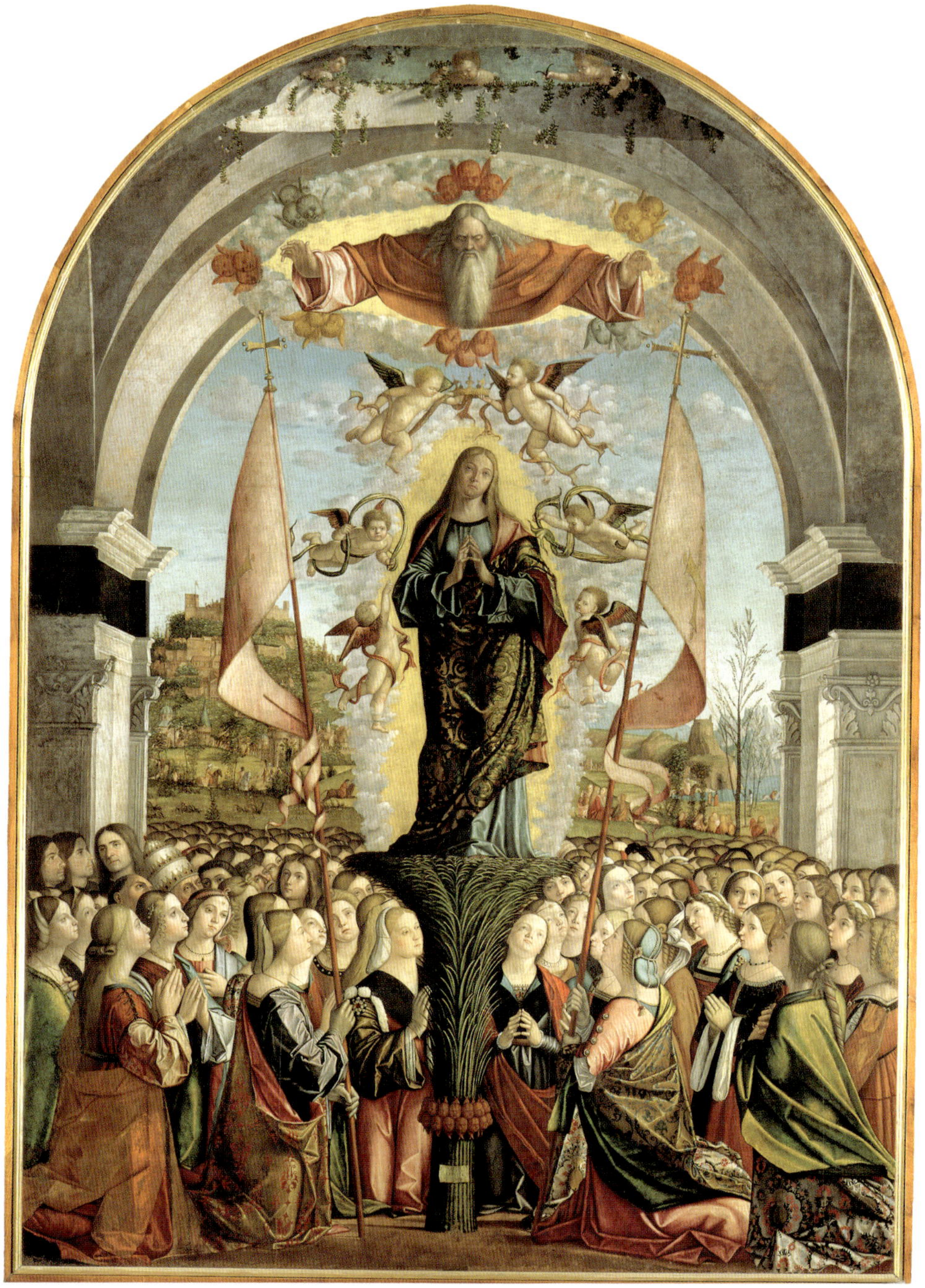

15 *THE GLORIFICATION OF ST URSULA*
Venice, Accademia.
Canvas, 481 x 336 cm. Inscribed: O P./VICTORIS / CARPATIO / MCCCCLXXXXI.

The altarpiece for the Scuola di S. Orsola, and thematically intended as the climax of the life cycle: after her virtuous life and martyrdom, St Ursula is crowned by angels in heaven. Accompanying her, in eternity as on earth, are her eleven thousand virgin companions, and also Pope Cyriacus. Although the canvas is dated 1491, many critics believe on stylistic grounds that it must have been repainted about a decade later.

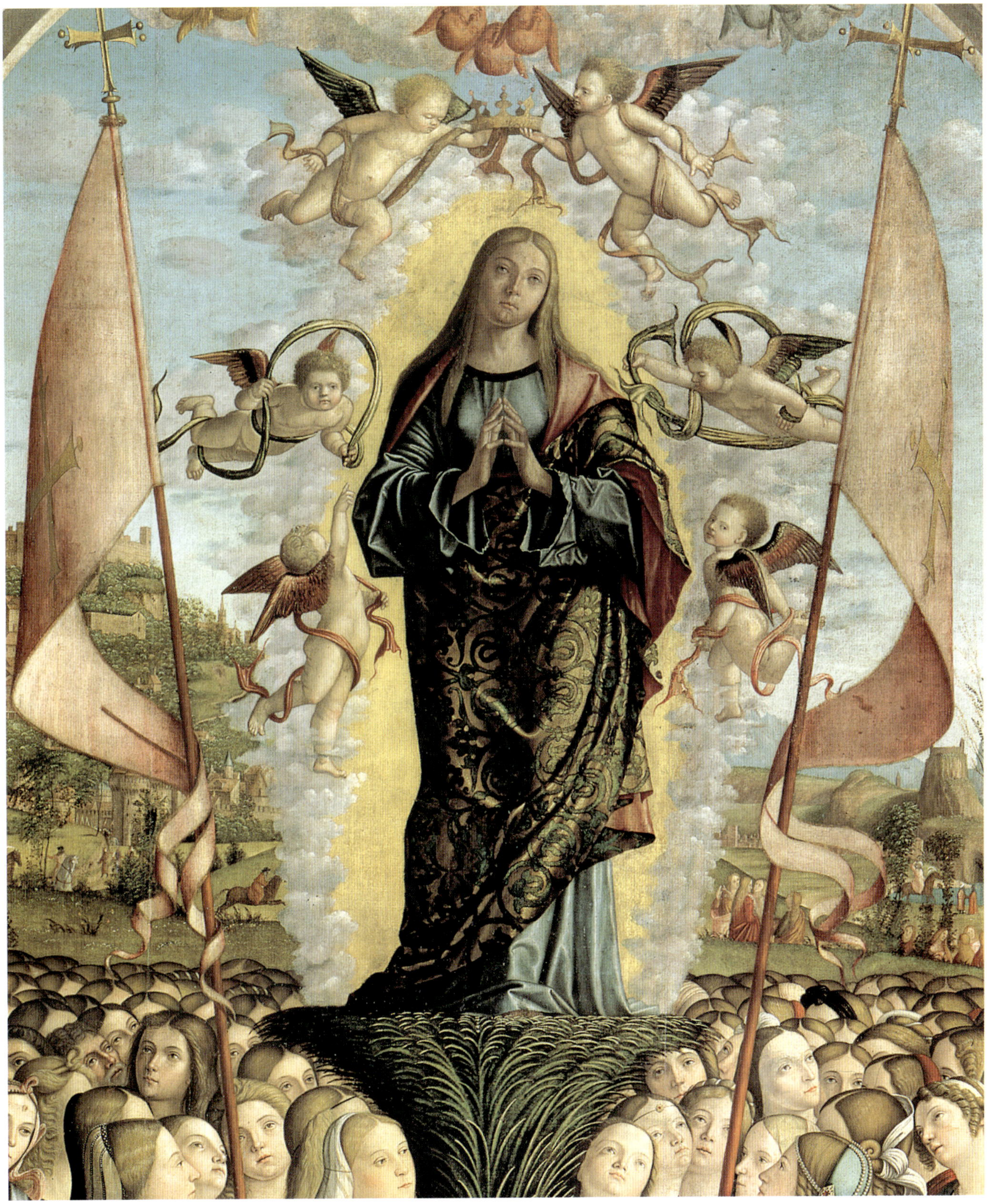

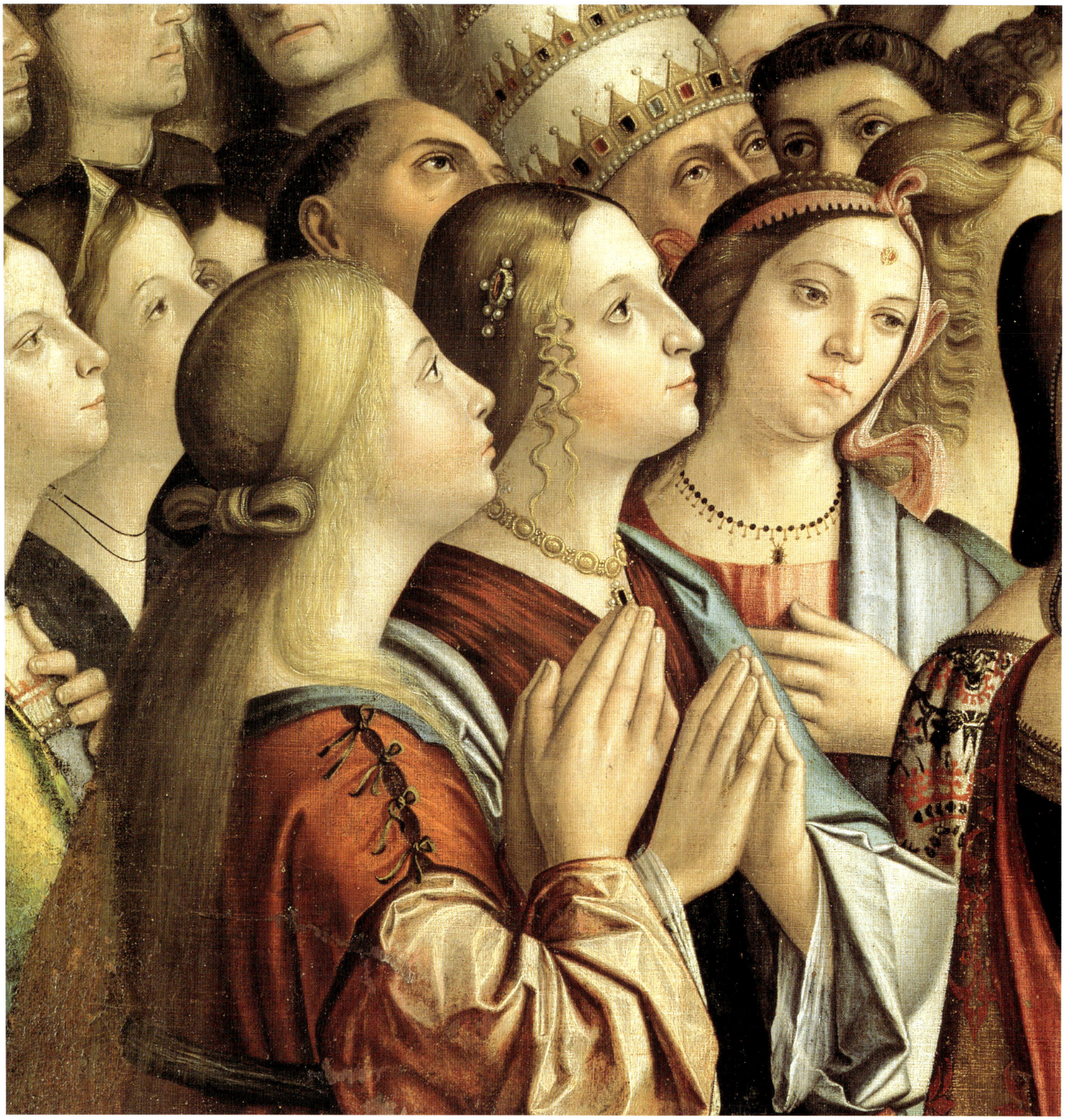

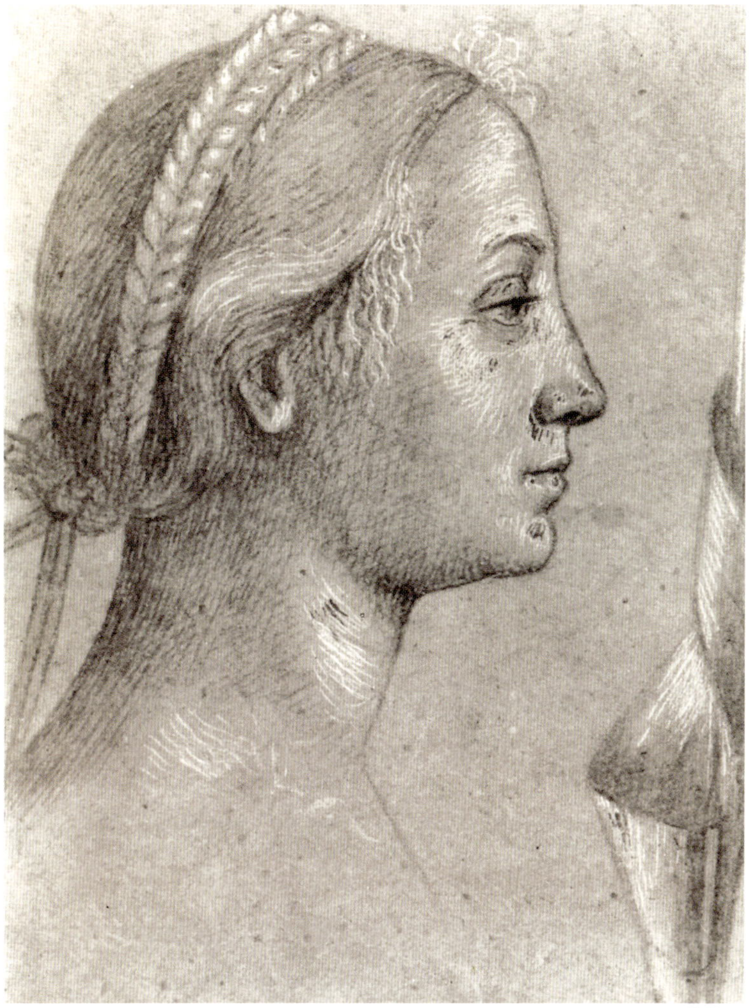

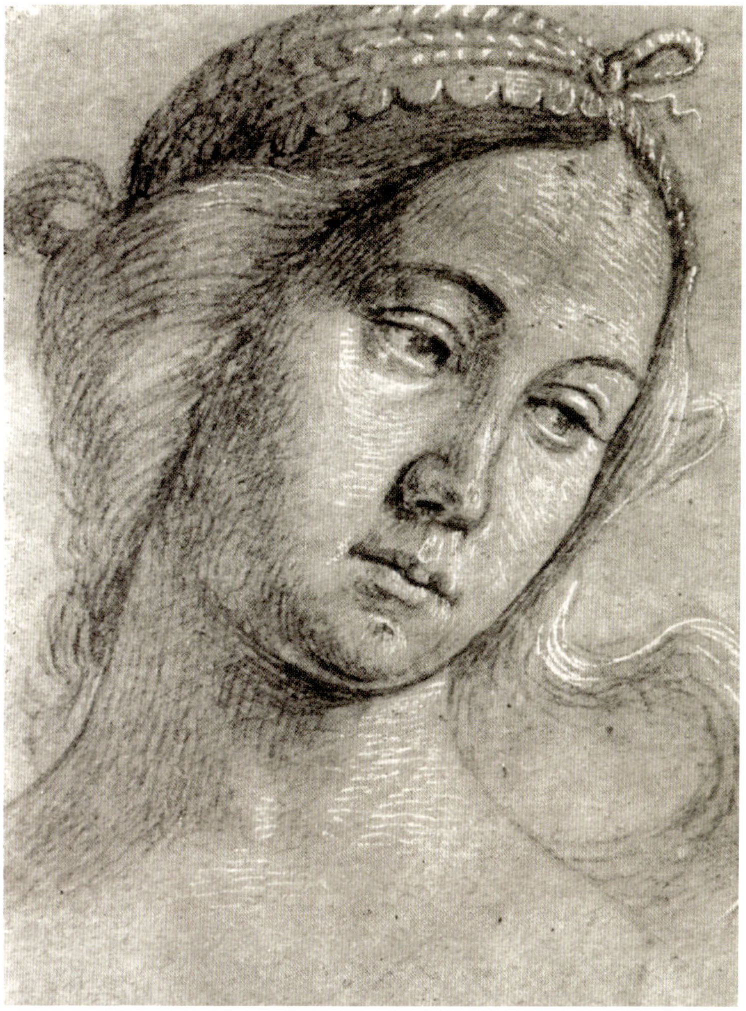

16 *HEADS OF WOMEN*
Oxford, Ashmolean Museum.
Brush, heightened with white, on blue paper, 239 x 181 mm.

The drawing above is a study for the head of one of the virgins in pl. 15. Carpaccio evidently kept the drawing in his studio for some years, since in 1510 he re-used it for one of the Madonna's companions in the *Presentation in the Temple.*

(left) Detail of pl.15.

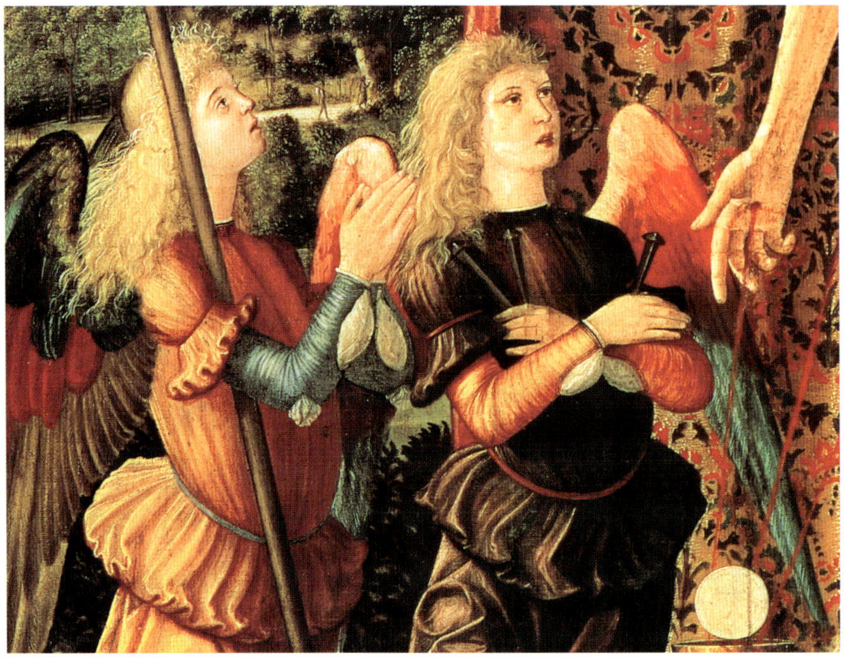

17 *THE BLOOD OF THE REDEEMER*
Udine, Museo Civico.
Canvas 162 x 160 cm. Inscribed: vjctorjs Charpatjo / uenetj opus / 1496.

From the church of S. Pietro Martire in Udine. The subject, which shows Christ pouring the blood from his wounds into an Eucharistic chalice, flanked by four angels holding the instruments of the Passion, strongly reflects the popular devotional interest in the physical sufferings of Christ, and the widespread cult of the Holy Blood. In its original position on a church altar, where mass would have been celebrated daily in front of it, the painting would also have provided a cogent exposition of the ecclesiological doctrine of the celestial liturgy, whereby every mass performed on earth has its counterpart in heaven, with Christ himself as celebrant and his angels as acolytes, distributing to the faithful the redemptive benefits of his sacrifice. Carpaccio has borrowed the central figure of Christ from a small panel of related subject-matter by Giovanni Bellini, *The Blood of the Redeemer* (National Gallery, London).

(above) Detail of pl. 17.

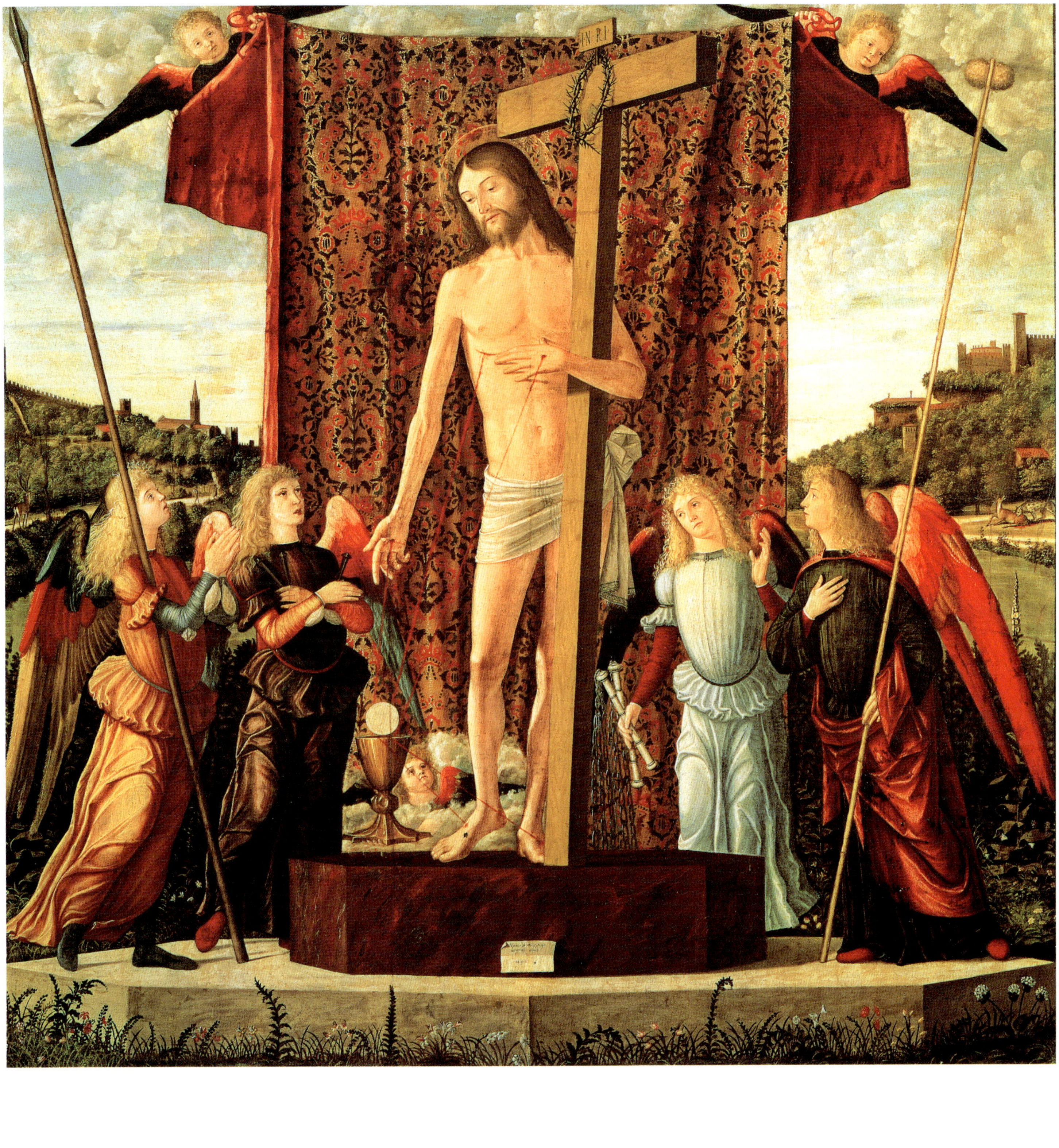

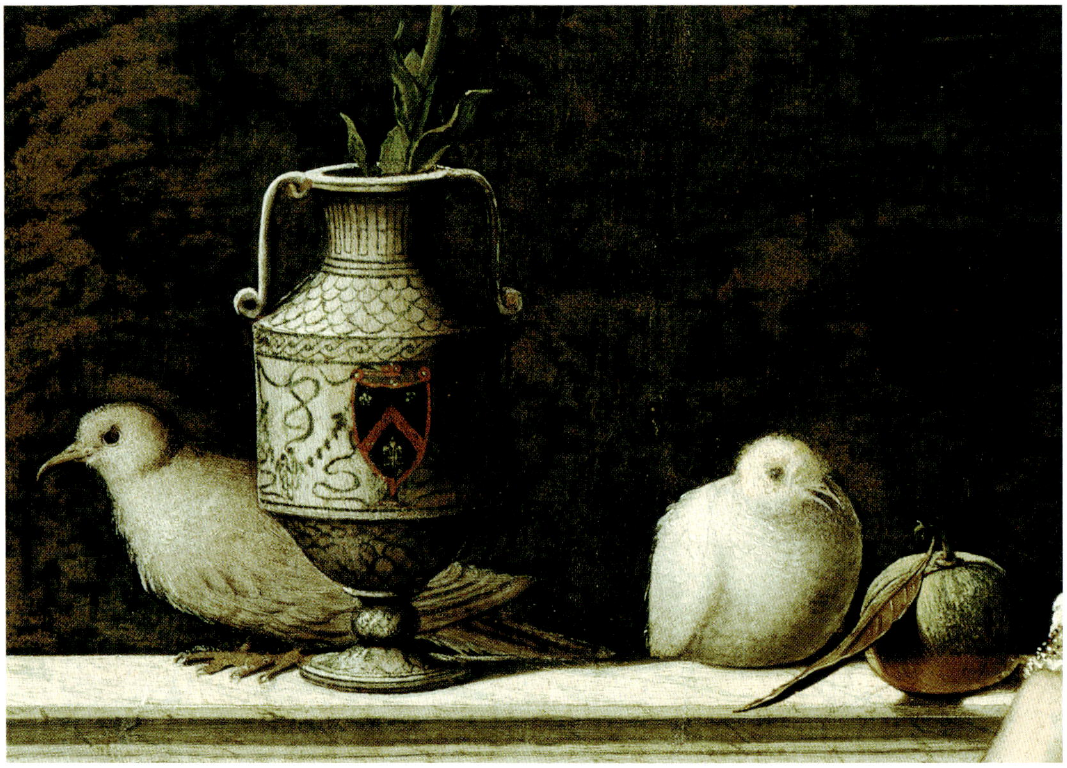

18 *TWO LADIES ON A BALCONY*
Venice, Museo Correr.
Panel, 64 x 94 cm. Inscribed: Opus Vjctorjs Carpatjo Venetj . . . (now illegible).

One of the most famous of Carpaccio's works, but in its fragmentary state also one of the most problematical. It has been variously interpreted as a genre scene, a double portrait, an allegory, and as part of a secular narrative. The popular title of *The Two Courtesans* does not have any firm historical justification, and seems to date from no earlier than the mid-nineteenth century. It has been argued that it was quite common for Venetian ladies of fashion to wear false hair and low necklines. In 1494 Canon Casola saw a large number of wigs and hair-pieces on sale in the Piazza San Marco, and was shocked to observe how low the women wore their dresses: 'Sometimes I marvelled that their clothes did not fall off their backs.' All the same, the painting's popular title does have a certain ring of poetic truth, and it is hard to imagine that Carpaccio's ladies are really portraits of two respectable Venetian noblewomen – despite the escutcheon of the Torelli Family on the vase of flowers. Although an interpretation of the painting as pure genre is probably also to be ruled out – such a concept would have been anachronistic at this early date – the courtesan-like appearance of the figures is perhaps not irreconcilable with an allegorical interpretation. It has been suggested, for instance, that the lady in the foreground, stretching out a stick towards the paws of a dog, alludes to the mythological figure of Circe, the lascivious sorceress who had the power to transform men into beasts. Whether or not this is so, John Ruskin was certainly unaware of any sexual allusion in the painting when he ranked it as 'the best picture in the world' with respect to its 'perfection of execution and artistic power of design . . . I know of no other which unites every nameable quality of the painter's art in so intense a degree – breadth with minuteness, brilliancy with quietness, decision with tenderness, colour with light and shade.' The dating of the painting is also controversial, but from the style of the costume it would seem to be earlier than 1500.

(above) Detail of pl. 18.

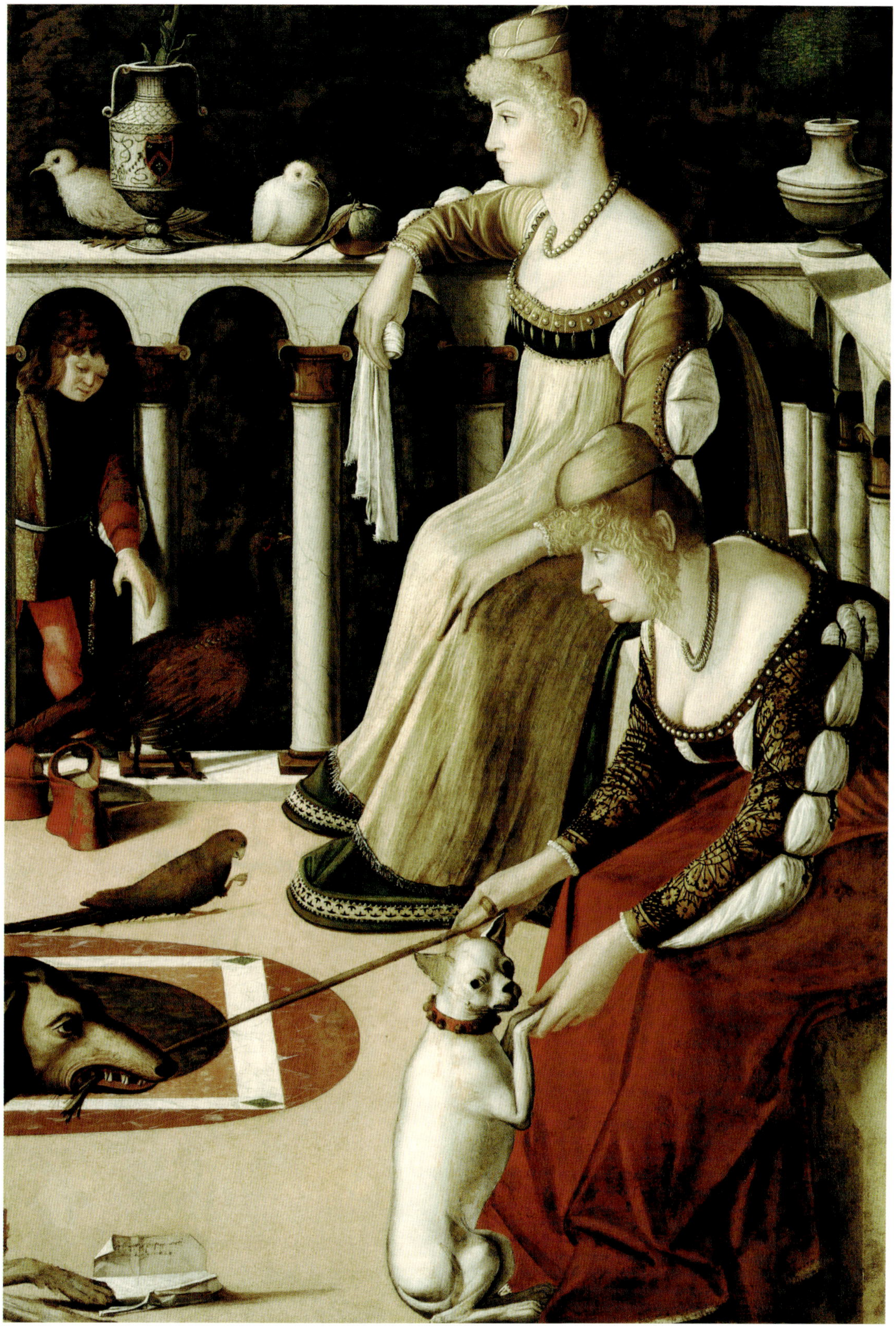

19 *THE CALLING OF ST MATTHEW*
Venice, Scuola di S. Giorgio degli Schiavoni.
Canvas, 141 x 115 cm. Inscribed: C (AR) PATIUS (VE)N(E)T(US) MDII.

From the inscribed date of 1502, apparently one of the first of the canvases for the Scuola di S. Giorgio to be executed. The episode, which is mentioned in all three synoptic gospels, was compared by St Jerome to a magnet attracting iron rings: 'The very splendour and majesty of His hidden godhead, which shone even in His human countenance, were enough to draw (the apostles) the first time they looked upon Him'. Carpaccio has interpreted Matthew in terms of the late fifteenth century as a Jewish money-lender: the yellow band he wears round his cap is one of the distinctive badges that Jews were customarily forced to wear. (Contrary to what is commonally supposed, however, the scene does not take place within the Jewish ghetto in Venice: this was instituted only in 1516, to accommodate the large number of refugees who had entered the city in 1509 during the war of Cambrai; and in 1502 the large Jewish community living under Venetian rule was still almost completely confined to cities of the mainland such as Mestre, Padua and Treviso. It may be the city gate of one of these that one sees in the background of Carpaccio's painting.) The head in profile immediately to the left of Matthew has been identified as a portrait of Sebastiano Michiel, Prior of the Knights of St John of Jerusalem, whose monastery adjoined the Scuola; it has also been suggested that the beak-like physiognomy of the head to the right of that of Christ is a portrait, perhaps of a confraternity officer. The escutcheon in the bottom left-hand corner is probably that of Michiel.

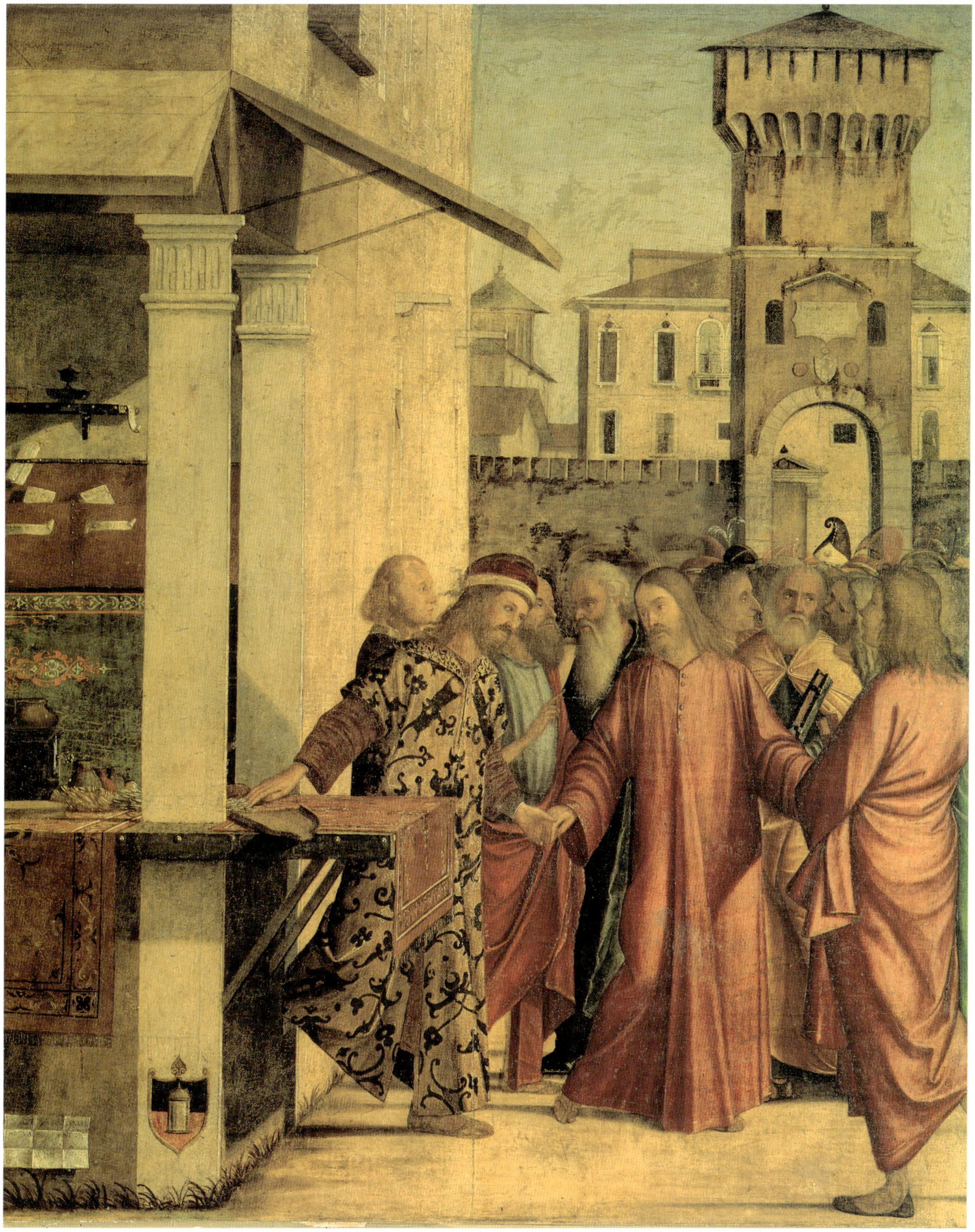

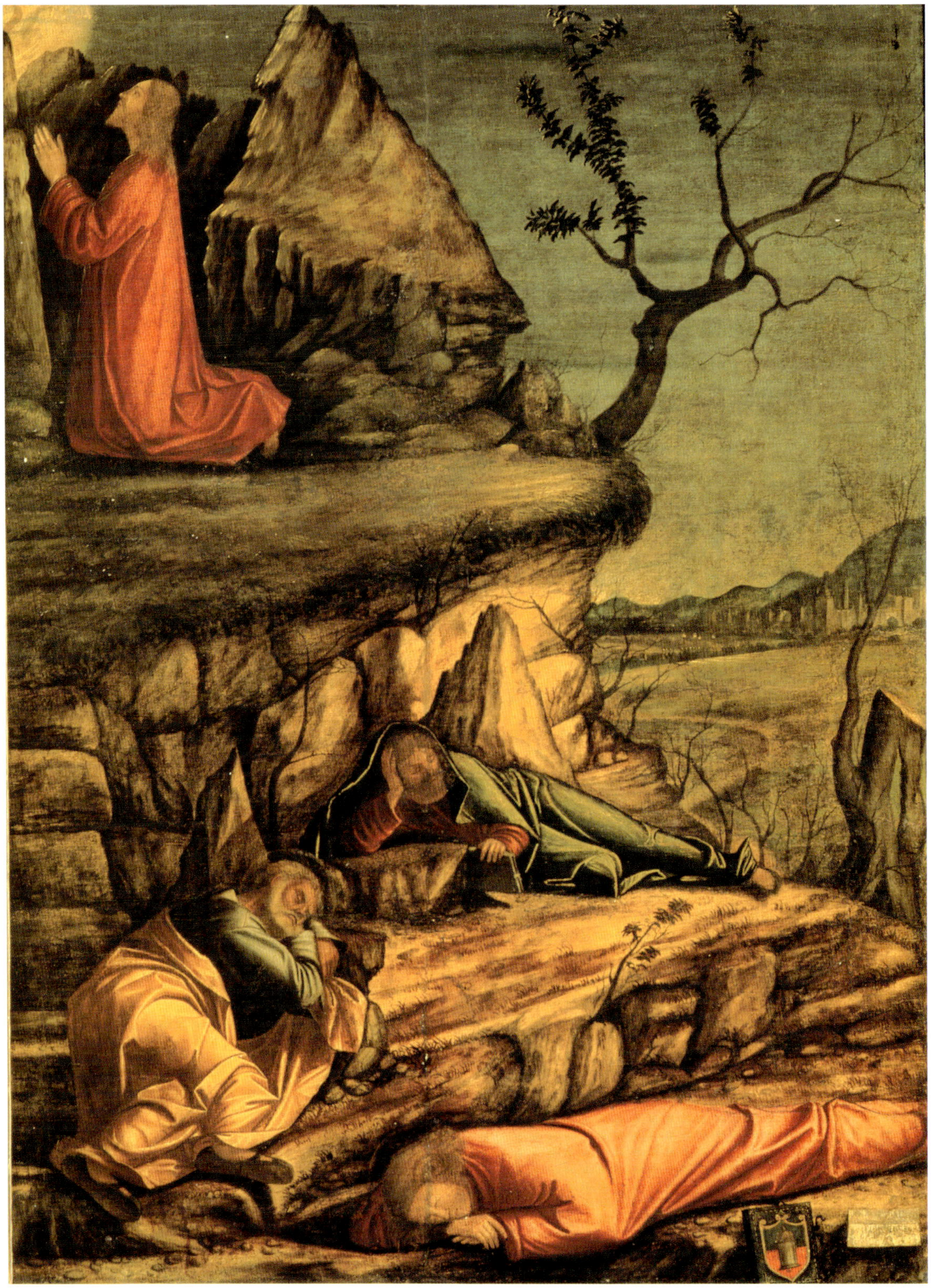

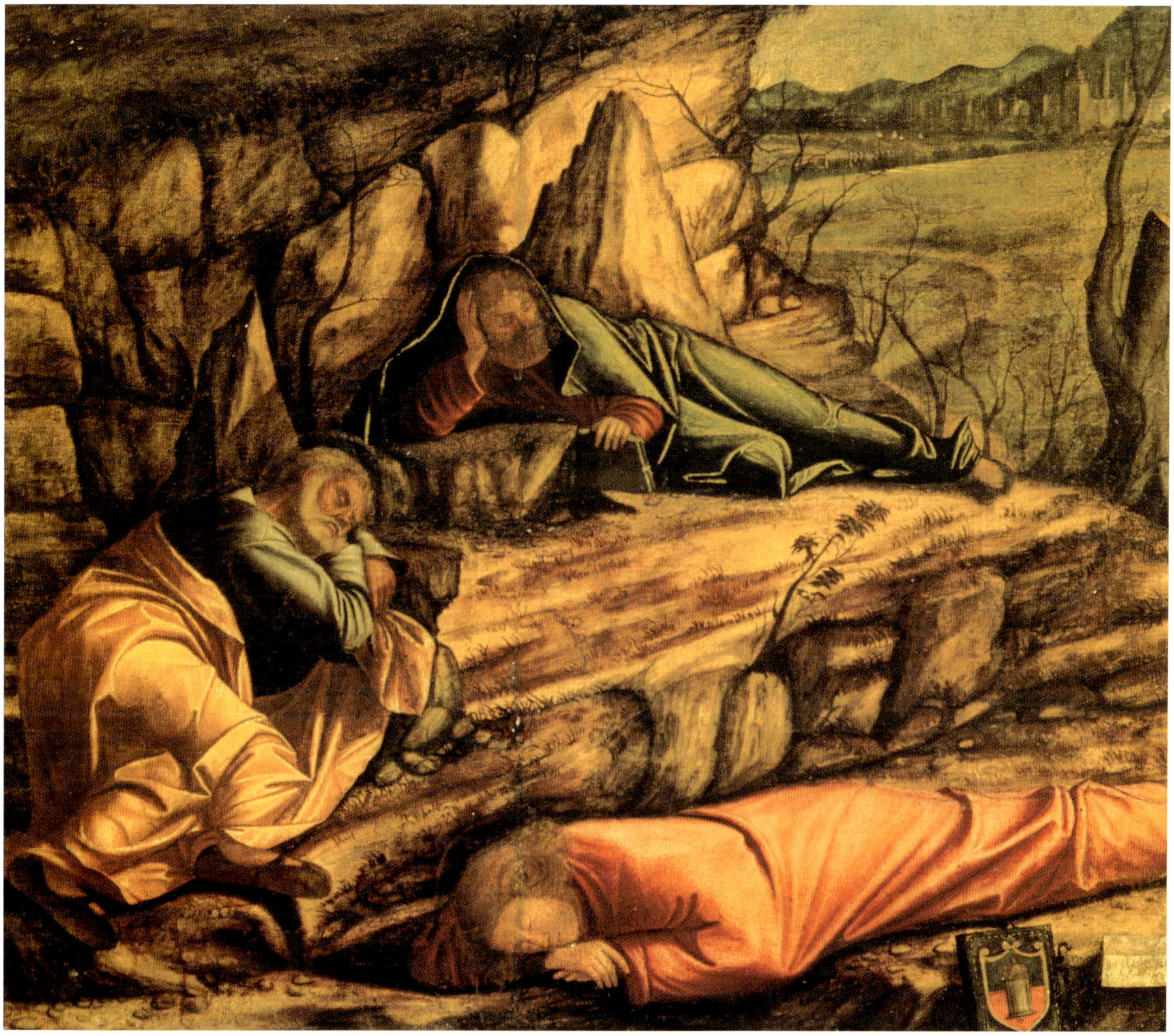

20 *THE AGONY IN THE GARDEN*
Venice, Scuola di S. Giorgio degli Schiavoni.
Canvas, 141 x 107 cm.

Apparently planned as a pendant to pl. 19 and of about the same date.

(above) Detail of pl. 20.

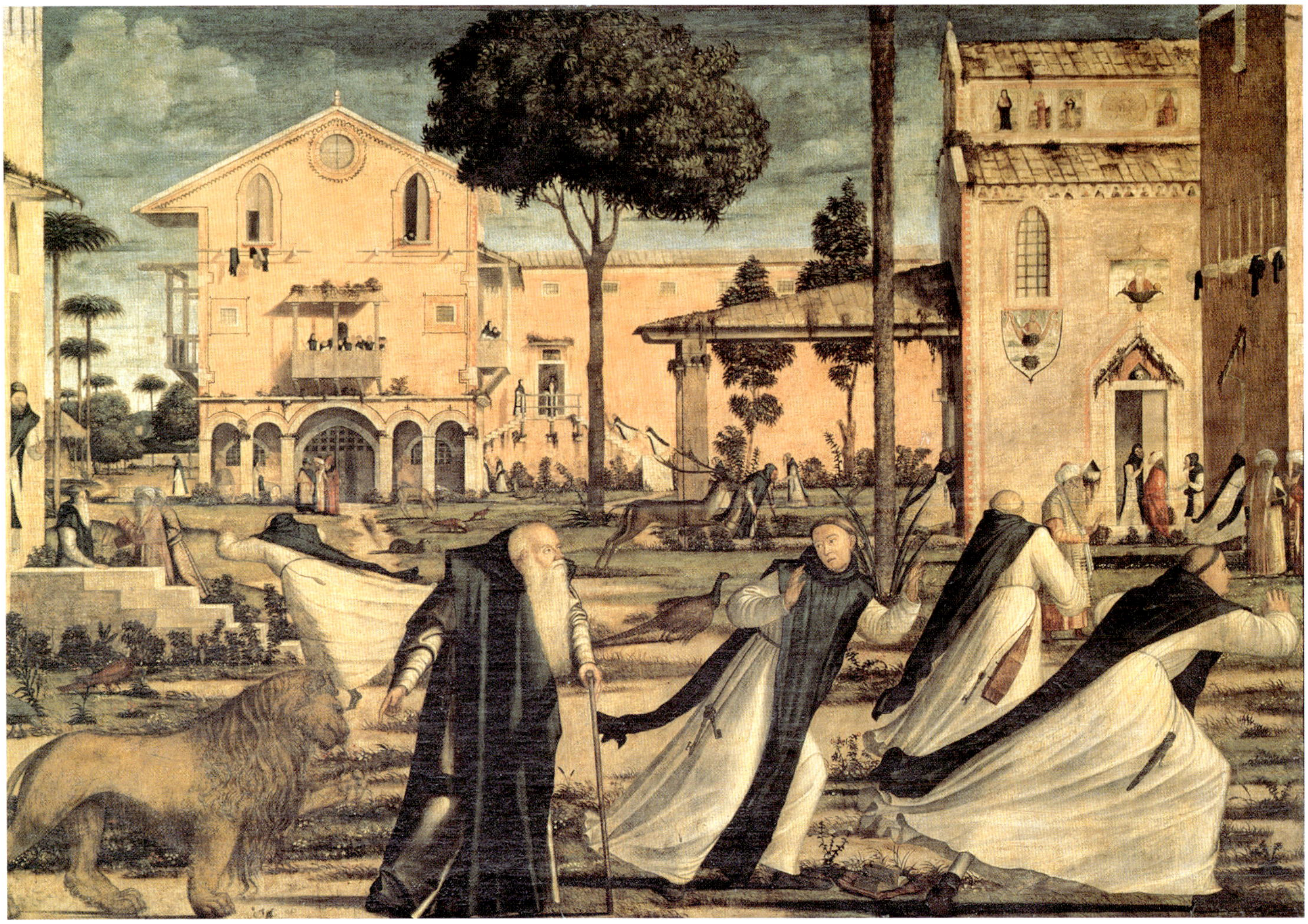

21 *ST JEROME LEADING THE LION INTO THE MONASTERY*
Venice, Scuola di S. Giorgio degli Schiavoni.
Canvas 148 x 215 cm.

The first of three scenes from the life of St Jerome, it shows a sense of humour rarely to be found in Italian Renaissance painting, with monks fleeing in terror as the saint leads a very docile-looking lion into the monastery. Even Ruskin was amused by the 'delicately smiling lion with his head on one side like a Perugino's saint, and his left paw raised, partly to show the thorn wound, partly in deprecation'. The buildings in the background have been identified as the Scuola di S. Giorgio as it appeared in Carpaccio's day, and to the right, the neighbouring church of the Knights of St John of Jerusalem. According to the eighteenth century critic Zanetti, Carpaccio's composition was based on the corresponding scene in another life cycle of St Jerome, painted by Alvise Vivarini for another confraternity, the Scuola di S. Girolamo; but this painting is unfortunately now lost.

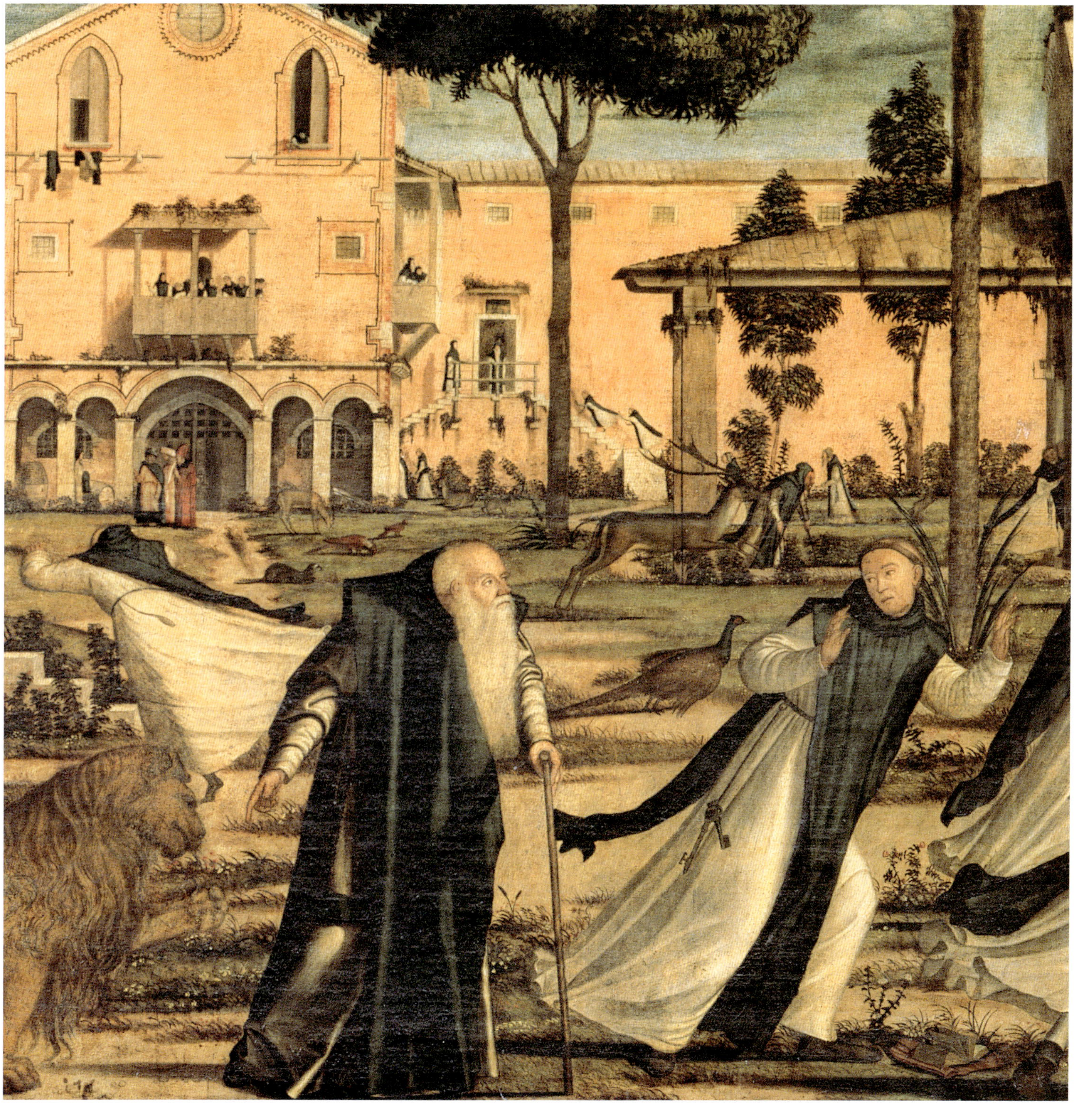

Detail of pl. 21.

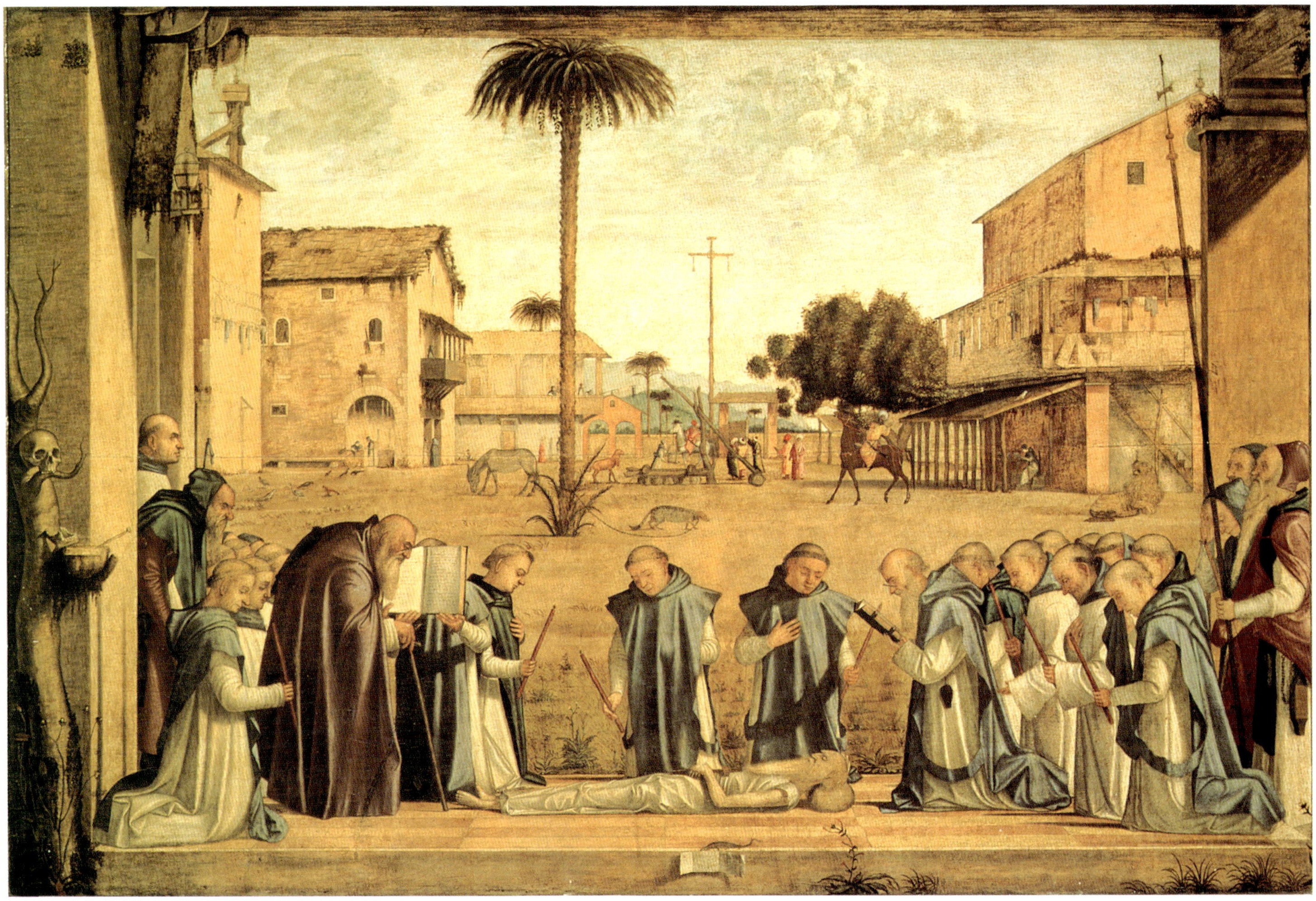

22 *THE FUNERAL OF ST JEROME*
Venice, Scuola di S. Giorgio degli Schiavoni.
Canvas, 144 x 210 cm. Inscribed: VICTOR CARPA THIUS/FINGEBAT/MDII.

The second of three scenes from the life of St Jerome, showing the funeral of the saint, mourned by the brethren of the monastery he founded in Bethlehem.

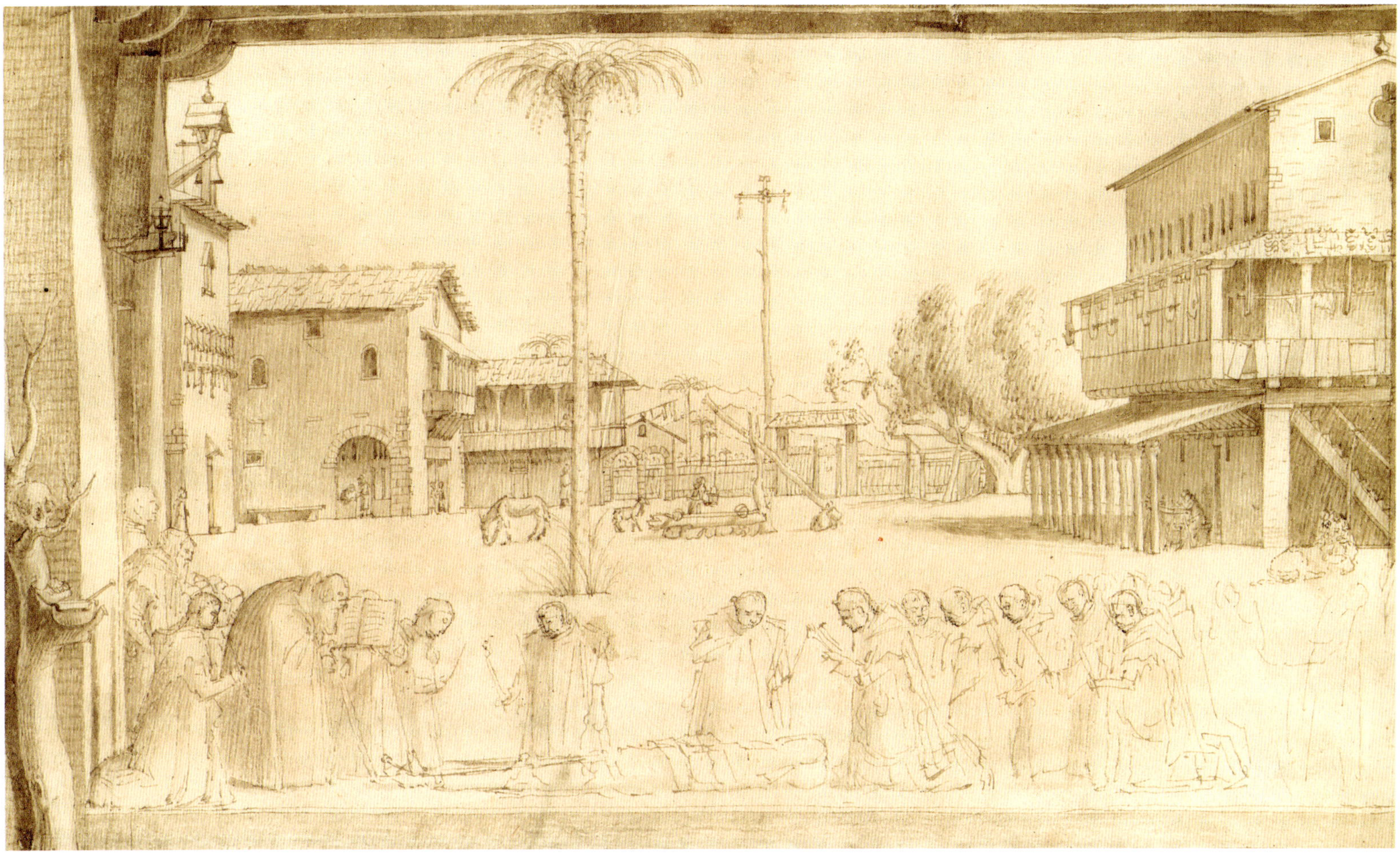

23 *THE FUNERAL OF ST JEROME*
Uppsala, University Library.
Pen and wash, 270 x 420 mm.

Preliminary study for pl. 22. As in his various other compositional sketches, the artist's main concern is to clarify the spatial environment, and the foreground figures are only very lightly indicated.

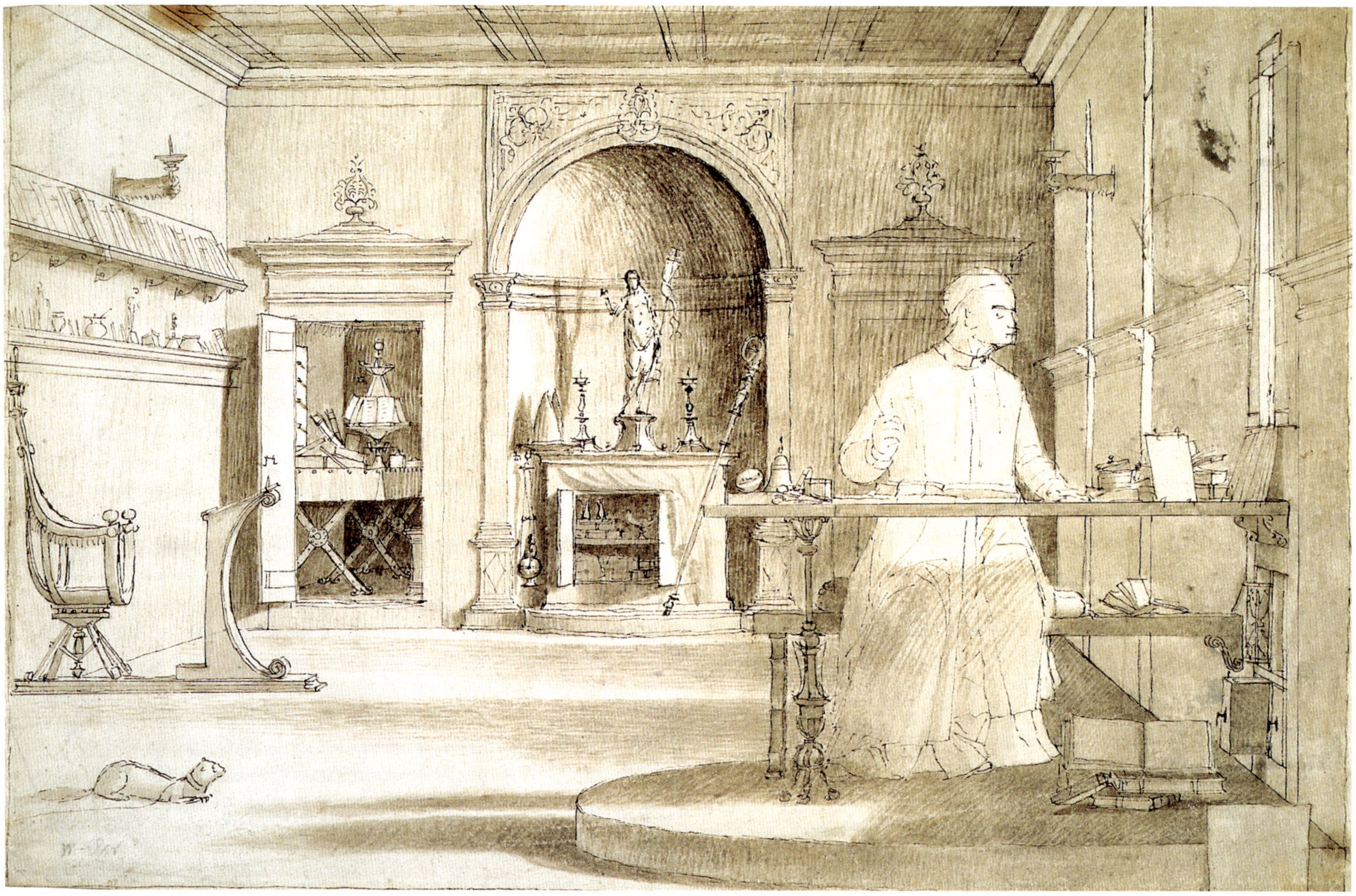

24 *ST AUGUSTINE IN HIS STUDY*
London, British Museum.
Pen and ink in outline, shaded with the point of the brush in brown, 277 x 427 mm.

Compositional drawing for pl. 25, opposite.

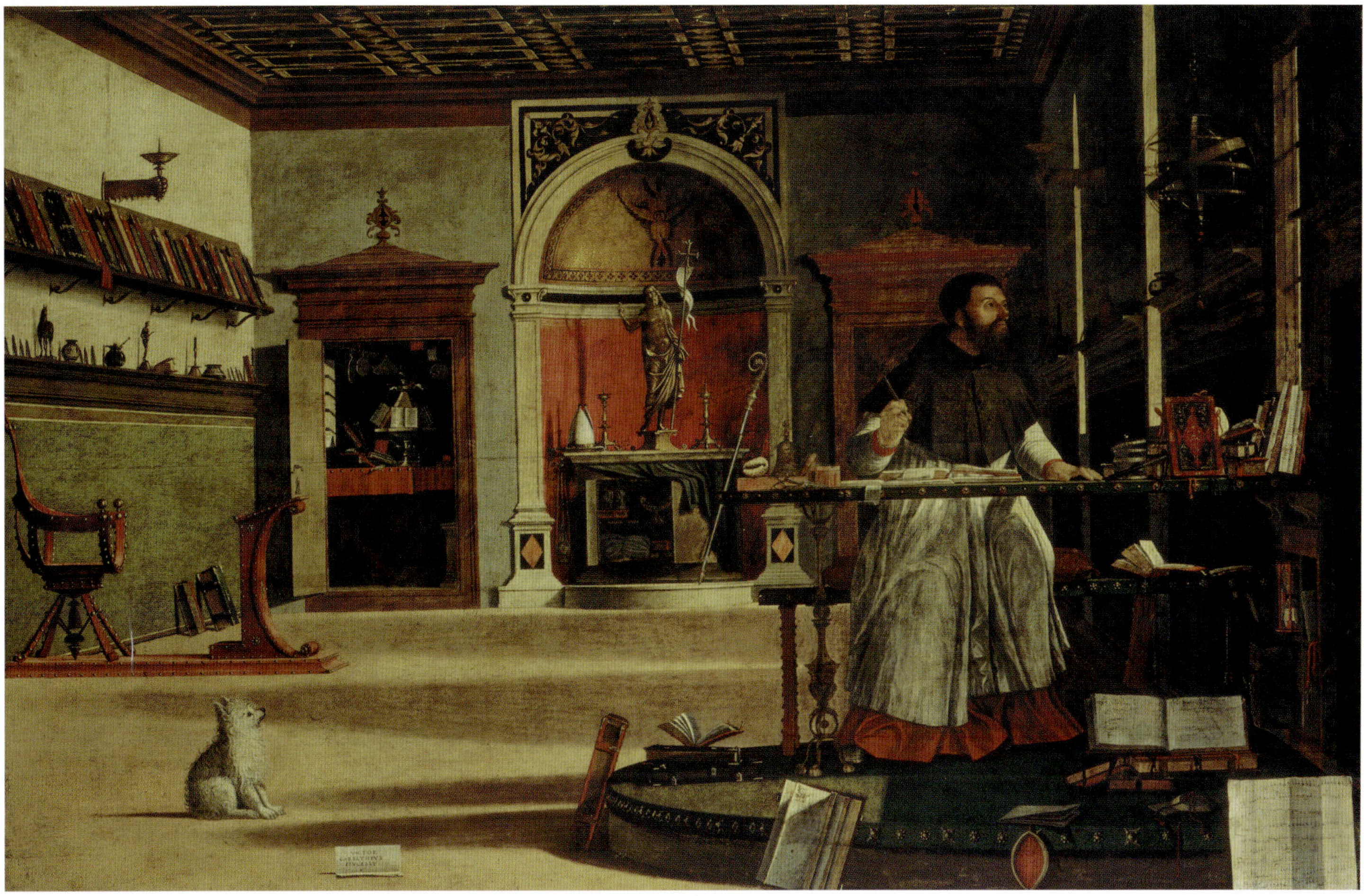

25 *ST AUGUSTINE IN HIS STUDY*
Venice, Scuola di S. Giorgio degli Schiavoni. Canvas, 141 x 210 cm. Inscribed: VICTOR CARPATHIUS FINGEBAT.

The third of the three canvases from the life of St Jerome shows not the saint himself, but his contemporary St Augustine, who at the very moment of Jerome's death experienced a vision while seated in his study at Hippo. According to an account purportedly written by Augustine himself, he had taken up his pen one evening to write a letter to Jerome, asking his opinion on the nature of heavenly bliss, when suddenly the room was filled with an extraordinary radiance, and he heard the voice of Jerome telling him that he had already ascended to Christ.

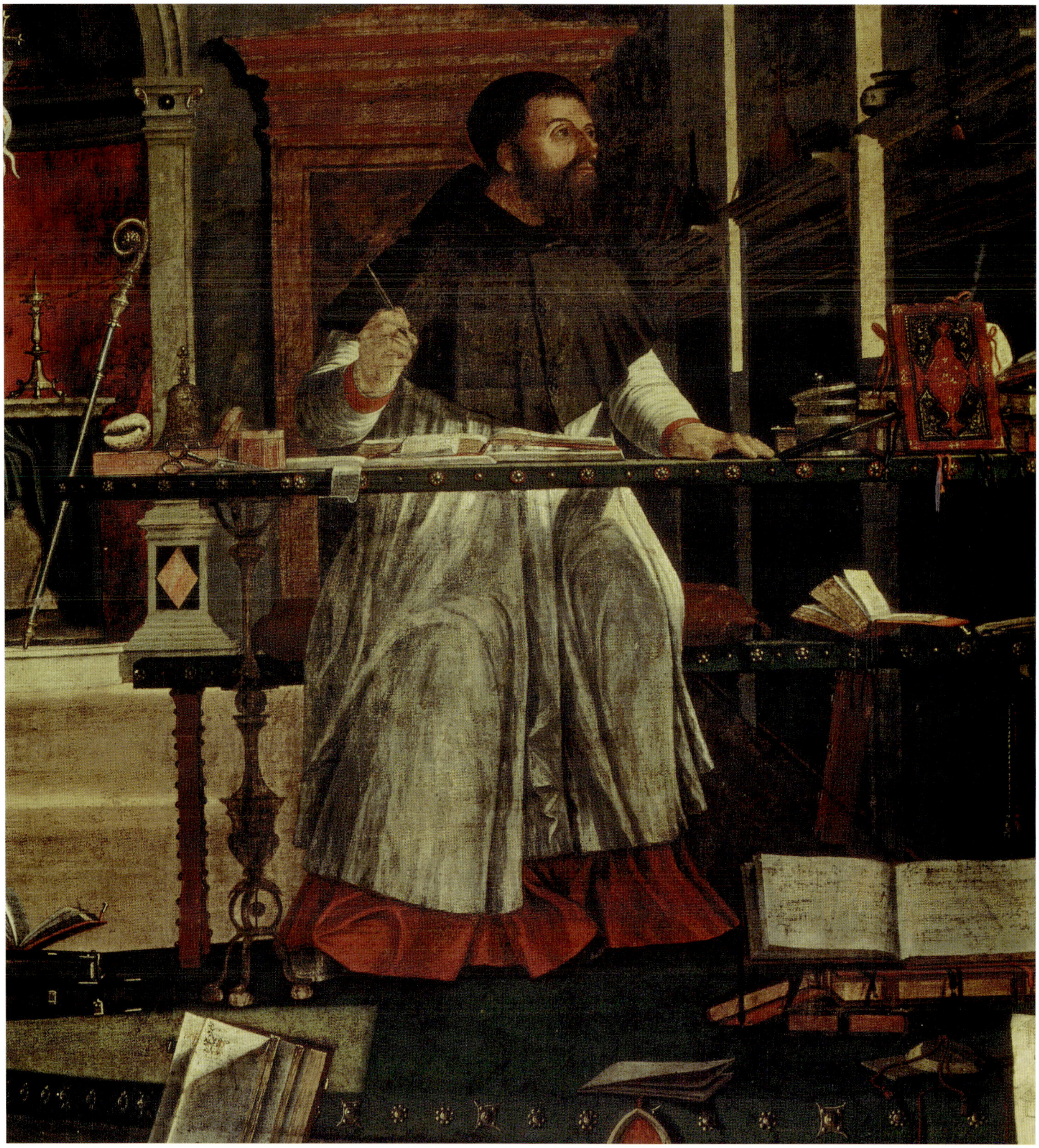

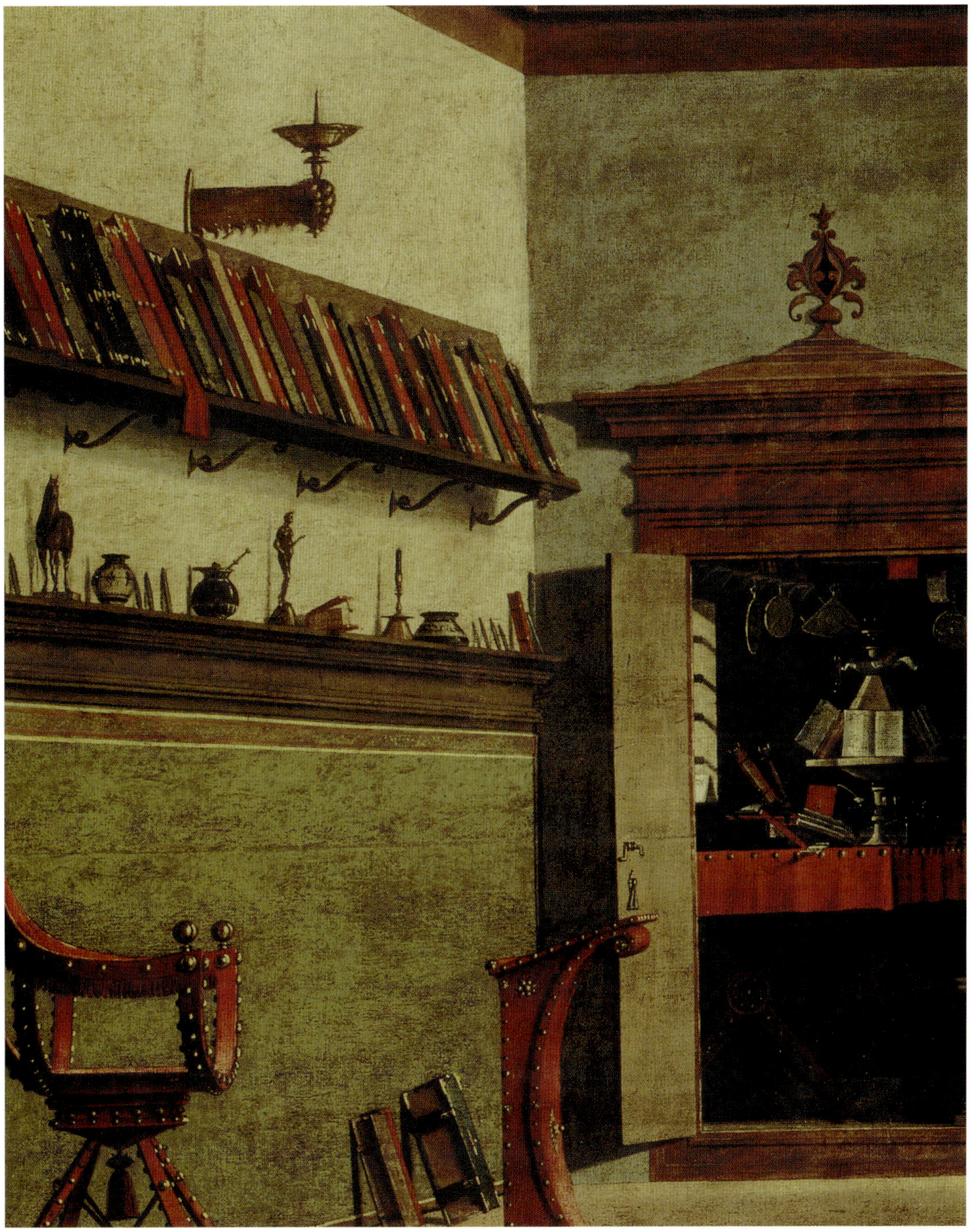

Details of pl. 25. The artist appears to have depicted the interior of the study of a contemporary learned man. The attributes of Renaissance learning are visible ranging from the astrolabe, upper right, to the collection of antiques and curiosities on the ledge below the shelves of books on the left.

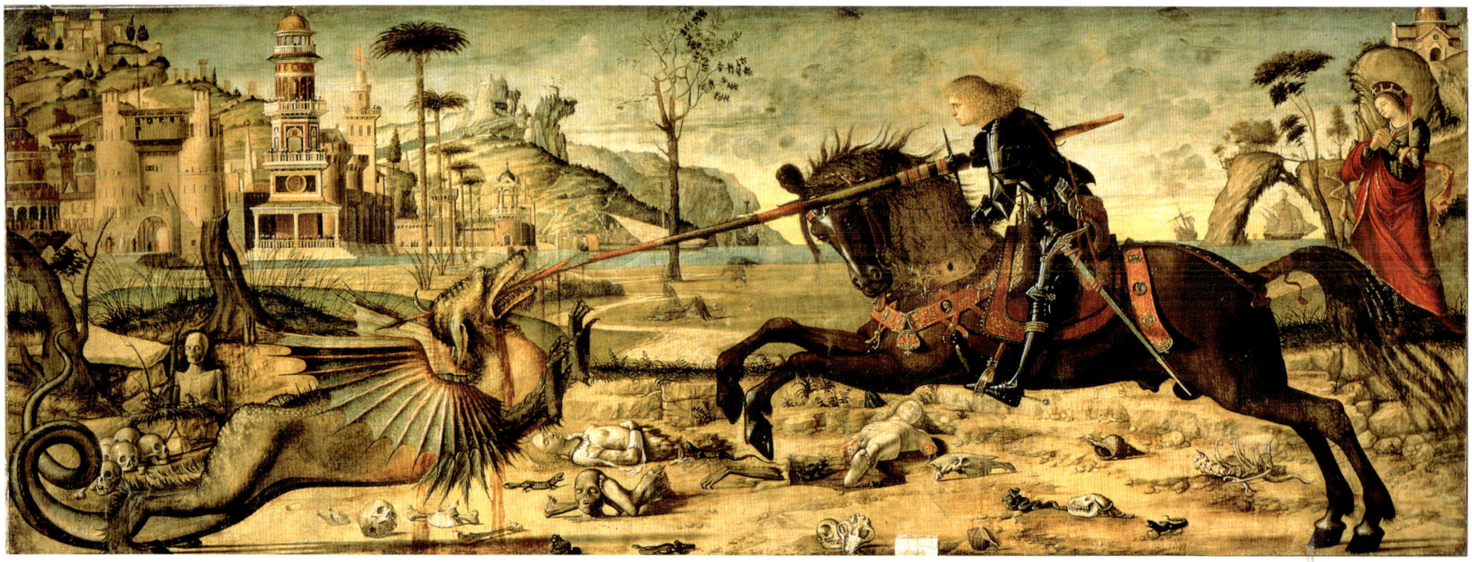

26 *ST GEORGE AND THE DRAGON*
Venice, Scuola di S. Giorgio degli Schiavoni.
Canvas, 141 x 360 cm.

Of the three episodes chosen to celebrate the titular saint of the confraternity, the scene of St George slaying the dragon is easily the most familiar. According to the *Golden Legend*, the citizens of the town of Silena in Libya were obliged to appease a fearsome dragon by providing him every day with a sheep, and later when his appetite became more voracious, with a human being. The daily victim was selected by a lottery from which not even the royal family was exempt; but on the day that the lot fell on the king's daughter, the errant St George happened to be passing, and true to the spirit of mediaeval chivalry, he attacked the dragon and mortally wounded it. Carpaccio may well have been inspired here by secular representations of knights jousting, such as those by Pisanello recently rediscovered in the ducal palace in Mantua; and as with Pisanello, his painting exudes a keen sense of nostalgia for a vanished age of chivalry. Such a sentiment may at first sight seem somewhat out of place in a maritime city-republic like Venice; but a taste for French Arthurian romances of the twelfth and thirteenth centuries was in fact quite widespread in Venetian literary circles in the later fifteenth century, and probably more than any other painter, Carpaccio was sensitive to its spirit of courtly fantasy.

(right) Detail of pl. 26.

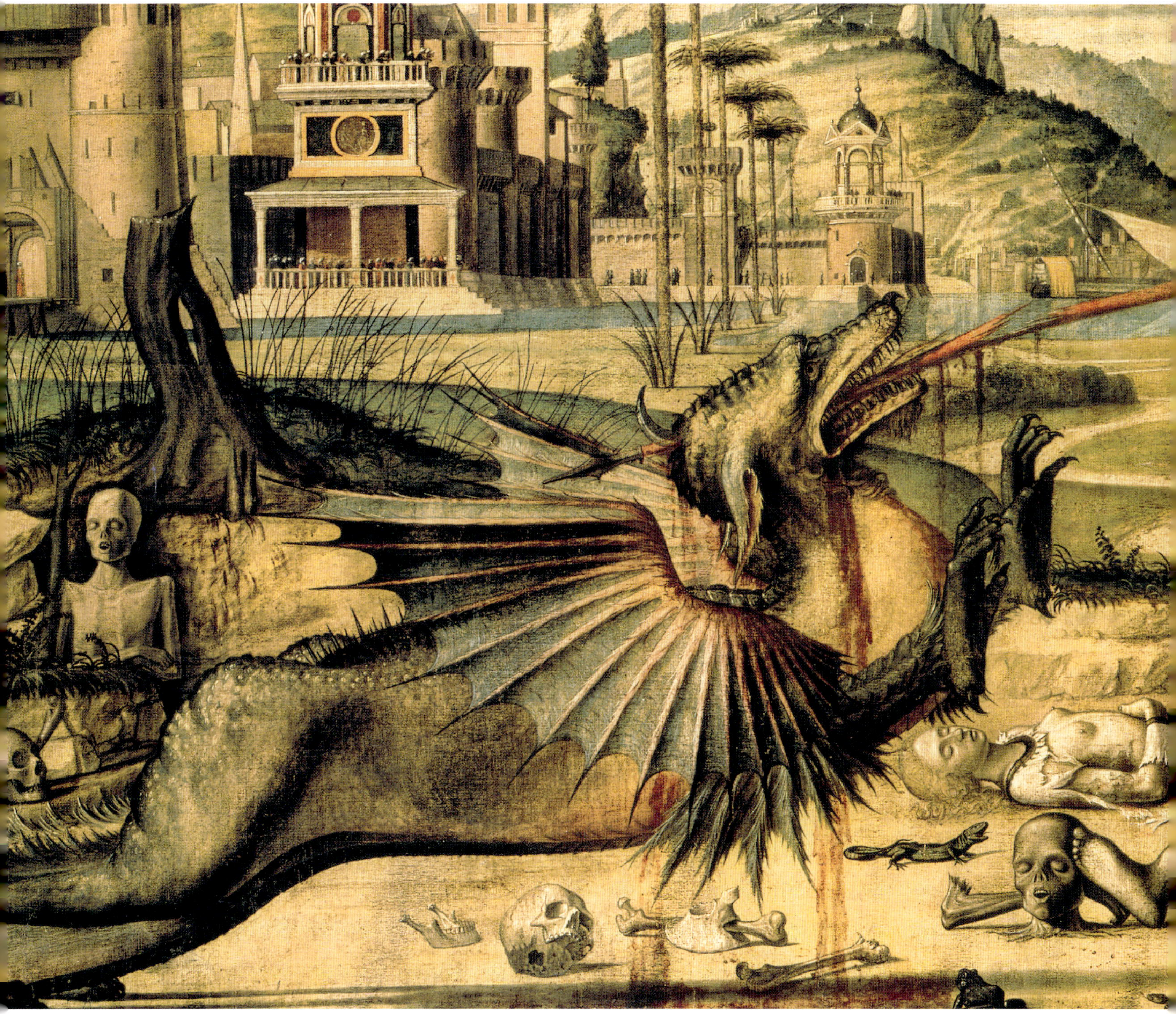

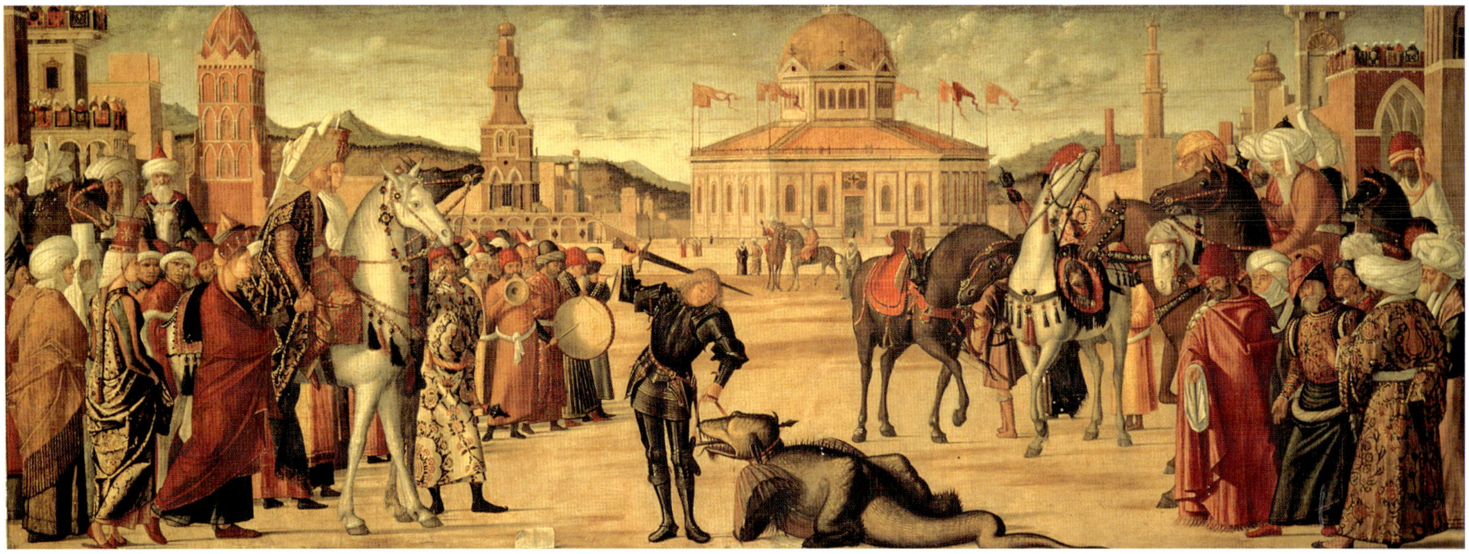

27 *THE TRIUMPH OF ST GEORGE*
Venice, Scuola di S. Giorgio degli Schiavoni.
Canvas, 141 x 360 cm.

After St George had defeated the dragon, it was so badly wounded that the princess was able to lead it into Silena on a leash. There the saint gave it the coup-de-grâce with his sword before the assembled populace.

(right) Detail of pl. 27. Two restless, richly caparisoned horses.

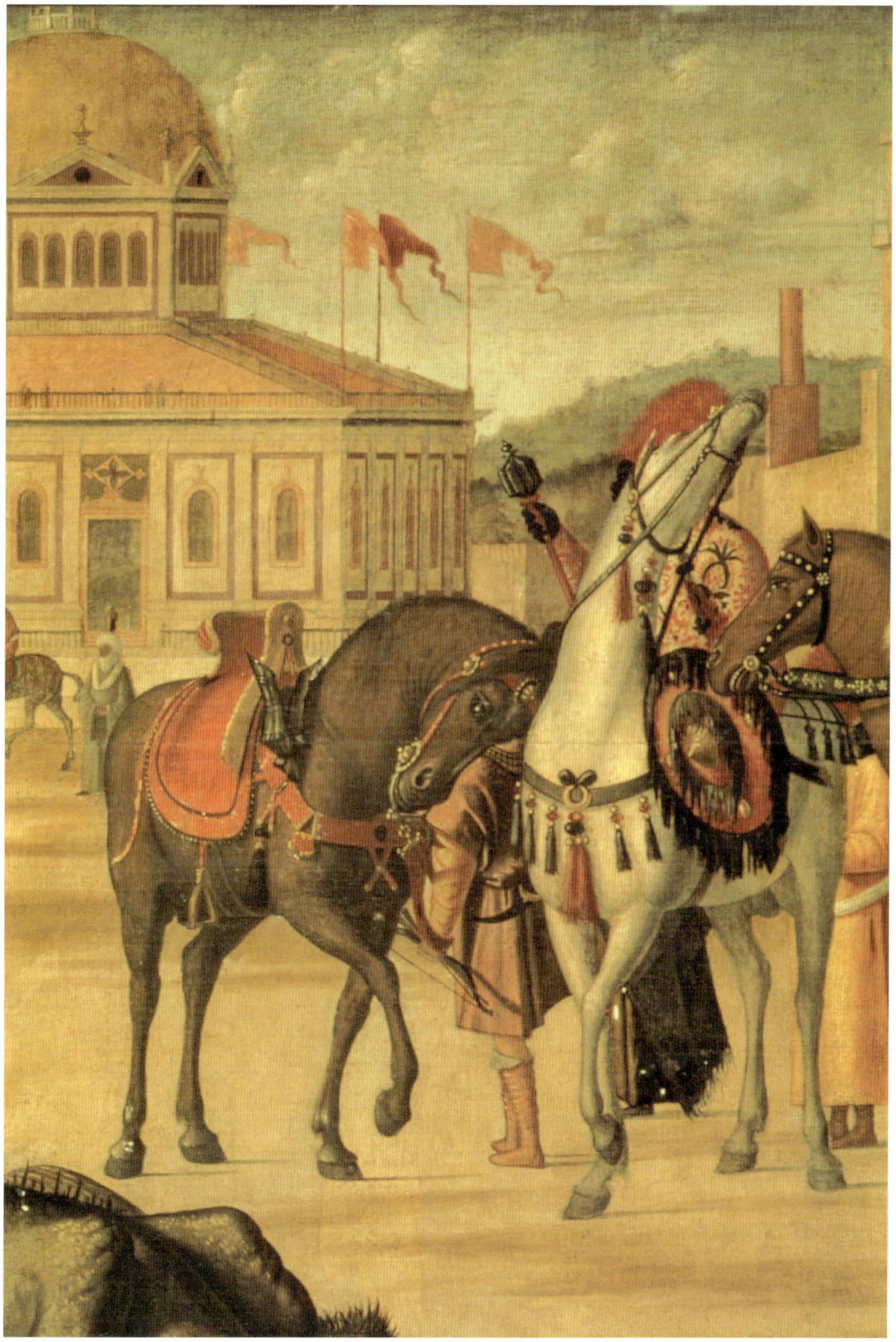

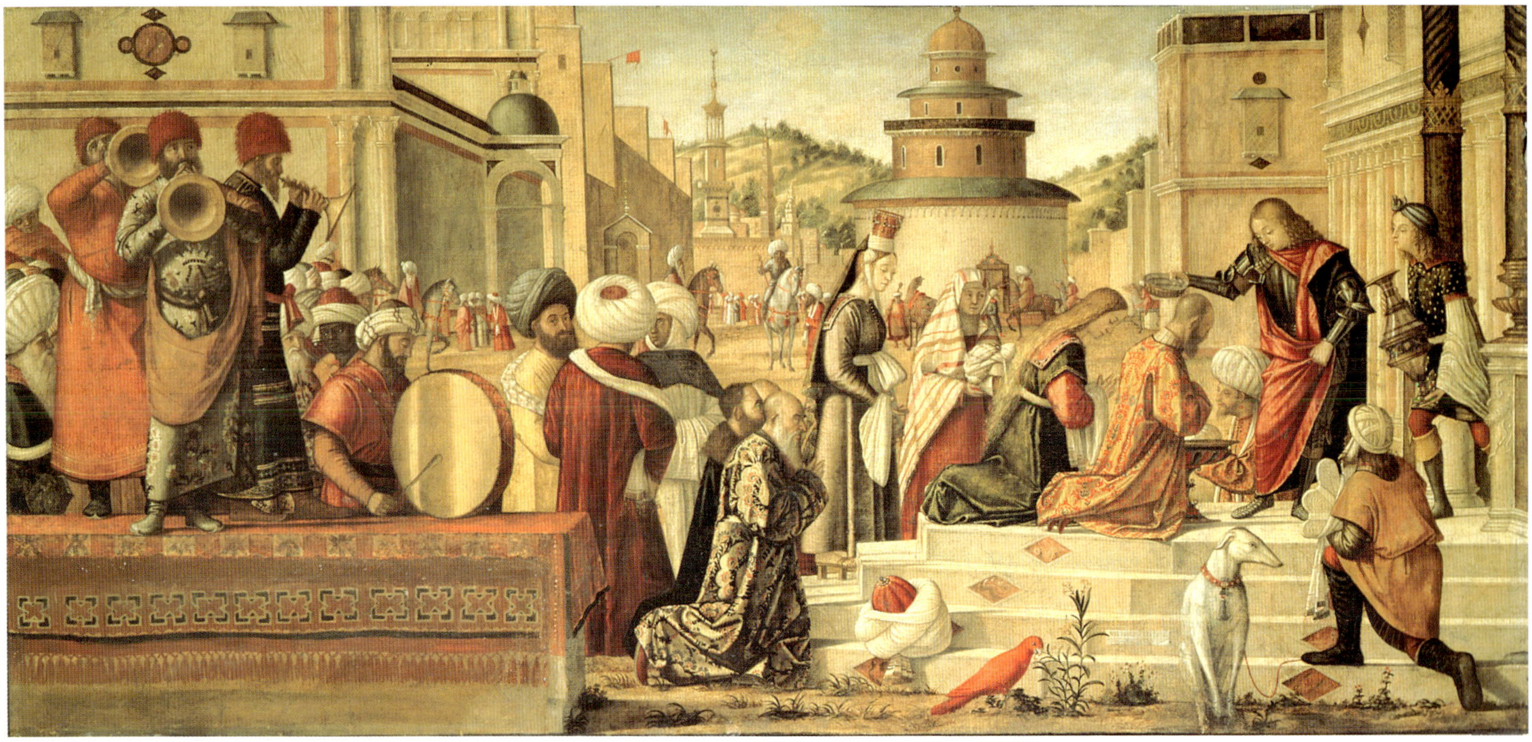

28 *ST GEORGE BAPTISING THE KING AND PRINCESS*
Venice, Scuola di S. Giorgio degli Schiavoni.
Canvas, 141 x 285 cm. Inscribed: VICTOR CARPA (TIUS)/M DVII (?)

Such was the gratitude of the King of Silena that he allowed himself and his subjects to be baptised by the saint in the Christian faith. Ruskin was particularly struck by the fastidiousness of the pose adopted by the saint as he performs the ceremony: 'He has taken a good platterful of water to pour on the Sultan's head. The font of inlaid bronze below is quite flat, and the splash is likely to be spreading. St George – carefullest of saints, it seems, in the smallest matters – is holding his mantle back well out of the way. I suppose, really and truly, the instinctive action would have been this, pouring at the same time so that the splash might be towards himself, and not over the Sultan'. Carpaccio's composition was deliberately devised to accommodate the top of a door, which originally cut into part of the bottom left-hand corner of the canvas.

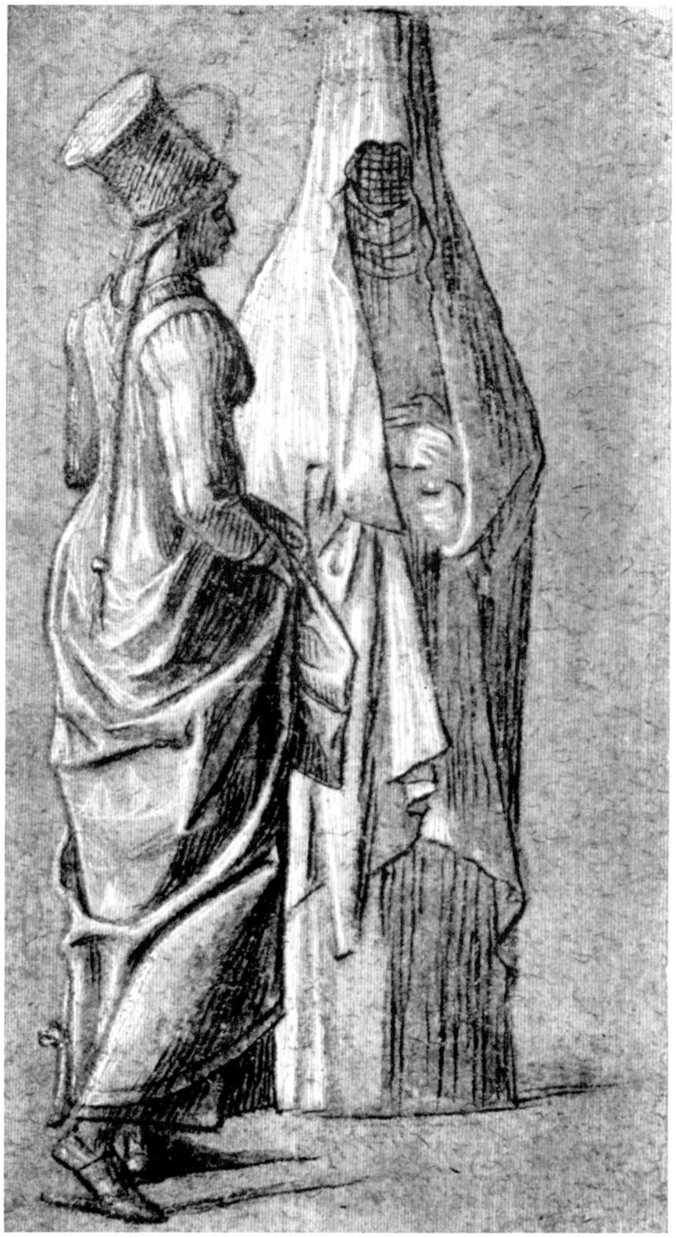

29 *TWO WOMEN IN TURKISH COSTUME*
Princeton, N.J., University Art Museum.
Pen and brush, washed with bistre, heightened with white, over a preliminary drawing in black chalk, 229 x 119 mm.

Costume studies related to the women in the retinue of the princess in pl. 28 borrowed from a woodcut by Reuwich. Carpaccio seems to have made further use of the drawing for some of the female figures in the Visitation of the Albanesi cycle and the *Ordination of St Stephen* of the S. Stefano cycle.

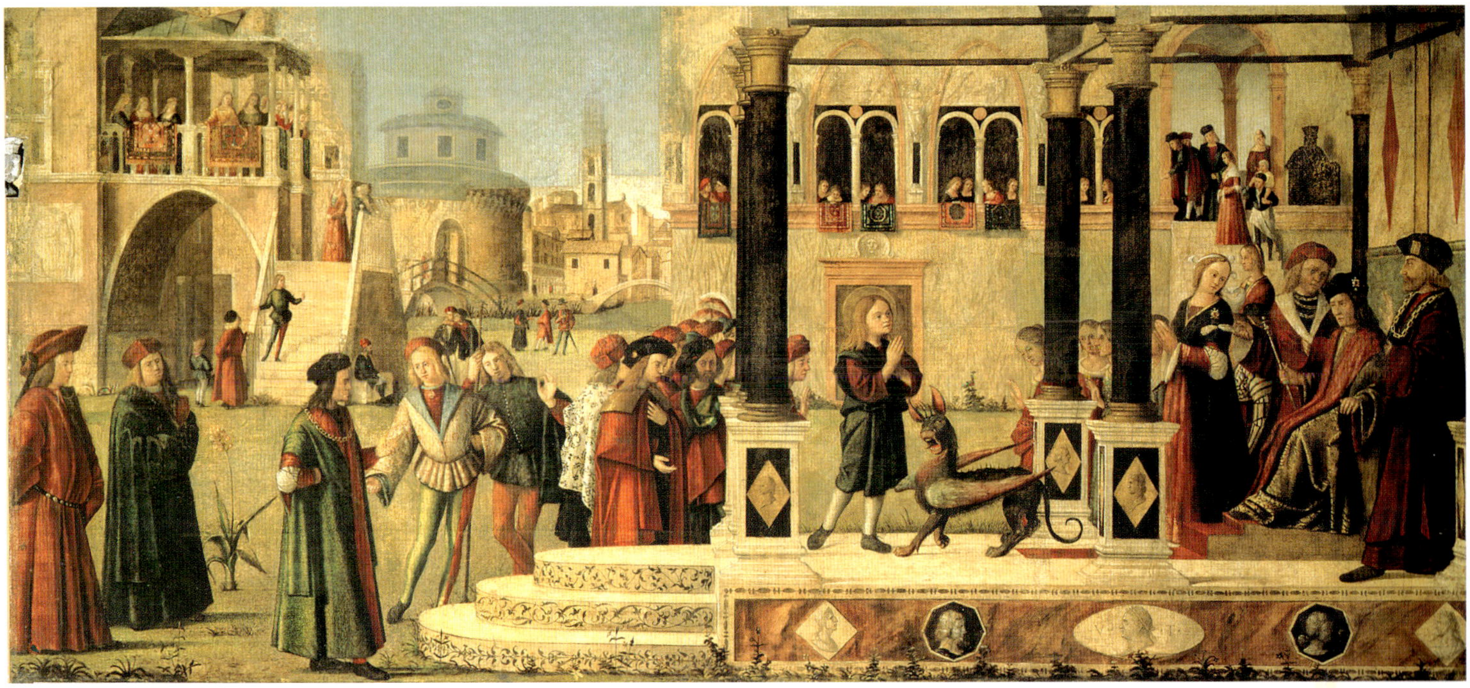

30 *ST TRYPHONIUS EXORCISING THE DEMON*
Venice, Scuola di S. Giorgio degli Schiavoni.
Canvas, 142 x 300 cm.

St Tryphonius, a rather obscure figure who lived in the third century, became patron saint of the Dalmatian city of Cattaro when his relics were brought there from Asia Minor by Venetian sailors. He is supposed to have had the power of working miracles from his earliest childhood, making a speciality of exorcising demons; and when the Roman Emperor Gordian heard of his fame, he sent for the boy to cure his daughter. Carpaccio depicts the moment in which the child-saint, having just cast out the demon from the princess, engages the monster in dialogue, forcing it to admit that it is the offspring of the devil, thus converting the pagan bystanders to Christianity. The classicising portrait reliefs in the foreground are probably intended as a reminder that the event took place in Rome, despite the very Venetian appearance of the background. Generally seen as one of the last of the S. Giorgio series, ca. 1507.

(right) Detail of pl. 30.

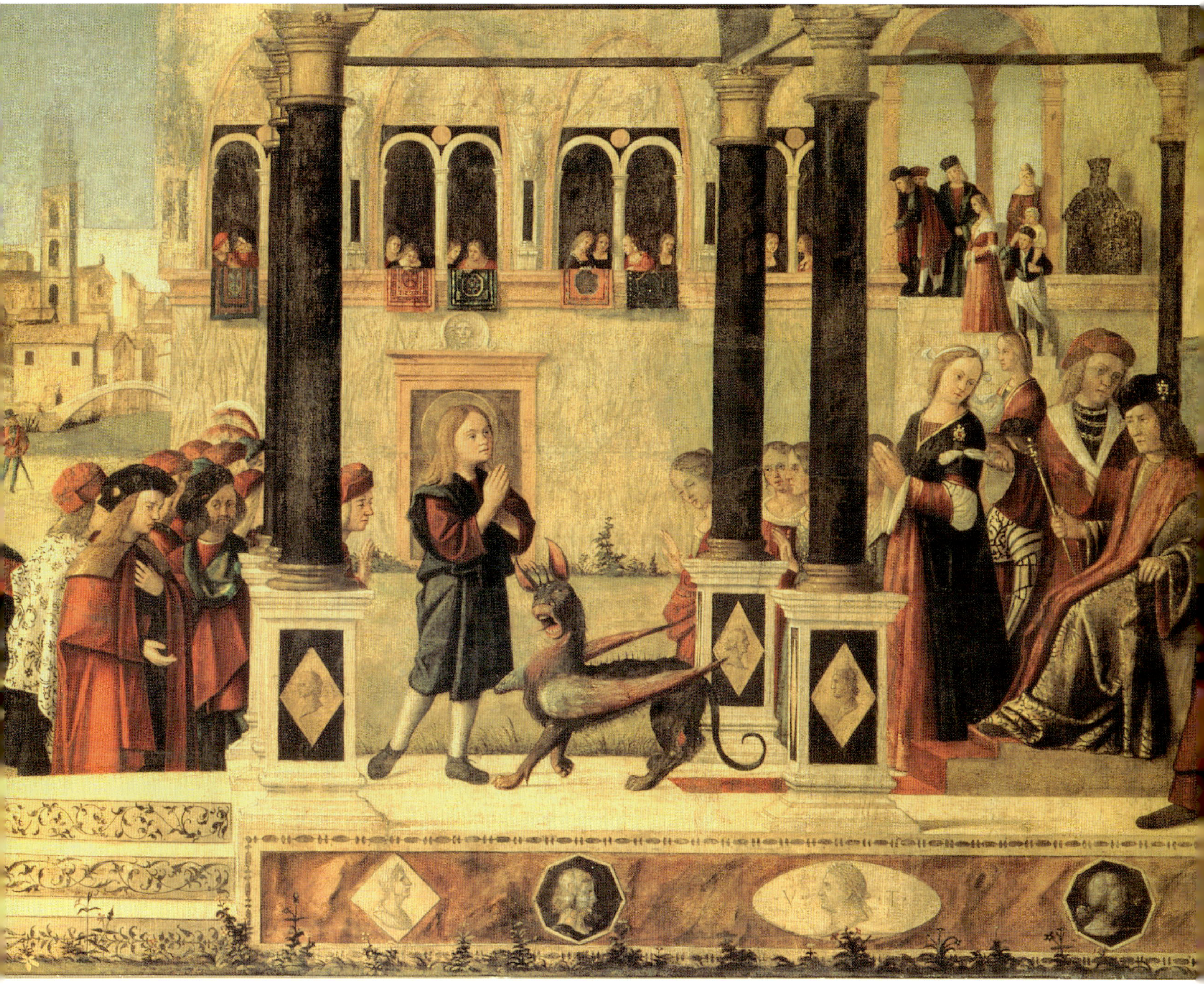

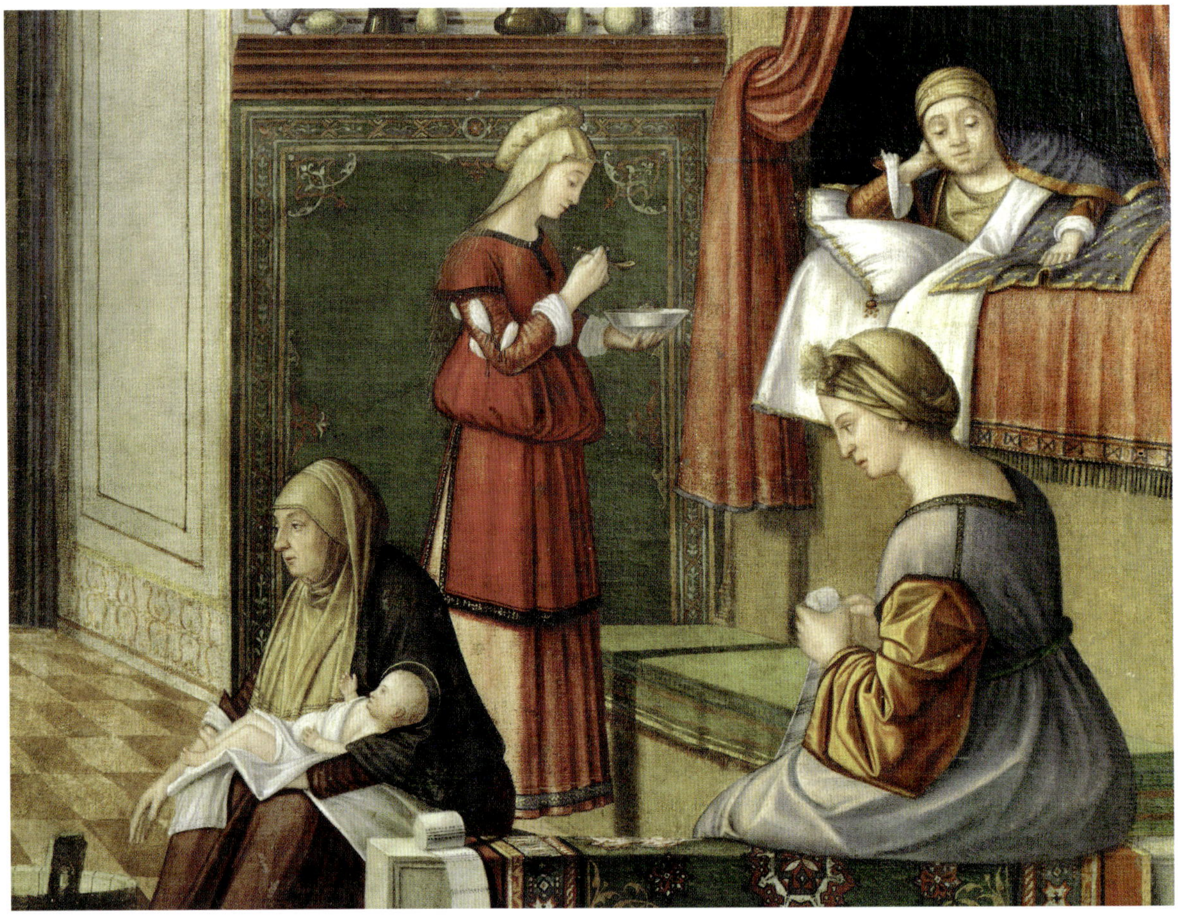

31 *THE BIRTH OF THE VIRGIN*
Bergamo, Accademia Carrara.
Canvas, 126 x 129 cm.

The first of a series of six canvases showing scenes from the life of the Virgin, painted for the Scuola degli Albanesi. This confraternity existed for the benefit of the many expatriate Albanians in Venice, many of whom were in the cloth trade. The birth of the Virgin is treated as a domestic event taking place in a Jewish household in Venice, with her mother Anna in the bed on her right, her earthly father Joachim standing on the left, and the infant herself in the arms of a nurse at the centre. It is possible that Carpaccio was influenced in this and the other scenes of the series by Jacopo Bellini's Life of the Virgin cycle, painted for the Scuola Grande di S. Giovanni Evangelista in the mid-fifteenth century.

(above) Detail of pl. 31.

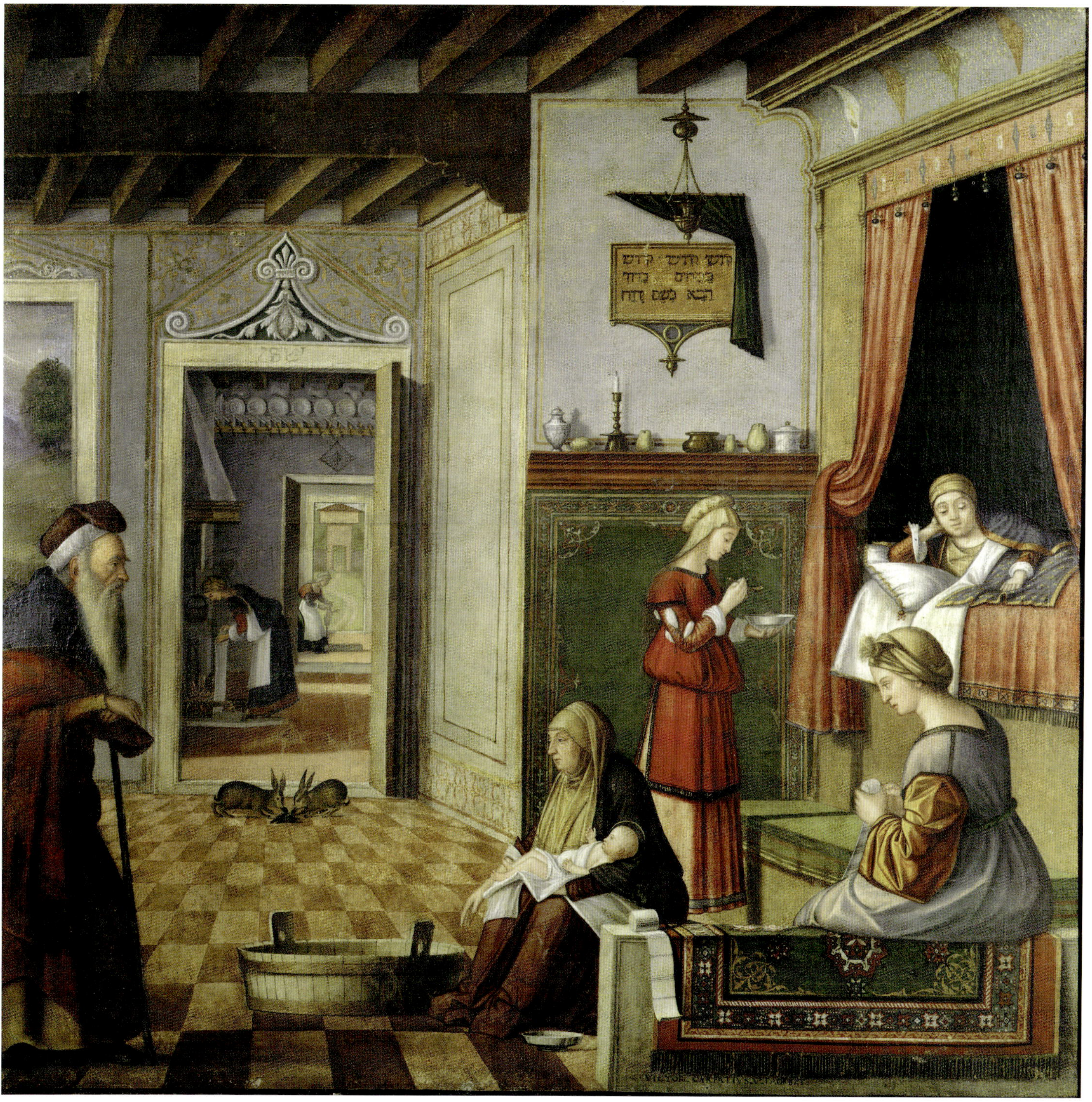

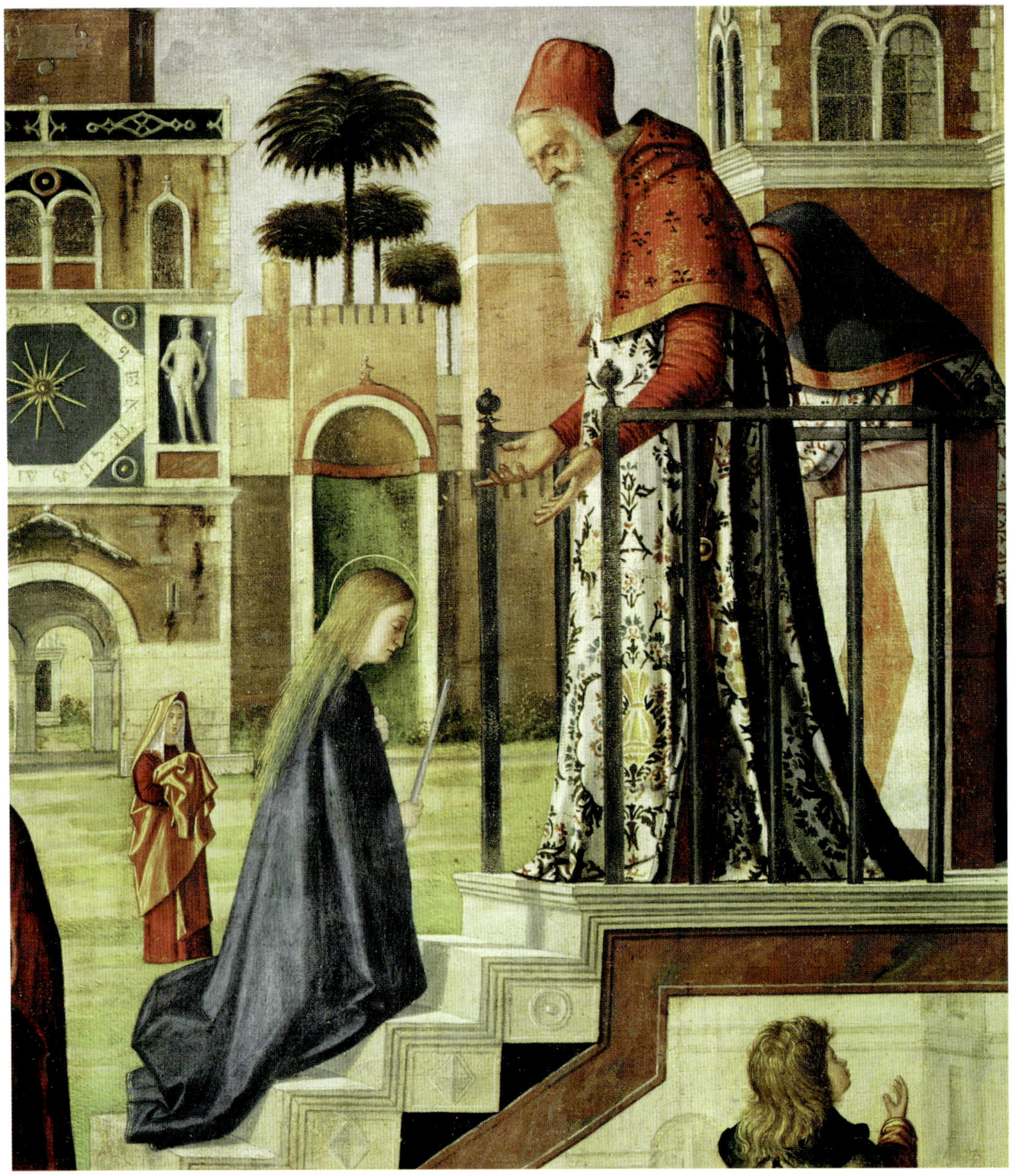

32 *THE PRESENTATION OF THE VIRGIN*
Milan, Brera.
Canvas, 137 x 130 cm.

According to the *Golden Legend*, the Virgin's parents dedicated her to the service of God, and when she had reached the age of three, they took her to the Temple in Jerusalem, where they gave her into the keeping of the High Priest. Carpaccio's composition is closely related to a rendering of the same subject by Cima da Conegliano now in Dresden, and it is probable that both are in some way related to a design made by Cima's pupil Pasqualino in 1504 for a large mural in the Scuola Grande della Carità. Pasqualino died before painting the mural, and the work was finally executed by Titian in the 1530s.

(above) Detail of pl. 32.

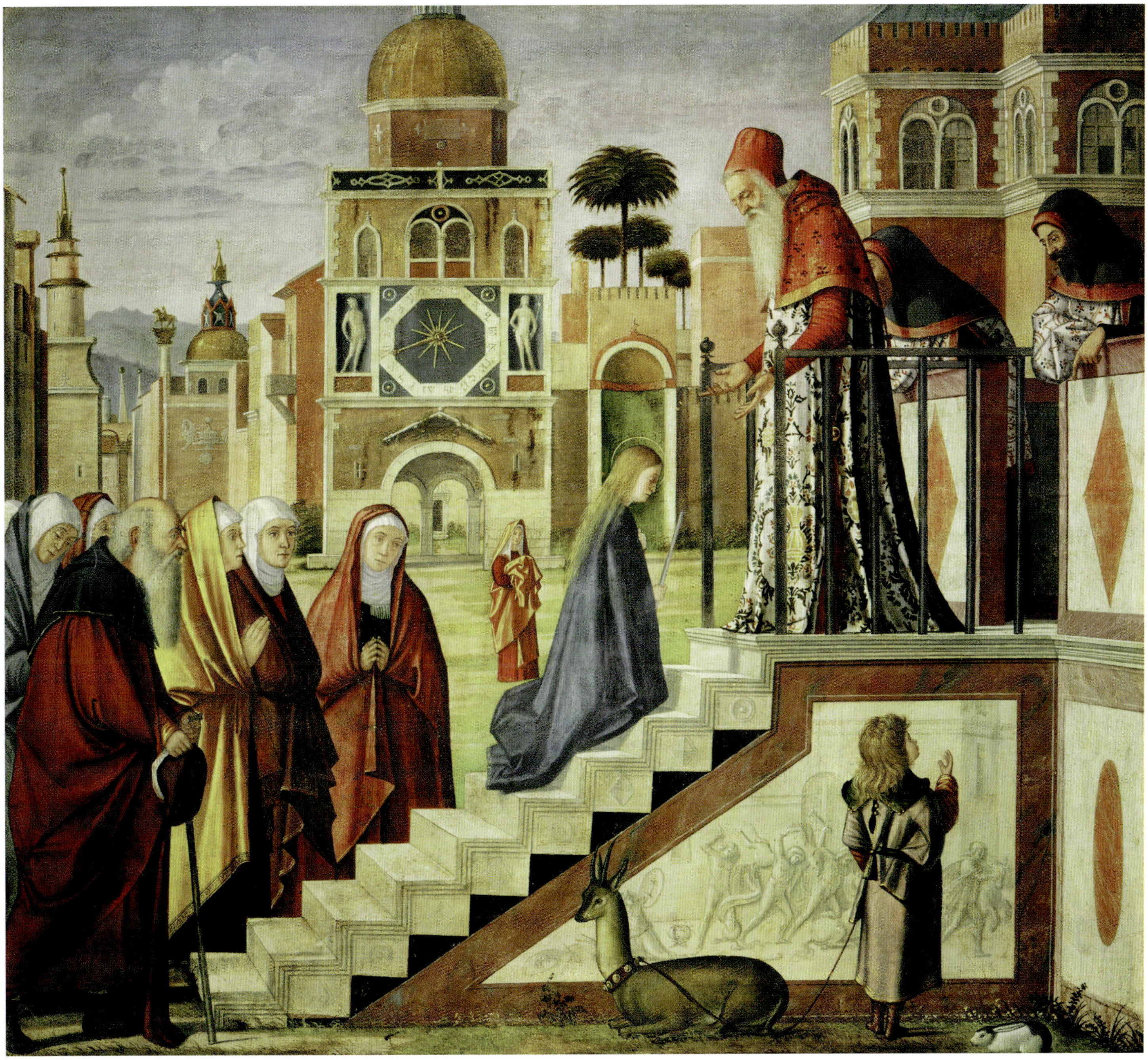

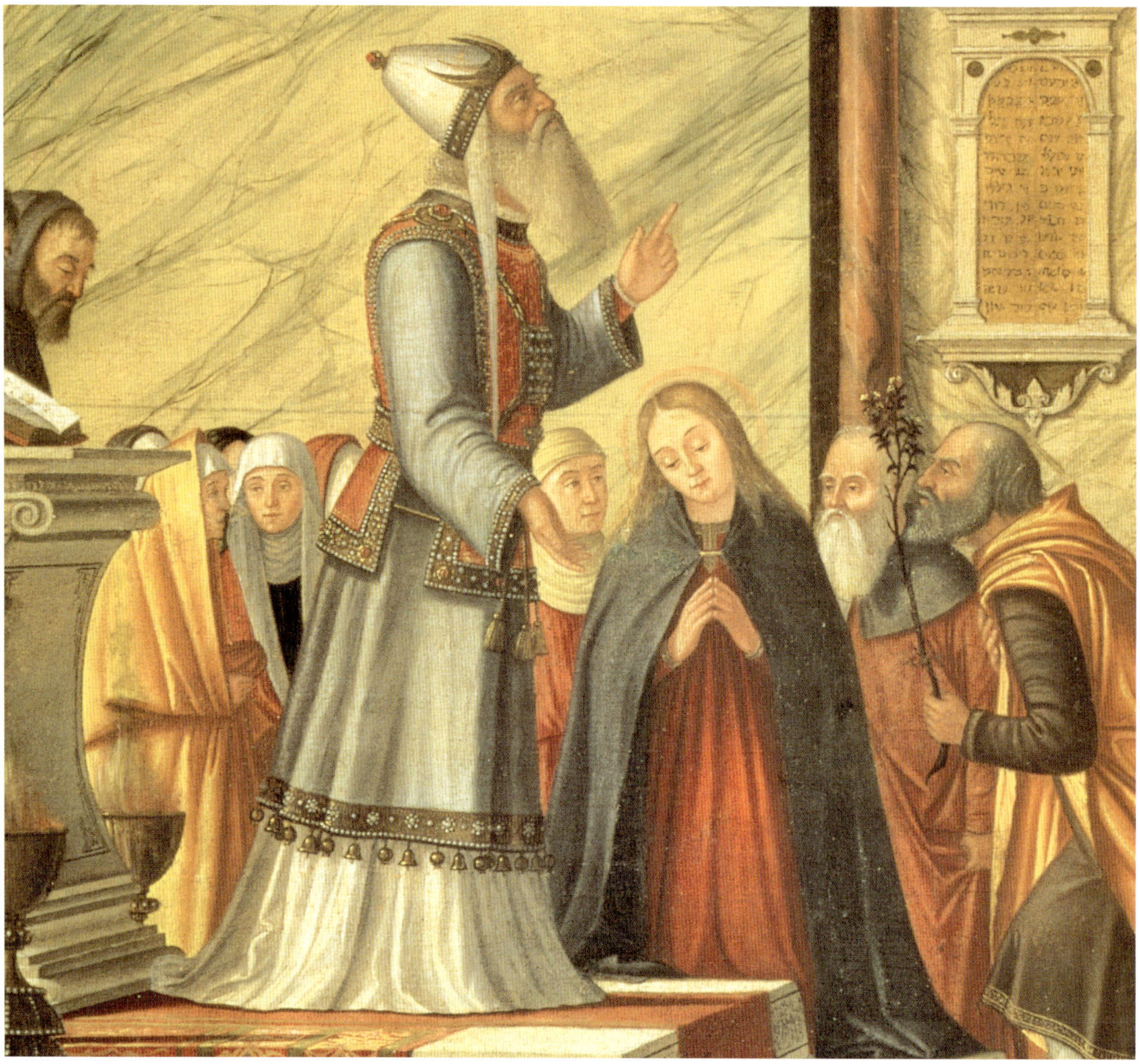

33 *THE MARRIAGE OF THE VIRGIN*
Milan, Brera.
Canvas, 140 x 130 cm.

The third of Carpaccio's canvases for the Scuola degli Albanesi shows the marriage of the Virgin to St Joseph. The many suitors for her hand were invited to place bare sticks on the altar of the Temple, and as a sign of his selection by Heaven, that of Joseph miraculously burst into flower. In the background on the right, the disappointed suitors are to be seen angrily breaking their bare sticks behind the Virgin are her parents, recognisable from their appearance in the *Birth* and *Presentation*. Carpaccio apparently went to great trouble to ensure that the liturgical furnishings of his temple were authentic: it has been shown that the seven-branched candlestick on the wall, the flaming brazier in the foreground, and the costume of the High Priest were all adapted from woodcuts found in printed books, illustrating Jewish ritual.

(above) Detail of pl. 33.

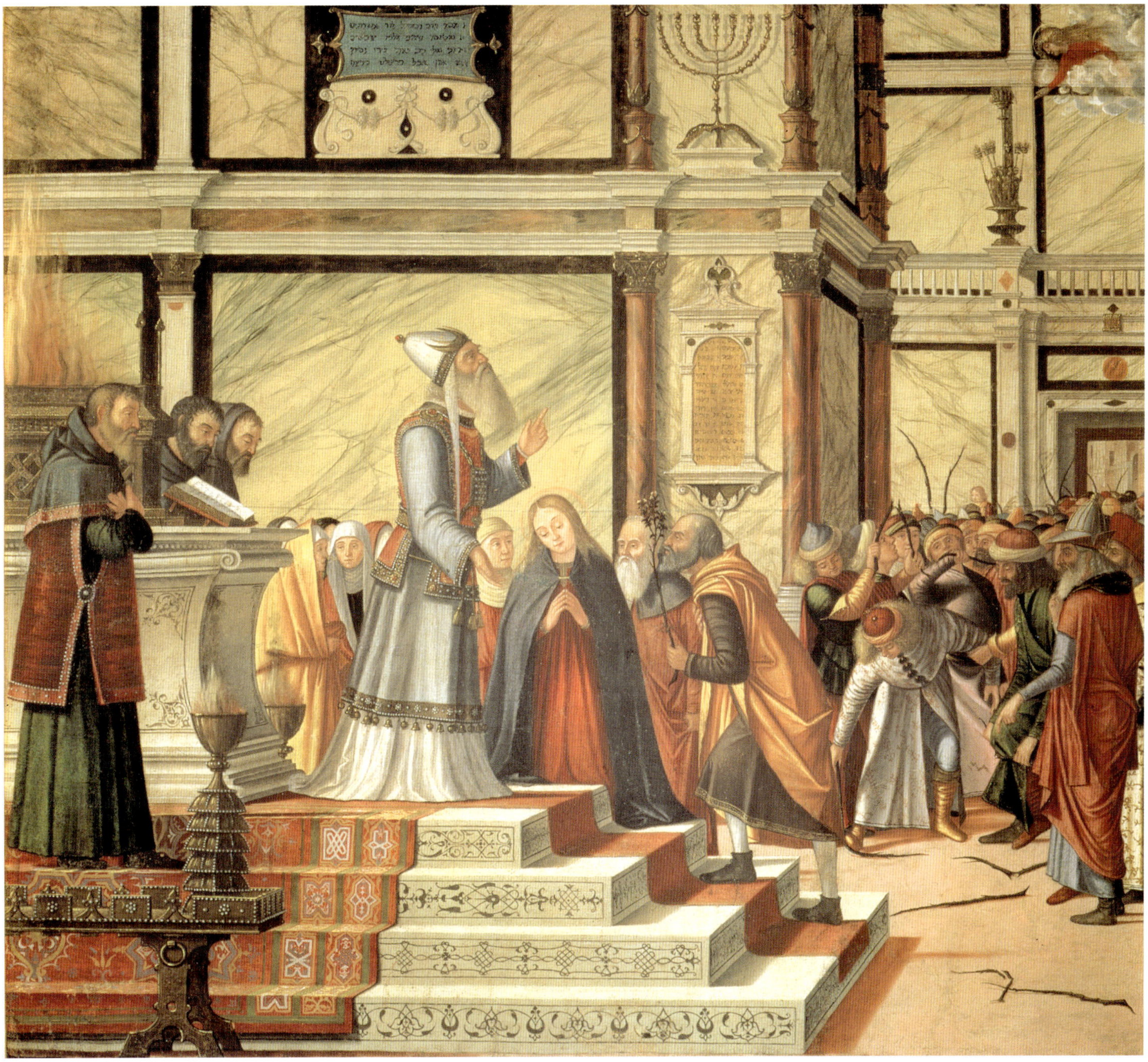

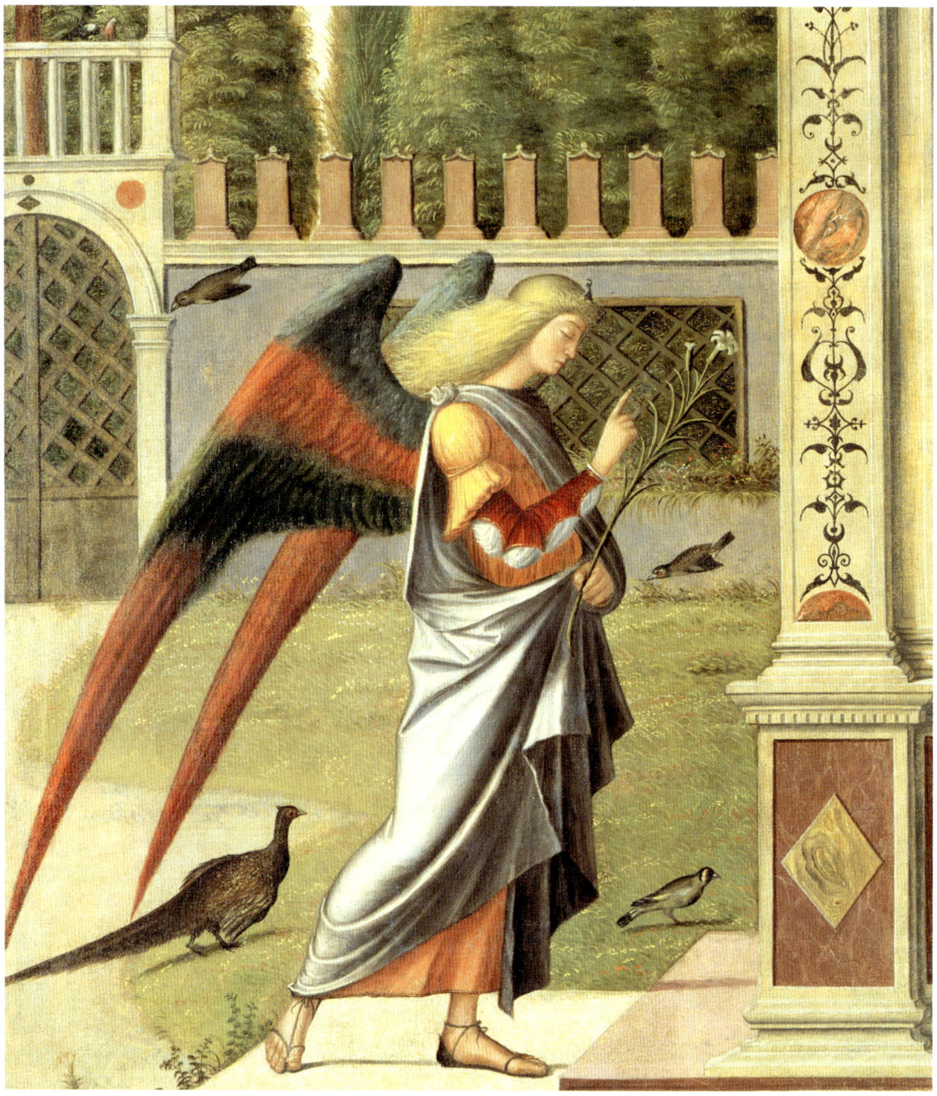

34 *THE ANNUNCIATION*
Venice, Ca'd'Oro.
Canvas, 127 x 139 cm. Inscribed: In tempo de Zuan de nicolo zimador e soi compagni. MCCCCCIIII del mese dapril.

From the cycle of the life of the Virgin painted by Carpaccio for the Scuola degli Albanesi. The inscription records that it was painted at the behest of one Zuan de Nicolo, a cloth-shearer and guardian of the confraternity, and that it was completed in April 1504. The spring-like freshness of Carpaccio's interpretation calls to mind the observation in the *Golden Legend* that Nazareth, where the Annunciation took place, means 'flower', accompanied by a quotation from St Bernard: 'The Flower willed to be born of flower, in flower, and in the season of flowers'. The walled garden in the background is probably intended as a reference to the *hortus conclusus* of the Song of Songs, traditionally understood as a metaphor for the Virgin's chastity. The Feast of the Annunciation was observed with particular solemnity in Venice, since it was traditionally believed that it was on March 25th, 421 that the lagoon on which the city is built miraculously rose from the waves of the Adriatic.

(above) Detail of pl. 34.

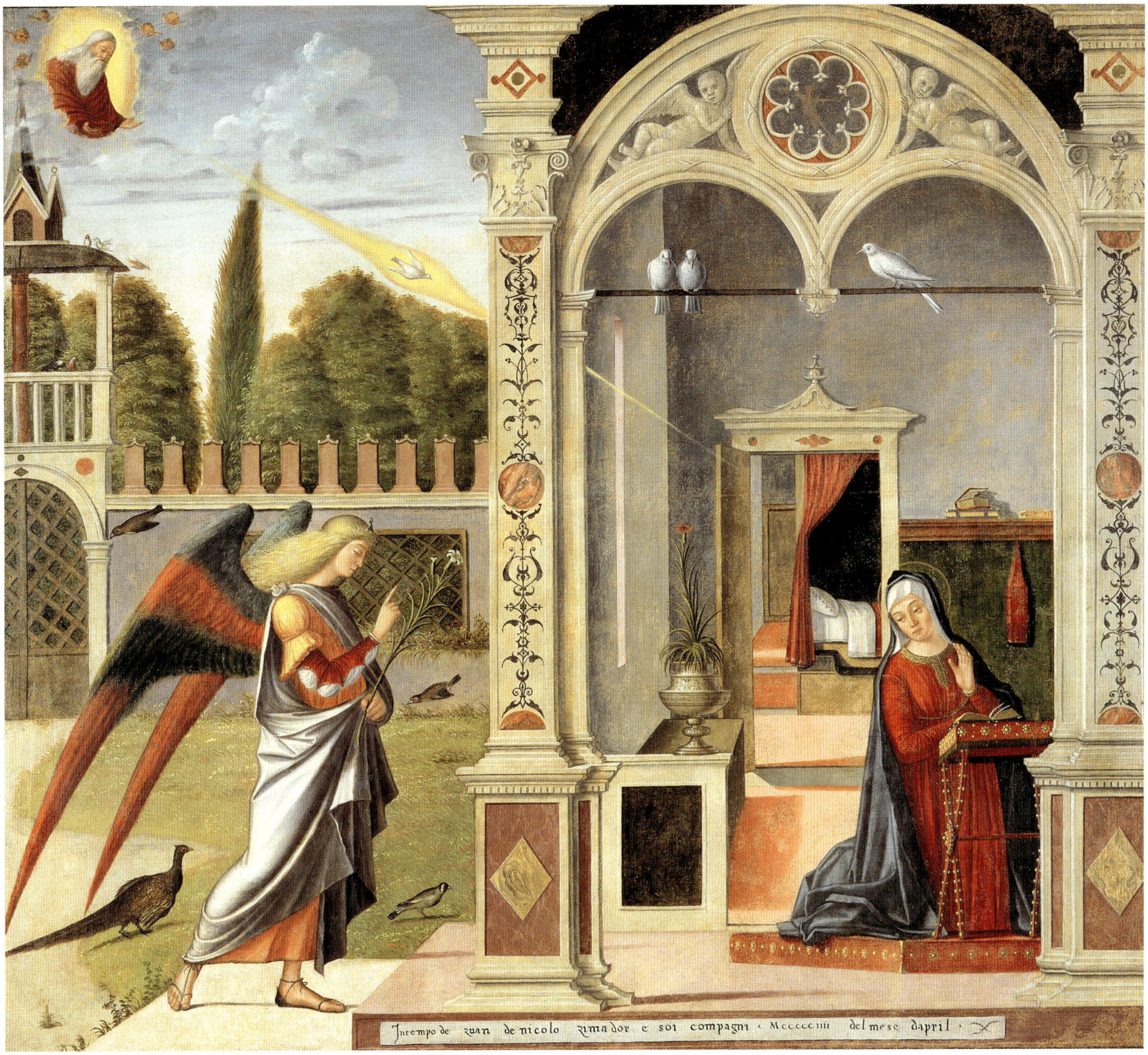
Intempo de zuan de nicolo zimador e soi compagni · Mccccciiii del mese dapril ·

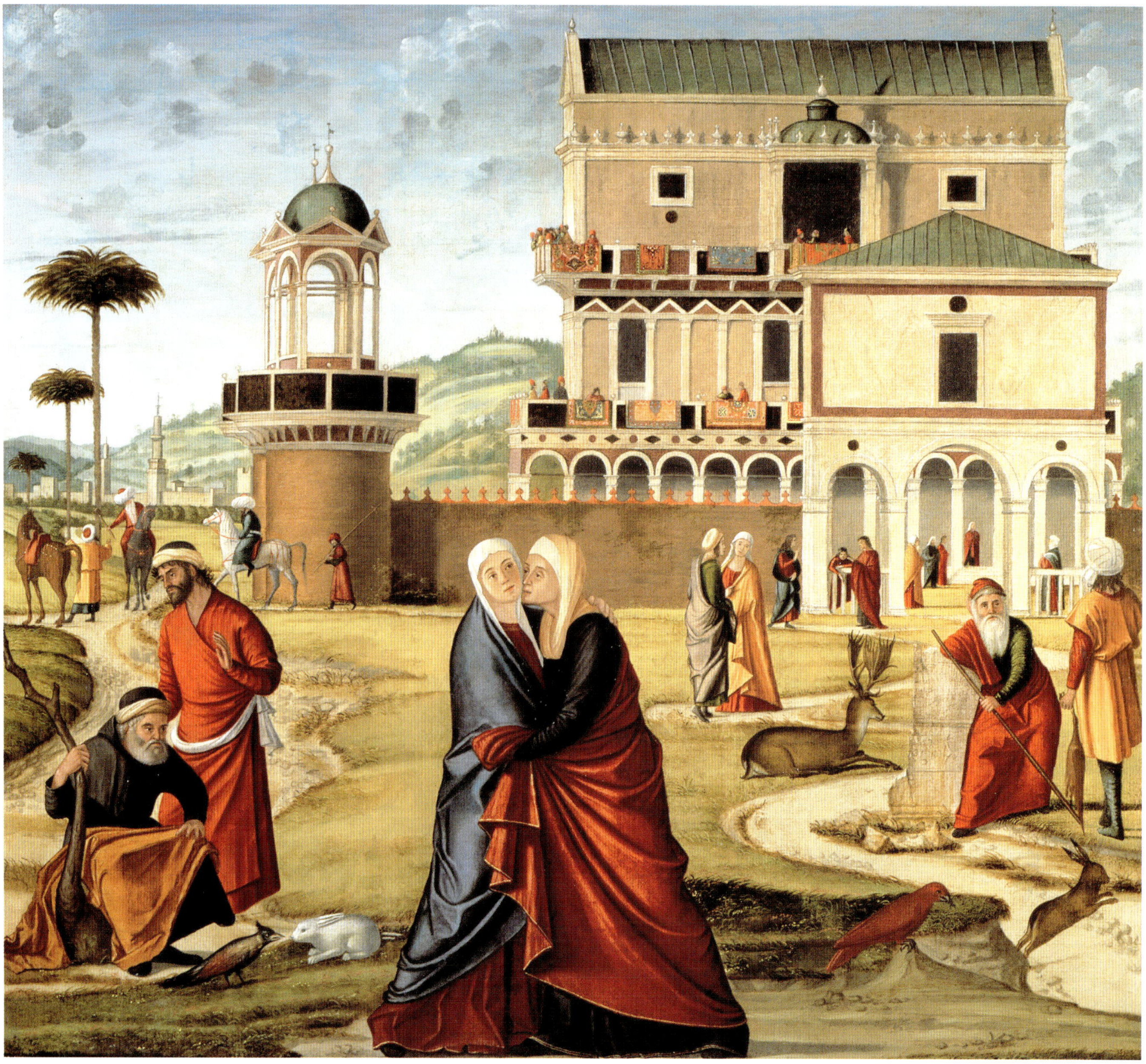

35 *THE VISITATION*
Venice, Museo Correr.
Canvas, 128 x 137 cm.

The angel of the Annunciation also gave the Virgin the news that her aged cousin Elizabeth was, by virtue of a miracle, six months pregnant, and St Luke's gospel tells of how the Virgin immediately went into the hills to visit her, and of how, as they embraced, the infant St John the Baptist leaped with joy in his mother's womb. It is interesting to notice that whereas the figures in the middle and background are dressed in an unmistakably oriental garb, in keeping with the exoticism of the scene as a whole, the two protagonists are given more classicising draperies, as an indication of their higher degree of sanctity.

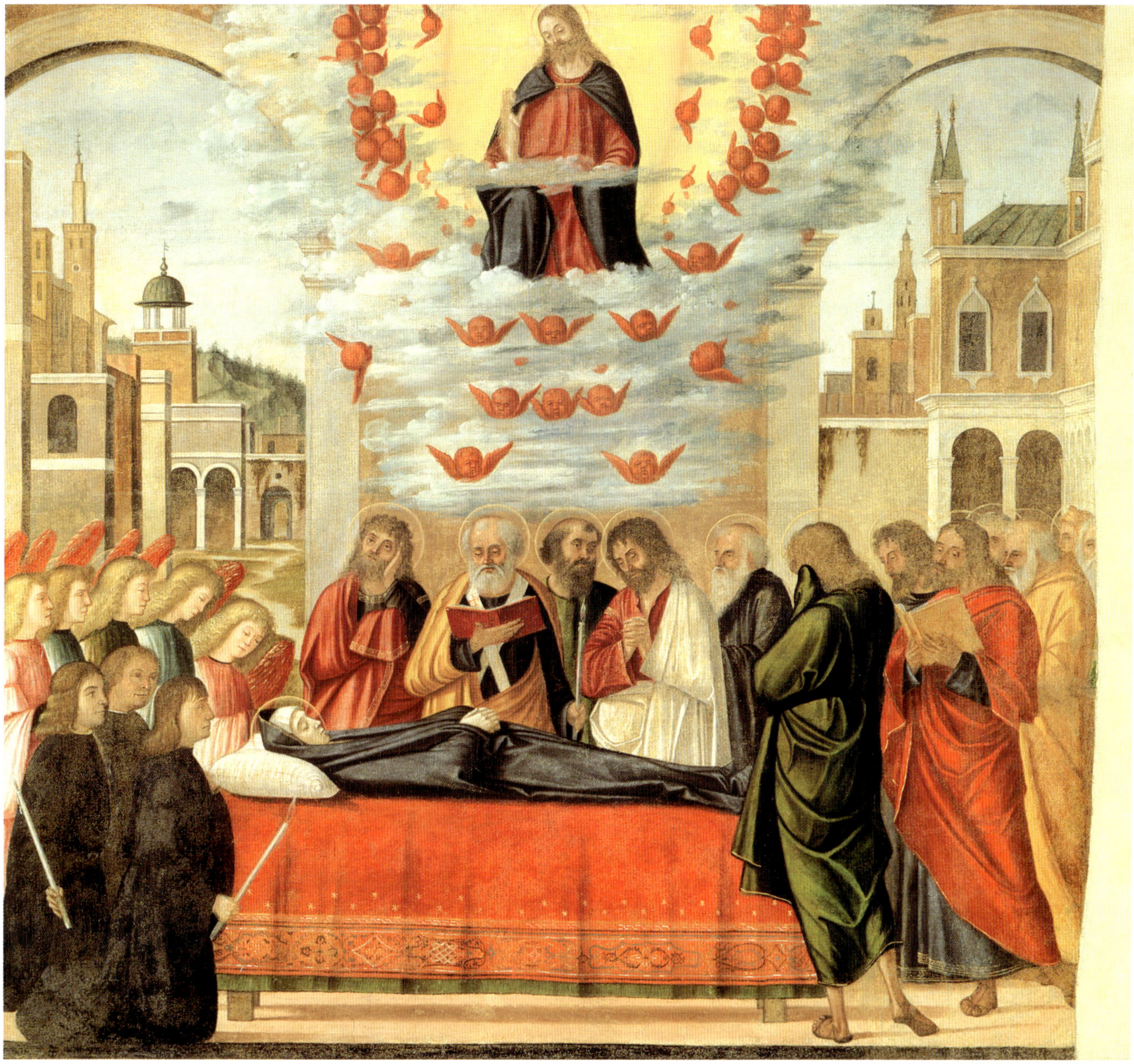

36 *THE DEATH OF THE VIRGIN*
Venice, Ca'd'Oro.
Canvas, 128 x 133 cm.

The last of the six canvases for the Scuola degli Albanesi shows the Virgin on her deathbed, mourned by angels and the apostles; in heaven, her soul is received by Christ. The three figures in the left foreground, wearing contemporary dress and holding lighted tapers, are probably portraits of governors of the confraternity. When in their original position, the canvases were arranged in a row down the left hand wall of the scuola chapel, and the profiles of the governors appropriately would have faced towards the chapel altar.

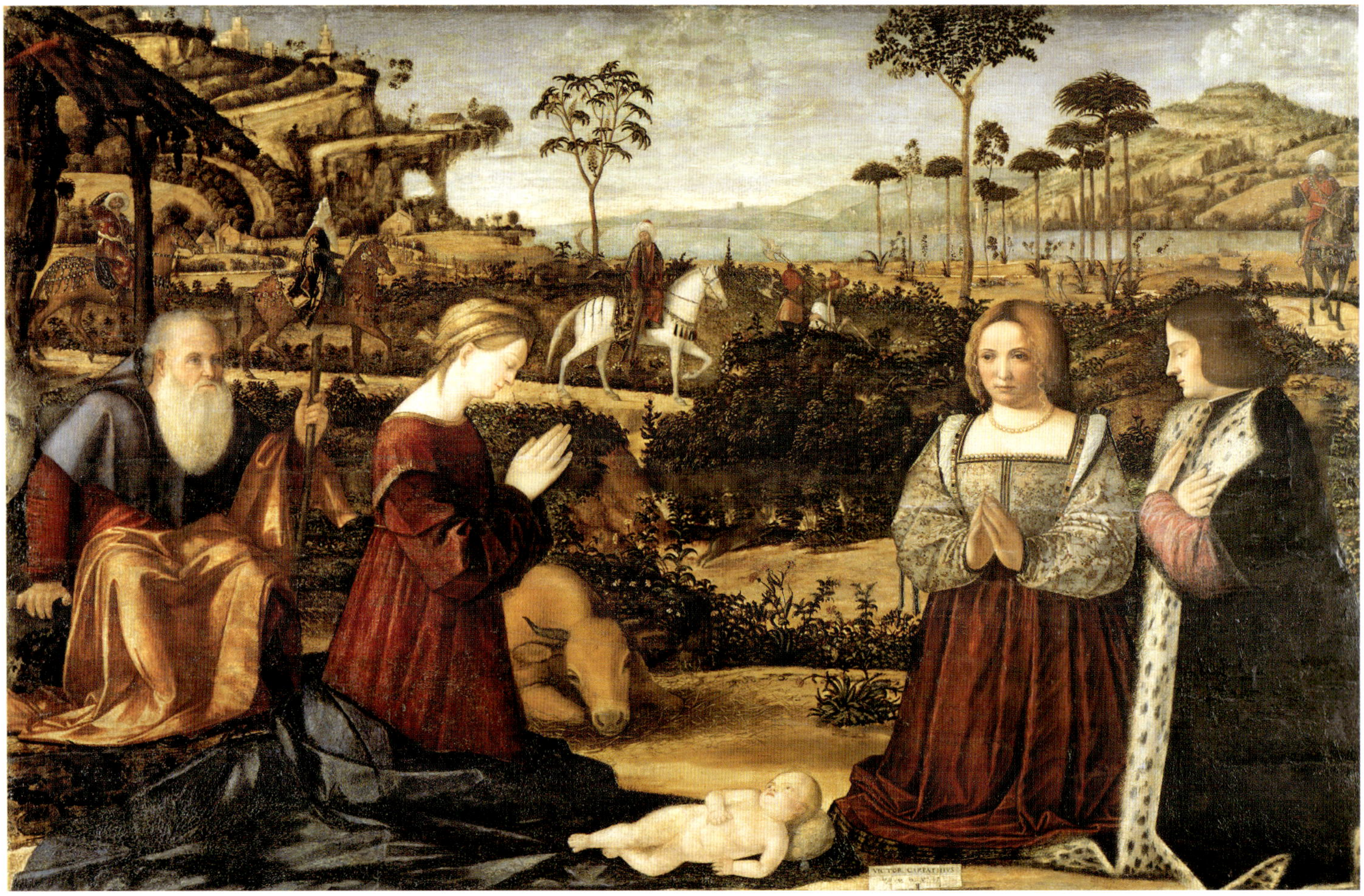

37 *THE ADORATION OF CHRIST WITH TWO DONORS*
Lisbon, Gulbenkian Foundation.
Panel, 90 x 134 cm. Inscribed: VICTOR CARPATHIUS / MDV

The two richly-dressed donors who adore the new-born Child have not been identified. In the background, the three Magi can be seen arriving. This painting, with its warm colours and its mood of a drowsy summer afternoon, has been seen as reflecting the influence of Giorgione.

38 *THE VIRGIN READING*
Washington D.C., National Gallery of Art, Kress Collection.
Panel, 78 x 51 cm.

Evidently a fragment of a larger painting, which probably once also included the Christ Child. A drawing now in New York may well record the original composition.
Datable to ca. 1505 on stylistic grounds.

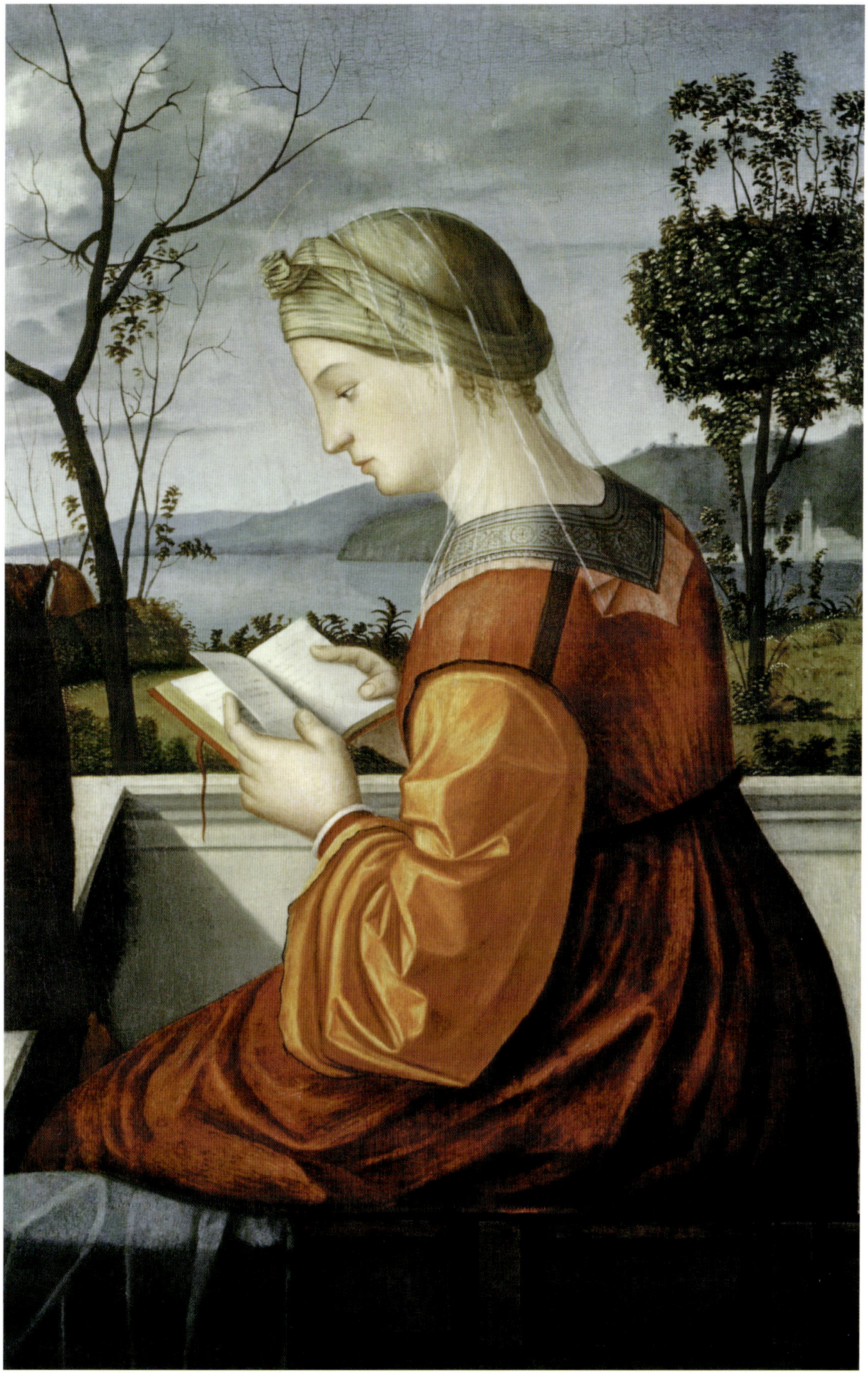

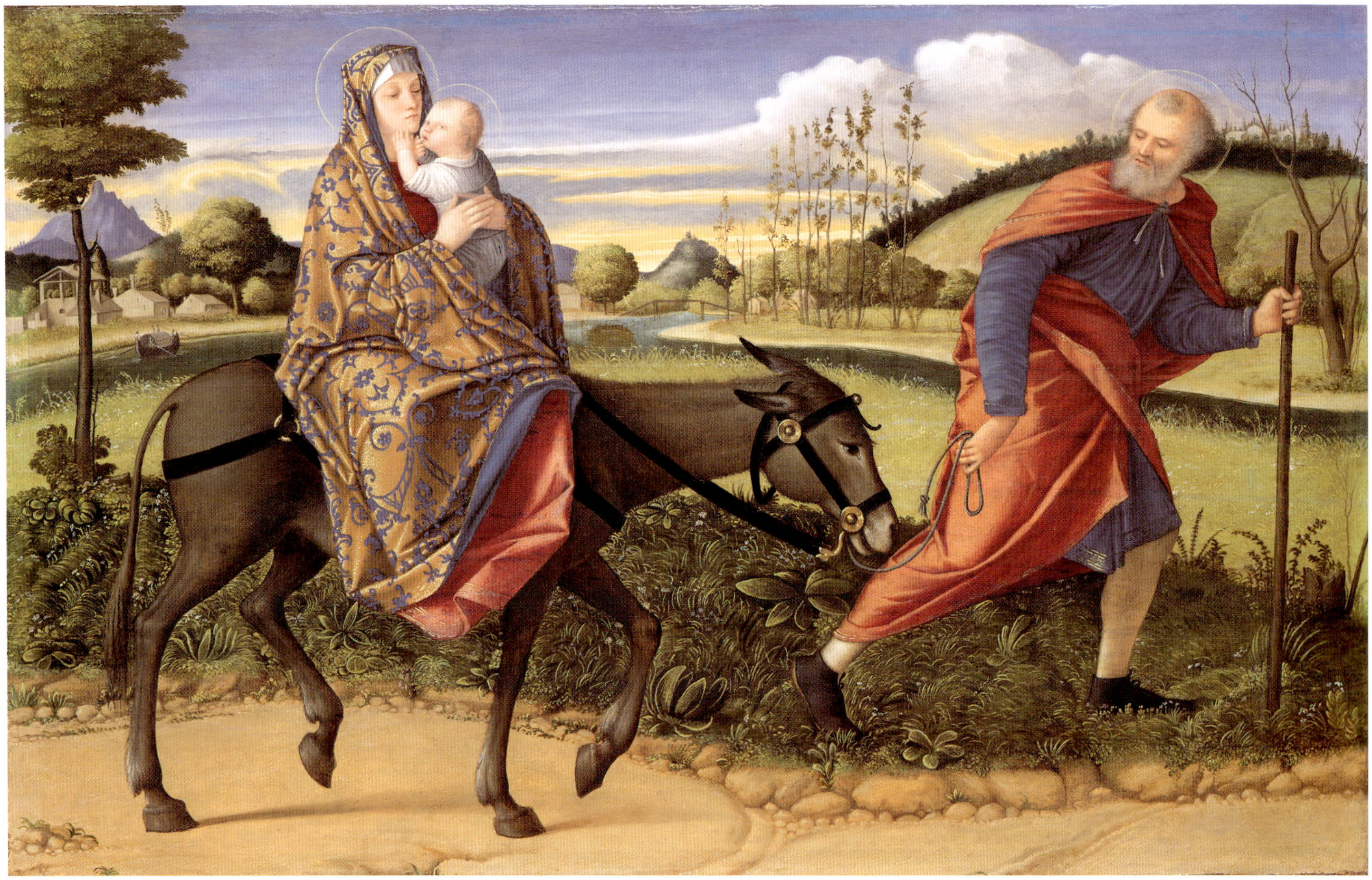

39 *THE FLIGHT INTO EGYPT*
Washington D.C., National Gallery of Art,
Mellon Collection.
Panel, 75 x 112 cm.

Still preserved in its original, wooden frame, adorned with two family escutcheons. These have not yet been identified, but it has been suggested they may have belonged to a husband and wife, to whom the painting was given as a wedding present. Probably datable to ca. 1505.

40 *VIRGIN AND CHILD IN A LANDSCAPE*
Washington D.C., National Gallery of Art,
Kress Collection.
Panel, 85 x 68 cm.

A devotional panel in the tradition of the many Madonna and Child representations by Giovanni Bellini (see Fig. G). Datable to ca. 1507.

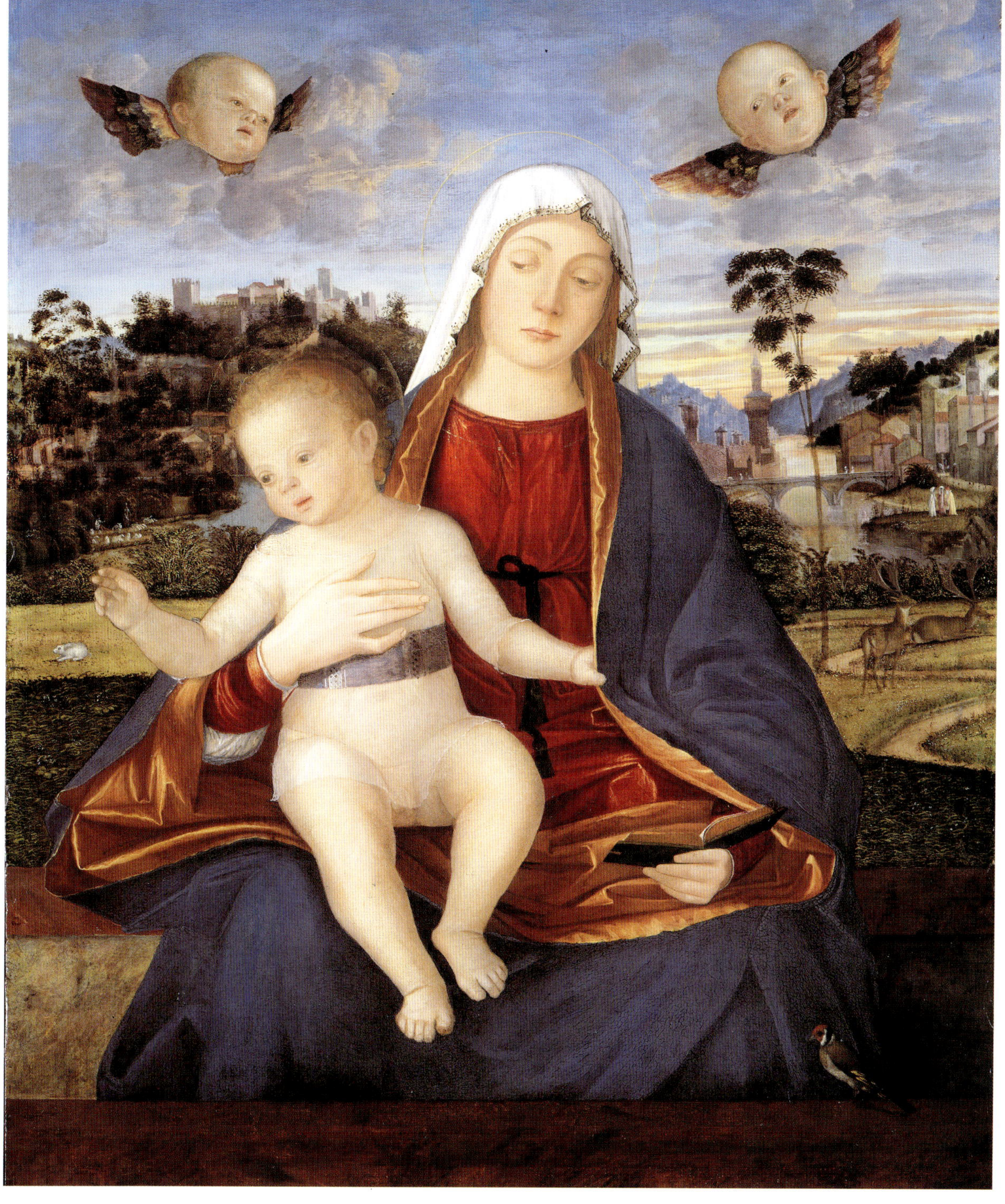

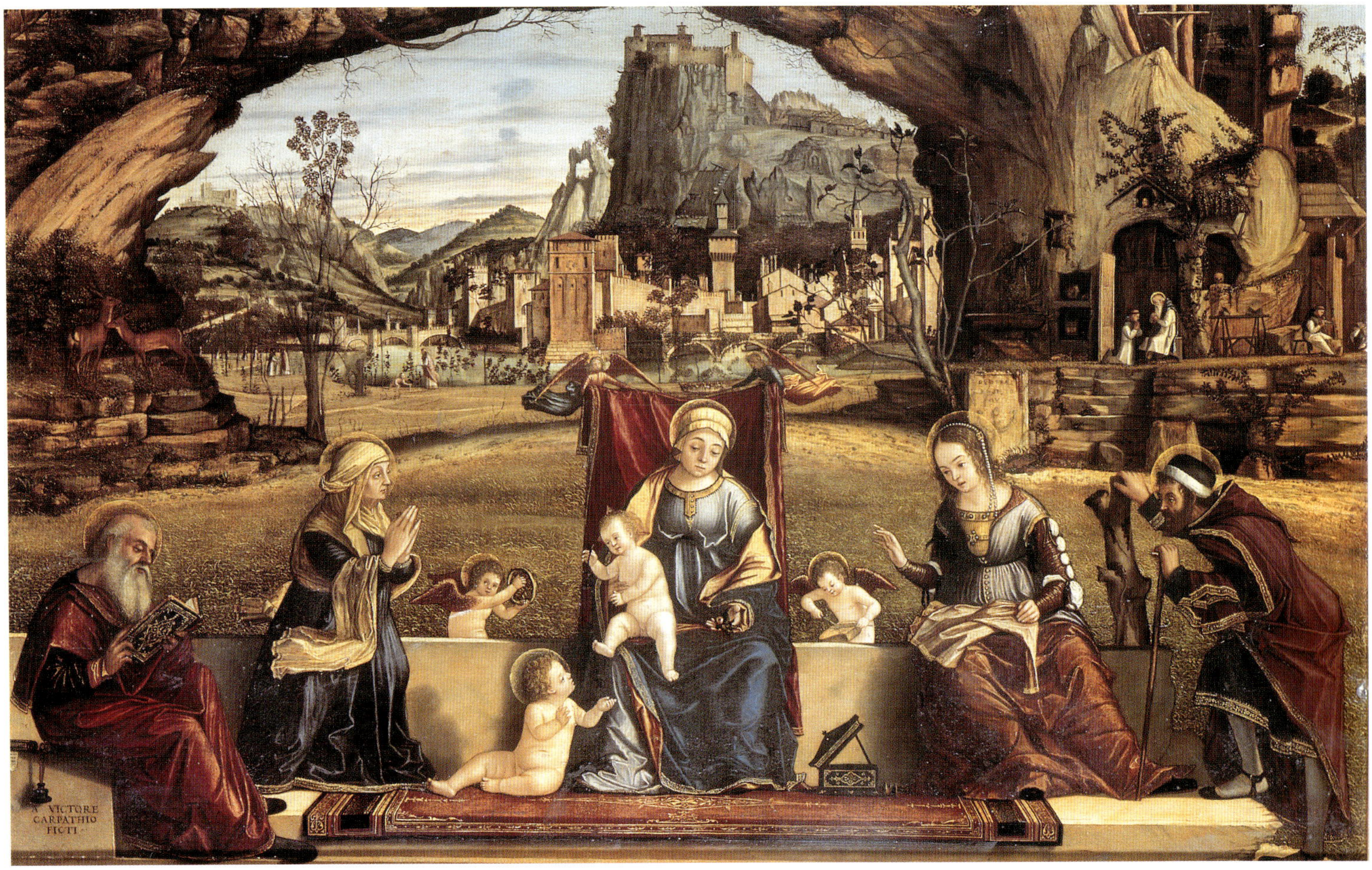

41 *HOLY FAMILY AND SAINTS*
Avignon, Musée du Petit Palais.
Panel, 98 x 127 cm. Inscribed: A VICTORE/CARPATHIO/FICTI.

The identities of the four saints flanking the central group of the Virgin, Child and St John the Baptist are not entirely clear. In all probability they are to be recognised as saints Joachim and Anna, the parents of the Virgin, on the left, and Mary Magdalen and Joseph on the right; but both pairs have also been interpreted as saints Elizabeth and Zachariah, the parents of the Baptist. In any case, the iconography is clearly related to Northern European representations of the theme of the Holy Kinship, a sort of enlarged Holy Family group, representing an array of Christ's cousins, uncles and aunts. Characteristic of this iconography is the mood of domestic harmony, showing the holy children at play and the mothers employed in household activities such as needlework; characteristic also is the setting of the figures within a sacred precinct closed off from the background landscape. It has been pointed out that whereas the background of Carpaccio's *Meditation on the Dead Christ* shows, in the top left-hand corner, a stag being cruelly devoured by a leopard, the left background here shows a tranquil scene of a stag being lovingly licked by a deer. Also in the background are to be seen various scenes from the lives of saints Jerome and Augustine.

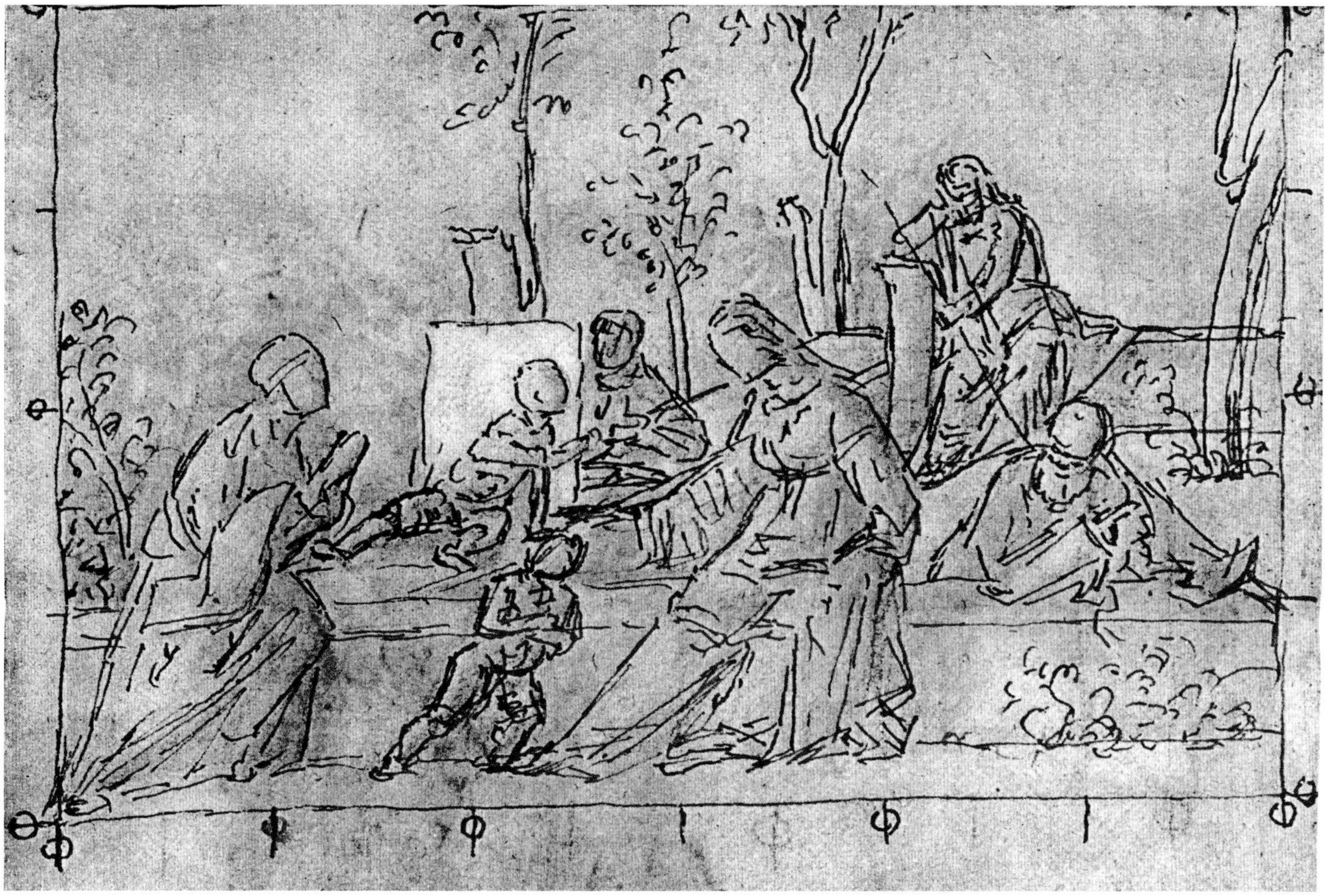

42 *STUDY FOR A HOLY FAMILY*
Florence, Uffizi.
Pen in brown ink and wash, 120 x 180 mm.

Perhaps an early draft for the composition of the *Holy Family and Saints* two adult figures in the foreground are very close in pose to their counterparts in the painting. Not all the saints are easy to identify, but it has been suggested that the figure in the left middleground – apparently seated at work behind an easel – represents St Luke.

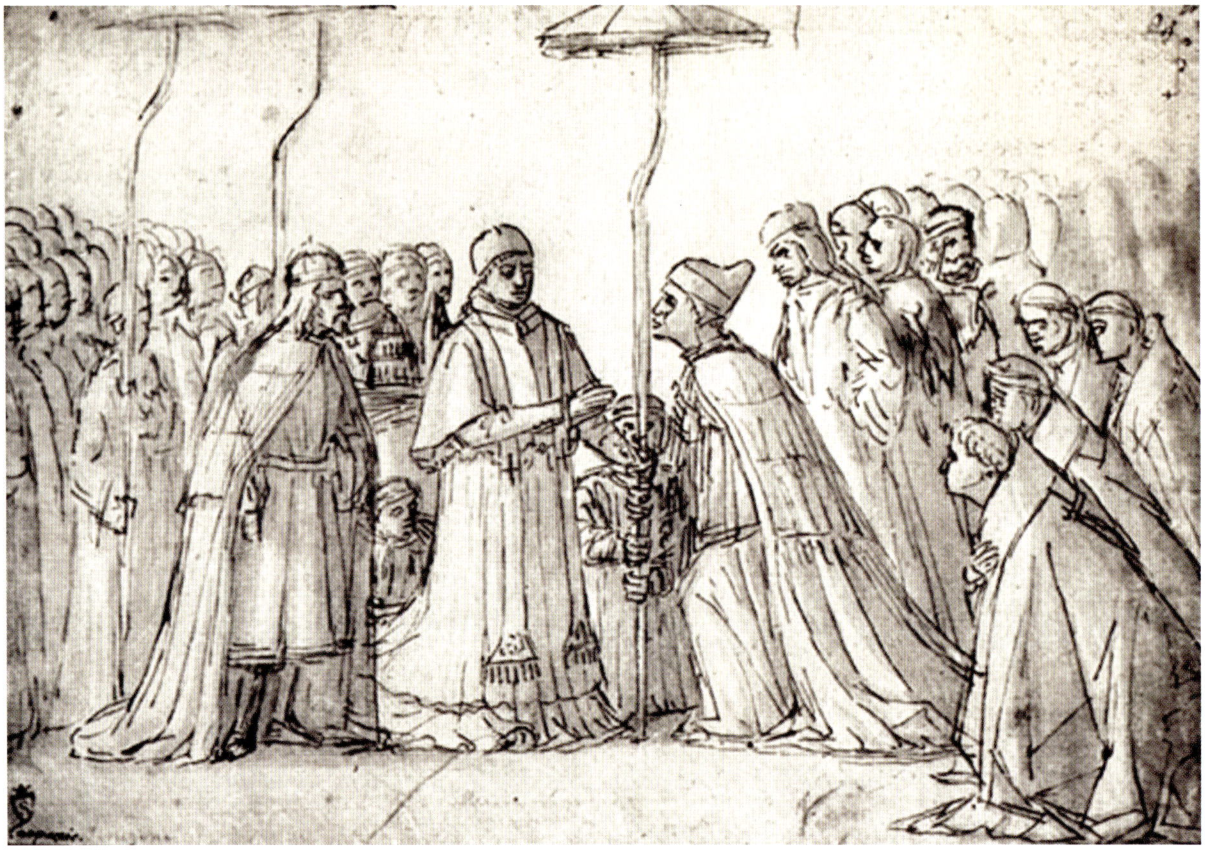

43 *POPE ALEXANDER III PRESENTS DOGE SEBASTIANO ZIANI WITH THE CEREMONIAL SUNSHADE*
Sacramento, Calif., E.B. Crocker Art Gallery.
Pen and wash, 210 x 295 mm.

A compositional sketch for a canvas painted by Carpaccio for the hall of the Great Council in the Doge's Palace in 1507. The scene shows the presentation of a ceremonial baldachin by Pope Alexander III to Doge Sebastiano Ziani, an event that took place at Ancona in 1177 in the presence of the Emperor Frederick Barbarossa. The presentation was of the highest symbolic significance for the dignity of the Venetian State, since it implicitly placed the doge and his successors on a footing equal to that of the pope and emperor, each of whom had his own baldachin. Carpaccio's canvas, which probably followed a general design by Giovanni Bellini, was destroyed by fire in 1577, together with the other historical narratives in the Hall. Some years later it was replaced by the version by Girolamo Gambarata, which is still in place today. Carpaccio also seems to have had a hand in another canvas of the cycle, *Pope Alexander III celebrating Mass in St Marks*, which according to literary sources contained a number of portraits of famous contemporaries; but no visual evidence of this has survived.

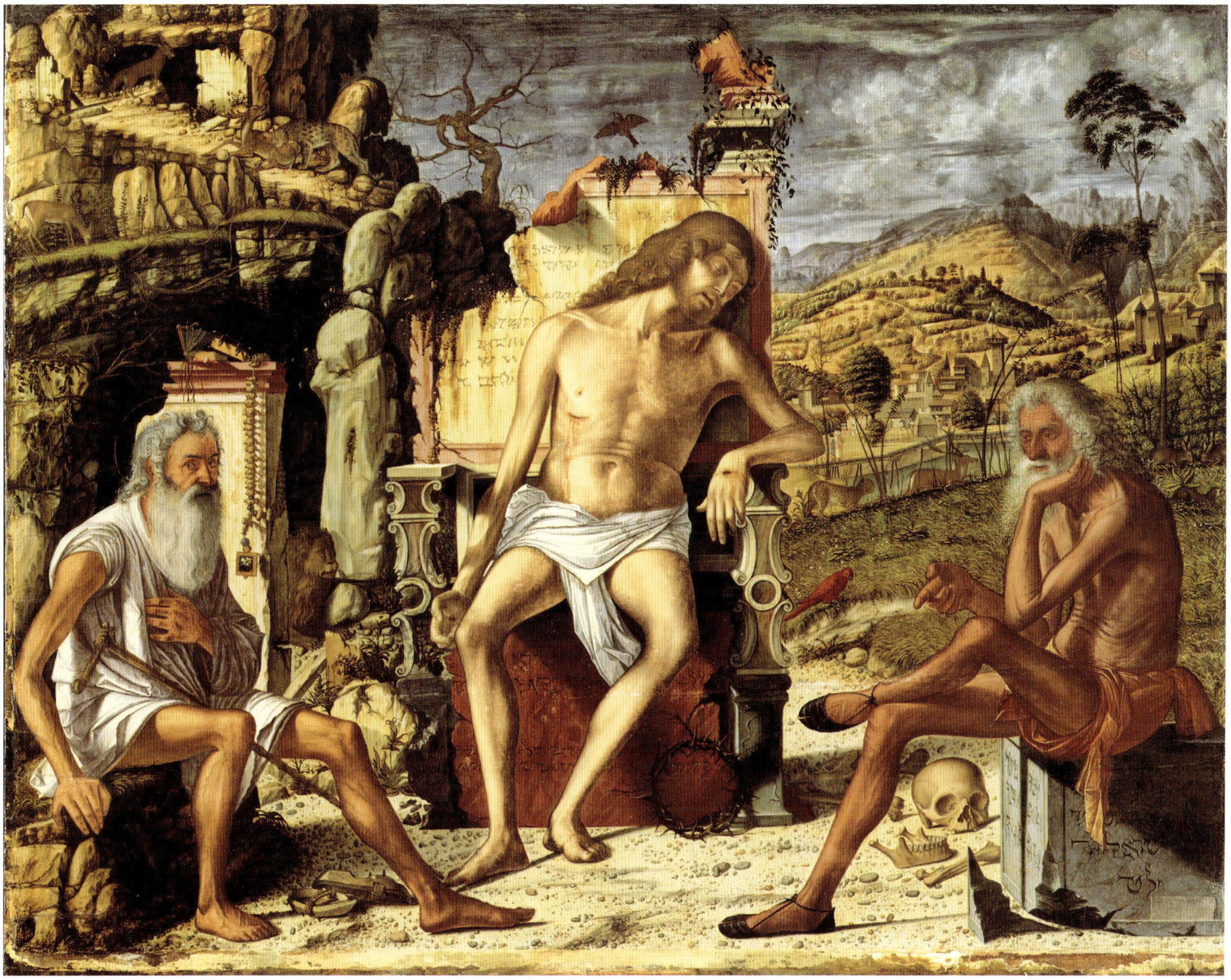

44 *MEDITATION ON THE DEAD CHRIST*
New York, Metropolitan Museum of Art.
Panel, 70.5 x 87 cm. Inscribed: vjctorjs carpattjj venettj opus.

The two figures on either side of the Dead Christ have been identified as St Jerome on the left, and as Job on the right. As an innocent man who bore his tribulations meekly and patiently, Job was often seen as a prototype of Christ, a comparison that is made explicit in the writings of St Jerome. It is as if St Jerome, with his eyes turned sharply towards the spectator, is inviting us to meditate on the inner meaning of Christ's Passion and death. The Hebrew inscription on the back of Christ's throne is taken from the famous text in the Book of Job 'I know that my Redeemer liveth'. The bird flying upwards immediately above it is a further allusion to the Resurrection. The dating of this painting is highly controversial, one body of opinion dating it ca. 1490, and another as much as twenty years later, ca. 1510.

(overleaf) Details of pl. 44.

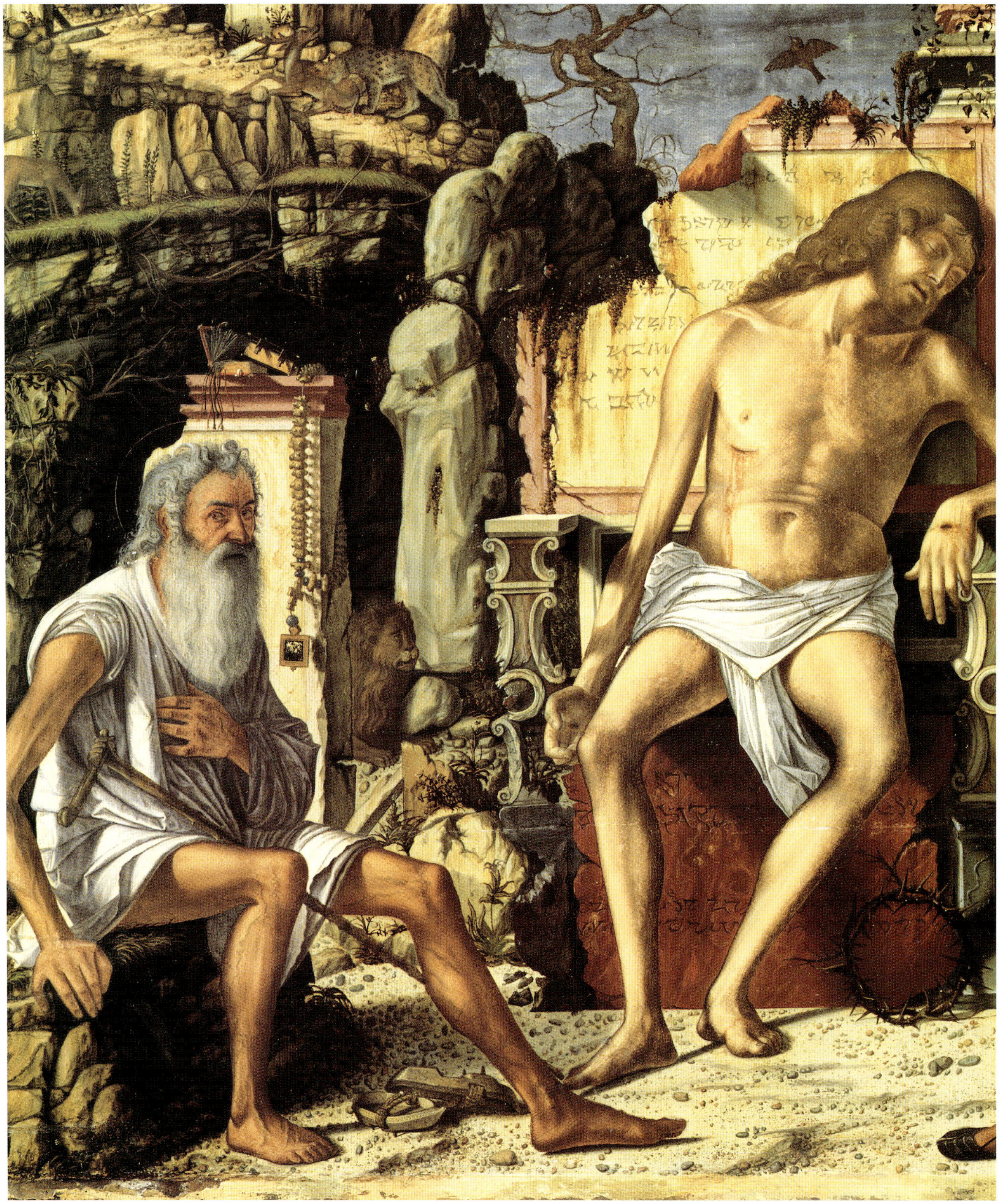

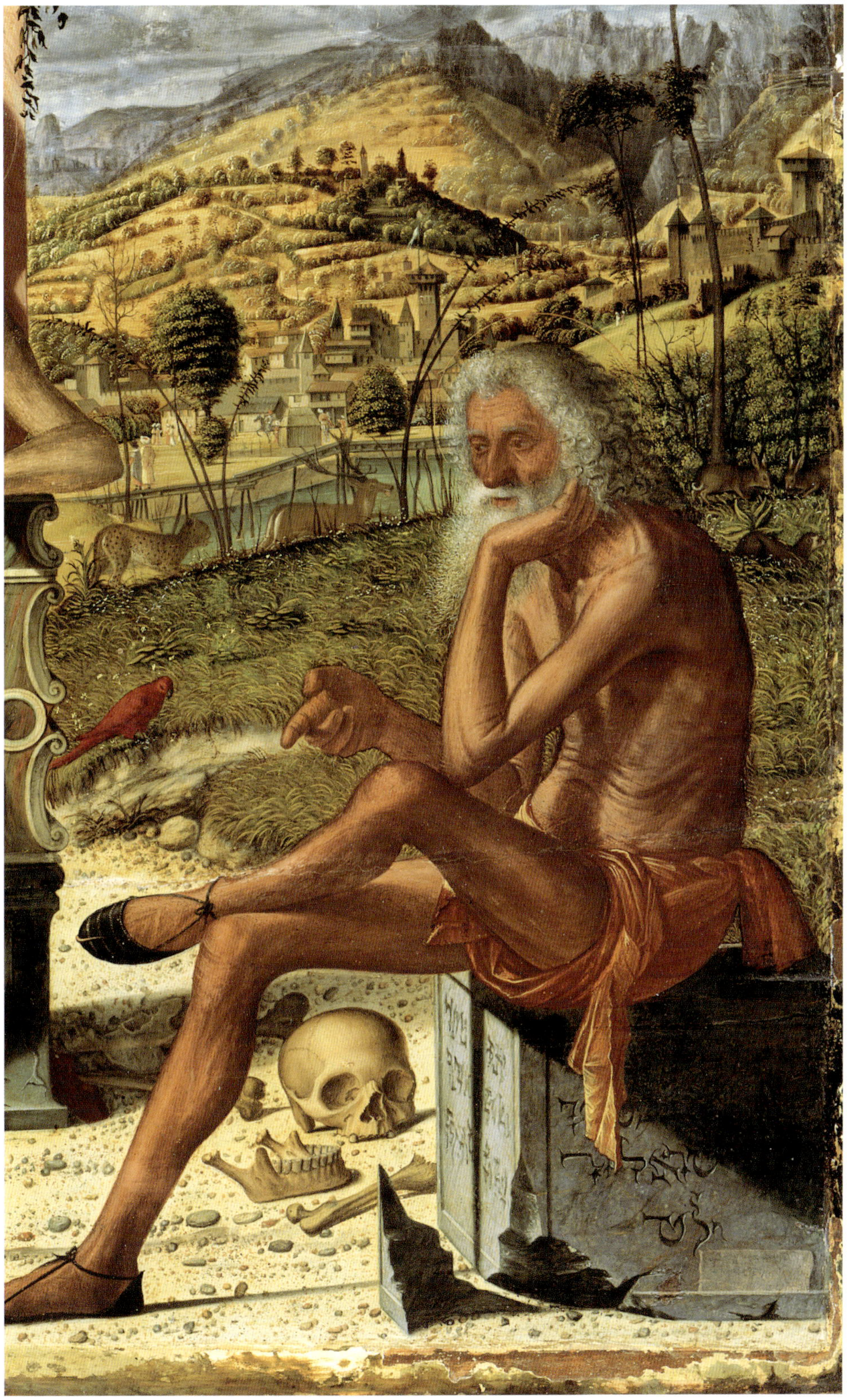

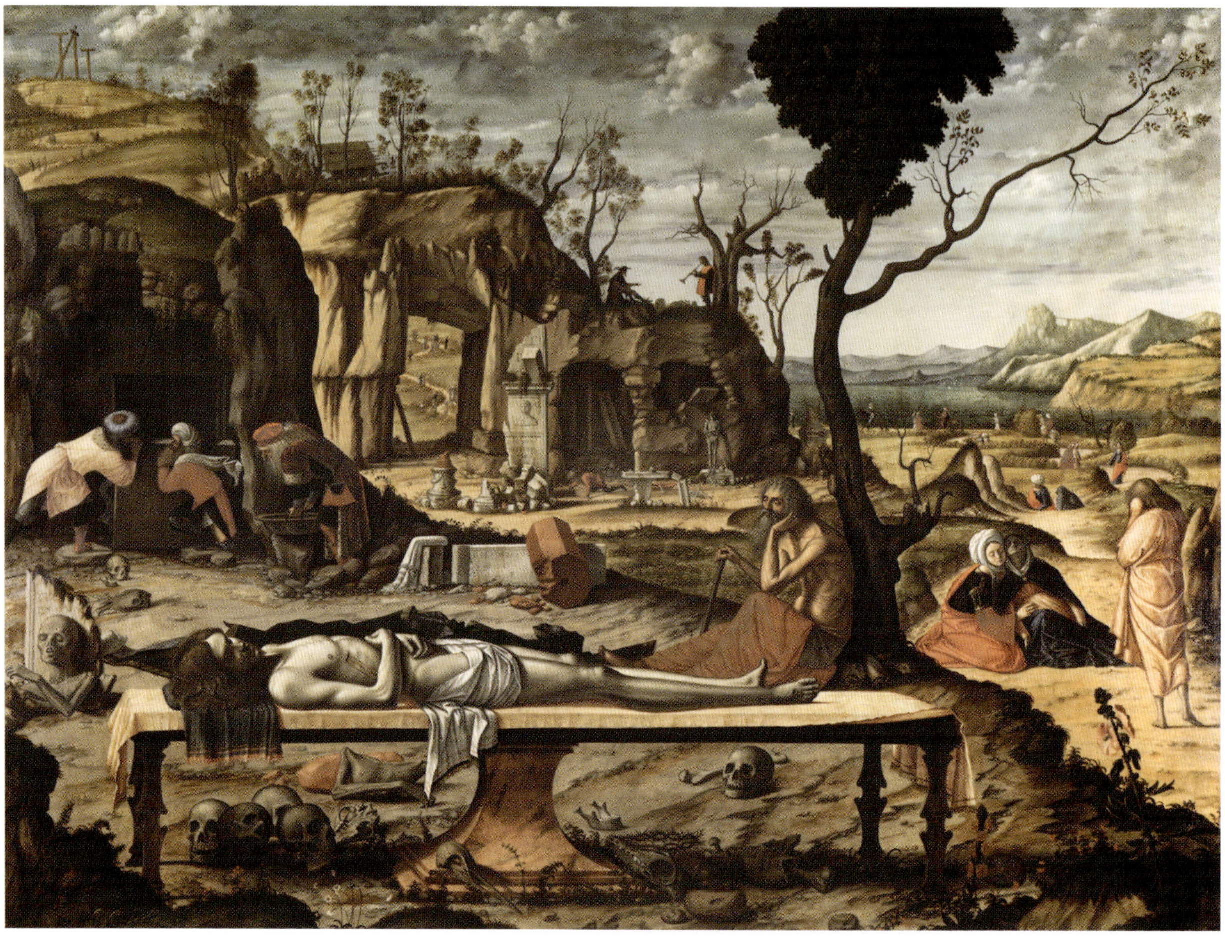

45 *THE ENTOMBMENT OF CHRIST*
Berlin, Gemäldegalerie.
Canvas, 145 x 185 cm.

Close in style and sentiment to pl. 44, and again the presence of Job – here seated under a tree in the middle-ground – invites the spectator to meditate on the meaning of Christ's Passion and death. Compared with the New York picture, the representation is more specifically historical, and is based on the sequence of events recounted in Matthew 27, 51–60: the earthquake at the moment of Christ's death, which rent rocks and opened up graves; the presence of the holy women; and the preparations of the rock sepulchre by Joseph of Arimiathea. The image of the Dead Christ in the foreground is based on the traditional Byzantine iconography of the *Epitaphios*, representing Christ's body stretched out on a stone slab to be anointed before burial. As is particularly apparent from a twelfth century rendering still preserved in the treasury of St Mark's in Venice, the theme had strongly Eucharistic implications, alluding to the constant renewal of the redemptive benefits of Christ's self-sacrifice in the celebration of the mass. The figure of the Virgin in the right background, swooning in the arms of the Magdalen, is derived from an engraving of the same subject by Mantegna. The motif of the swoon – an obvious metaphor for death – also seems to have a theological meaning, based on the doctrine of the Virgin as an active co-operant in the Passion – and hence also in the Resurrection. Most critics are agreed that the painting dates from the first decade of the sixteenth century.

(right) Detail of pl. 45.

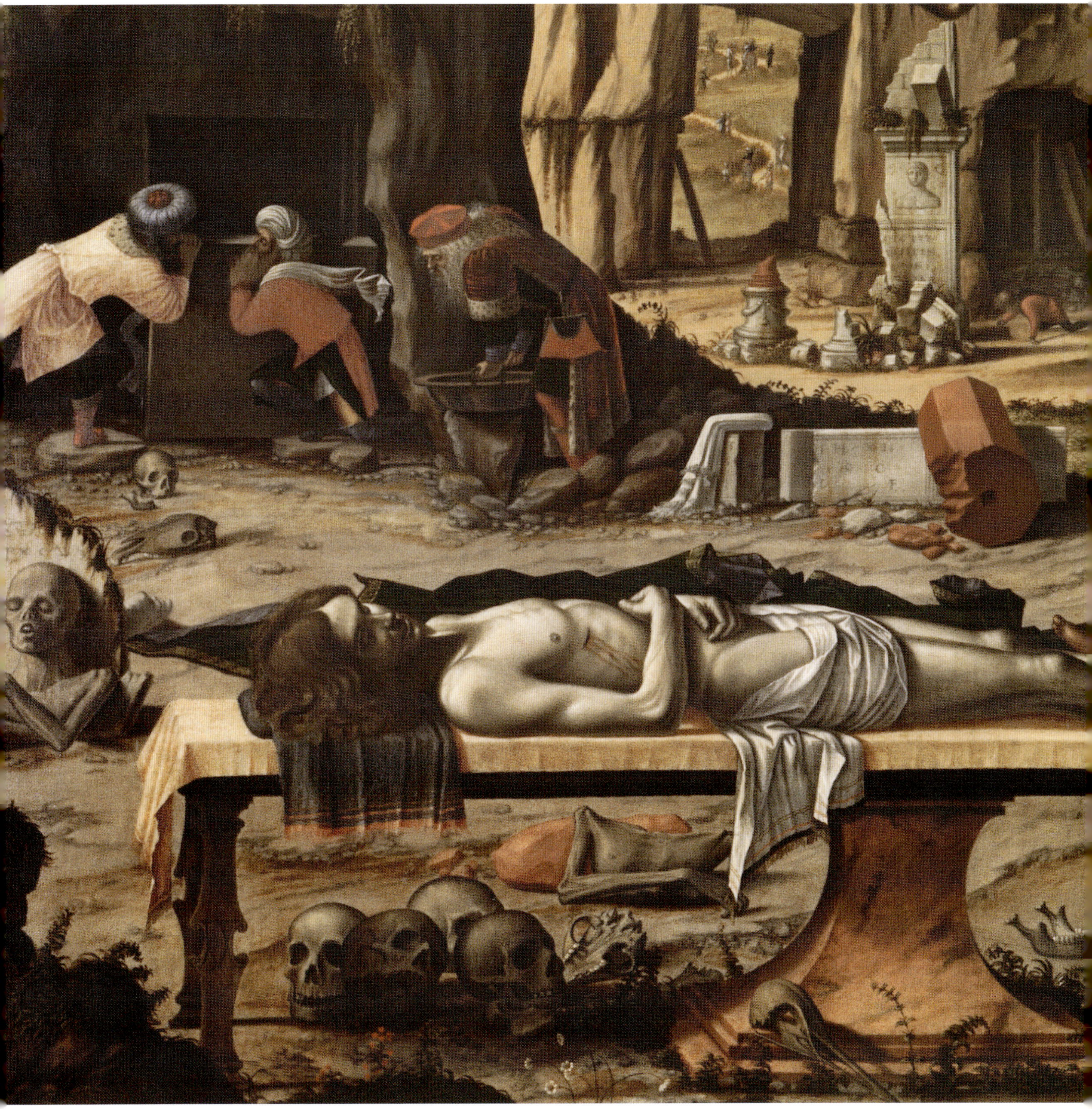

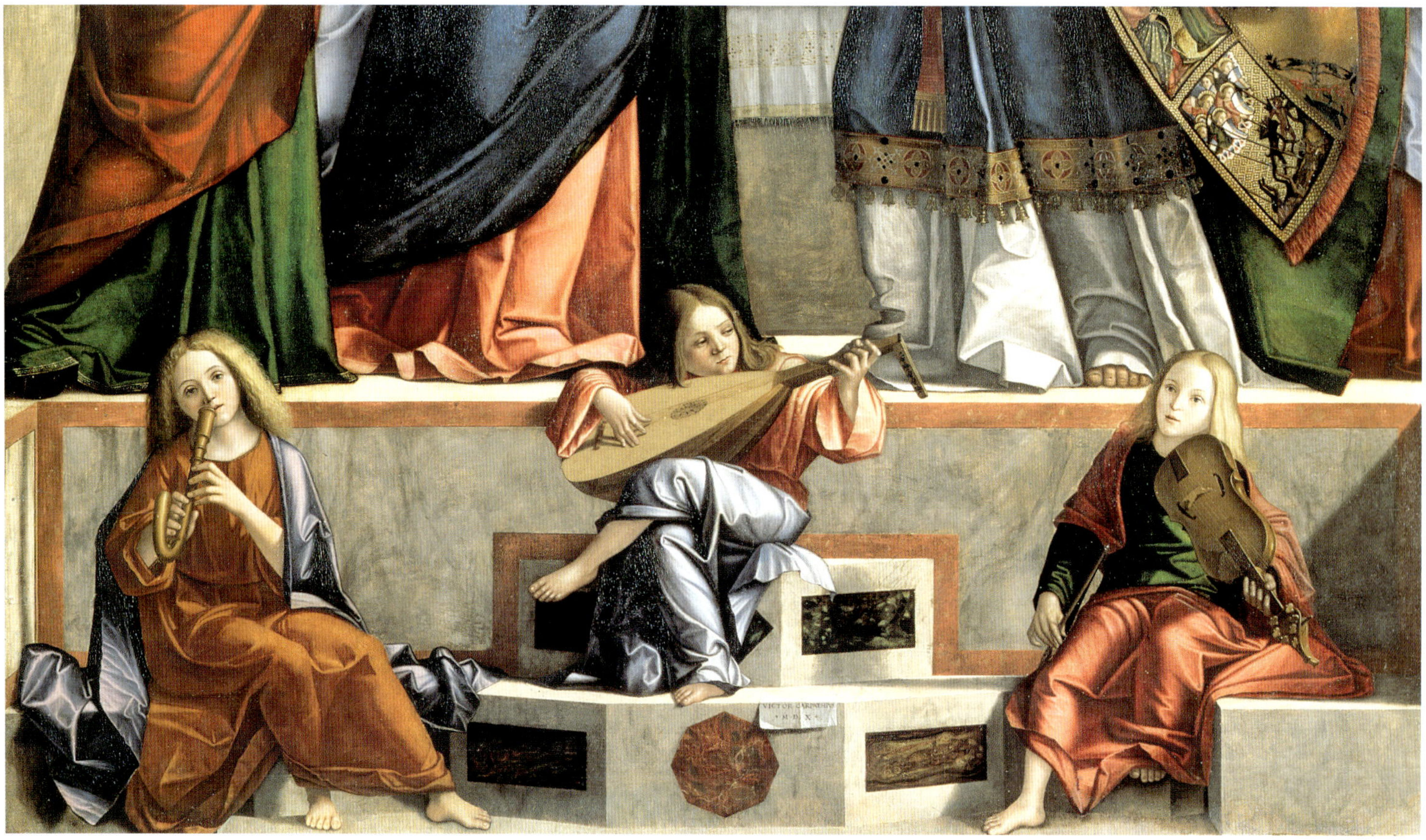

46 *THE PRESENTATION OF CHRIST IN THE TEMPLE*
Venice, Accademia.
Panel, 421 x 236 cm. Inscribed: VICTOR CARPATHIUS / M.D.X.

Formerly placed on the altar of the Sanudo Family in the church of S. Giobbe in Venice, where the original stone frame still survives *in situ*. Old Testament law required of every mother who bore a son to bring her child to the Temple forty days after giving birth; and in accordance with this custom, the Virgin duly presented the infant Christ before the high priest Simeon, bringing with her a pair of turtle doves as an offering. The embroidered orphreys on Simeon's cope show various scenes from the Creation, perhaps intended as a reminder of the Redemption of mankind through Christ's Incarnation.

(above) Detail of pl. 46.

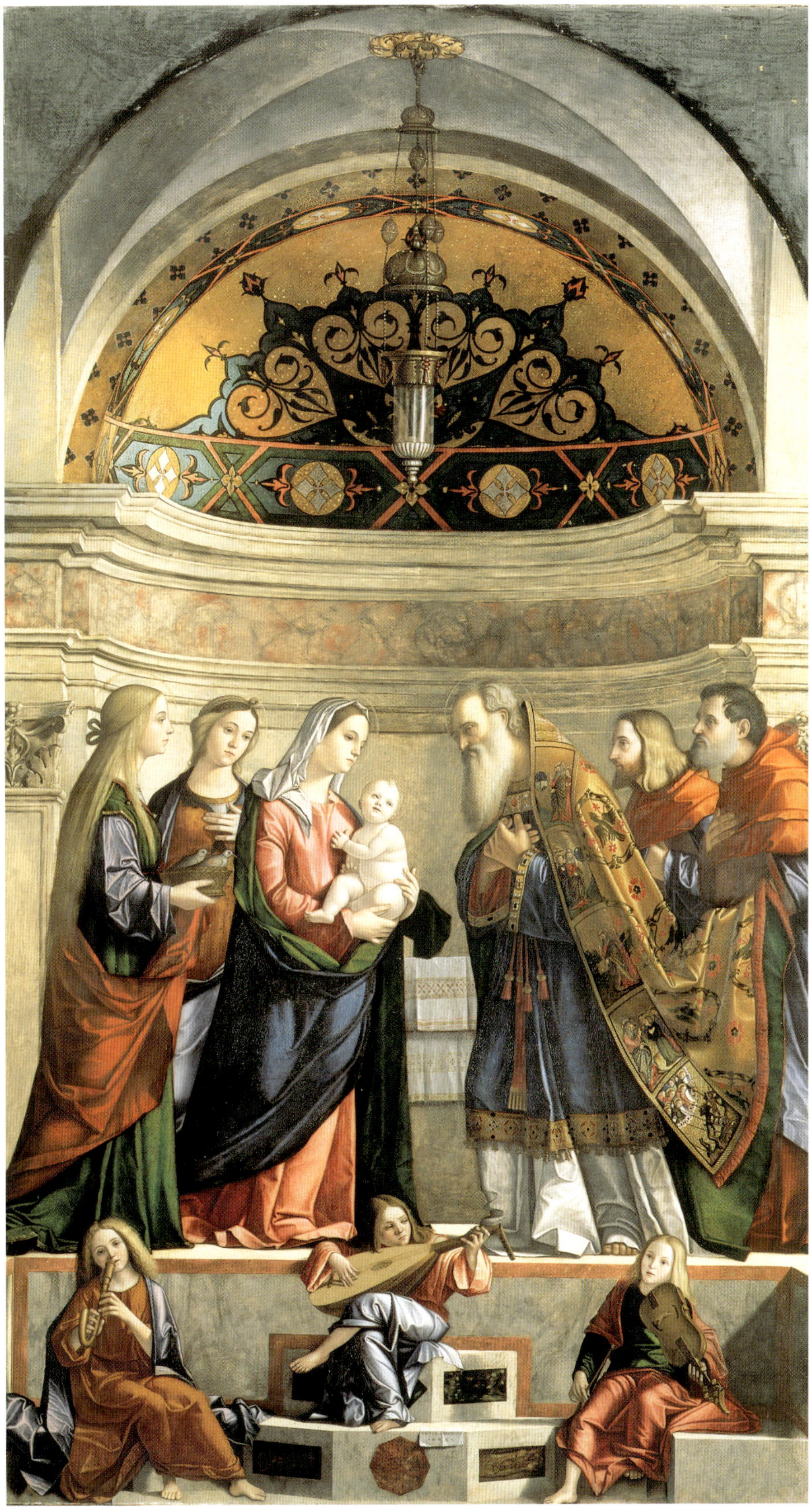

47 *PORTRAIT OF A YOUNG KNIGHT*
Madrid, Museo Thyssen-Bornemisza.
Canvas, 218 x 151 cm. Inscribed: VICTOR CARPATHIUS / FINXIT / M.D.X and MALO MORI / QUAM / FOEDARI.

The sitter for this portrait has been persuasively identified as the young Duke of Urbino, Francesco Maria della Rovere, who from his earliest childhood was passionately interested in the arts of war, and in descriptions of deeds of valour in ancient and mediaeval literature. The ermine in the bottom left hand corner, and the motto immediately above it ('Rather Dead than Spotted') are heraldic references to a Neapolitan order of chivalry, the Order of the Ermine, of which Francesco Maria's maternal grandfather, Duke Federigo da Montefeltro, had been a founder-member. The various plants and animals that fill the landscape are stylistically quite close to woodcuts by Dürer such as the *Holy Family with three Hares* (Fig. H), but they may also allude symbolically to the sitter's many virtues. The dog, for instance, was a traditional symbol of fidelity, and the lily – as well as the ermine – of unspotted purity; and similarly, the aerial combat between the heron and the falcon in the top left-hand corner may refer to Francesco Maria's military prowess. It is likely that the portrait was commissioned from Carpaccio at the time of the Duke's wedding to Eleonora Gonzaga in 1509; by the time it was completed, he had been appointed by his paternal uncle, Pope Julius II, to lead the papal troops against Venice in the war of Cambrai.

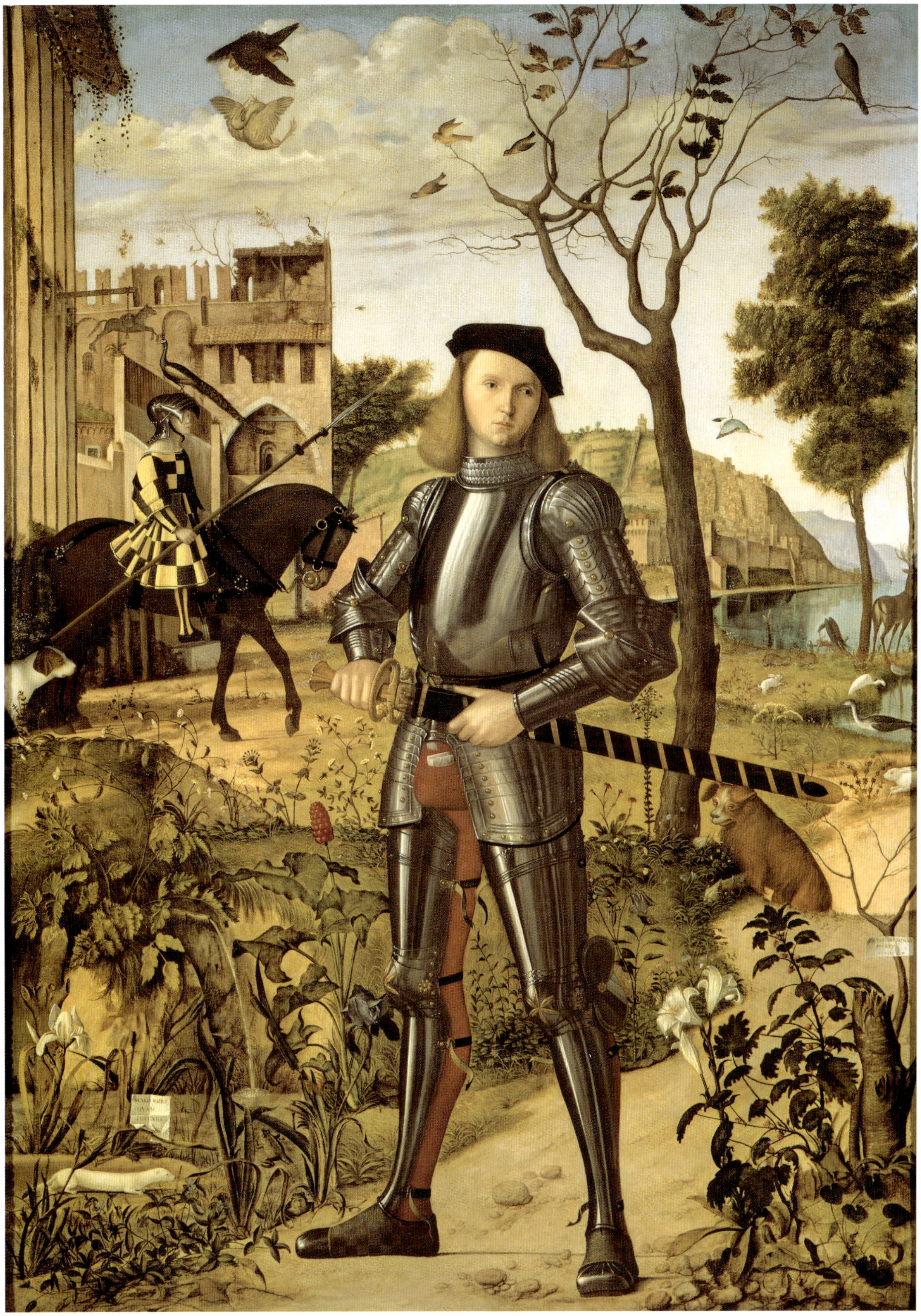

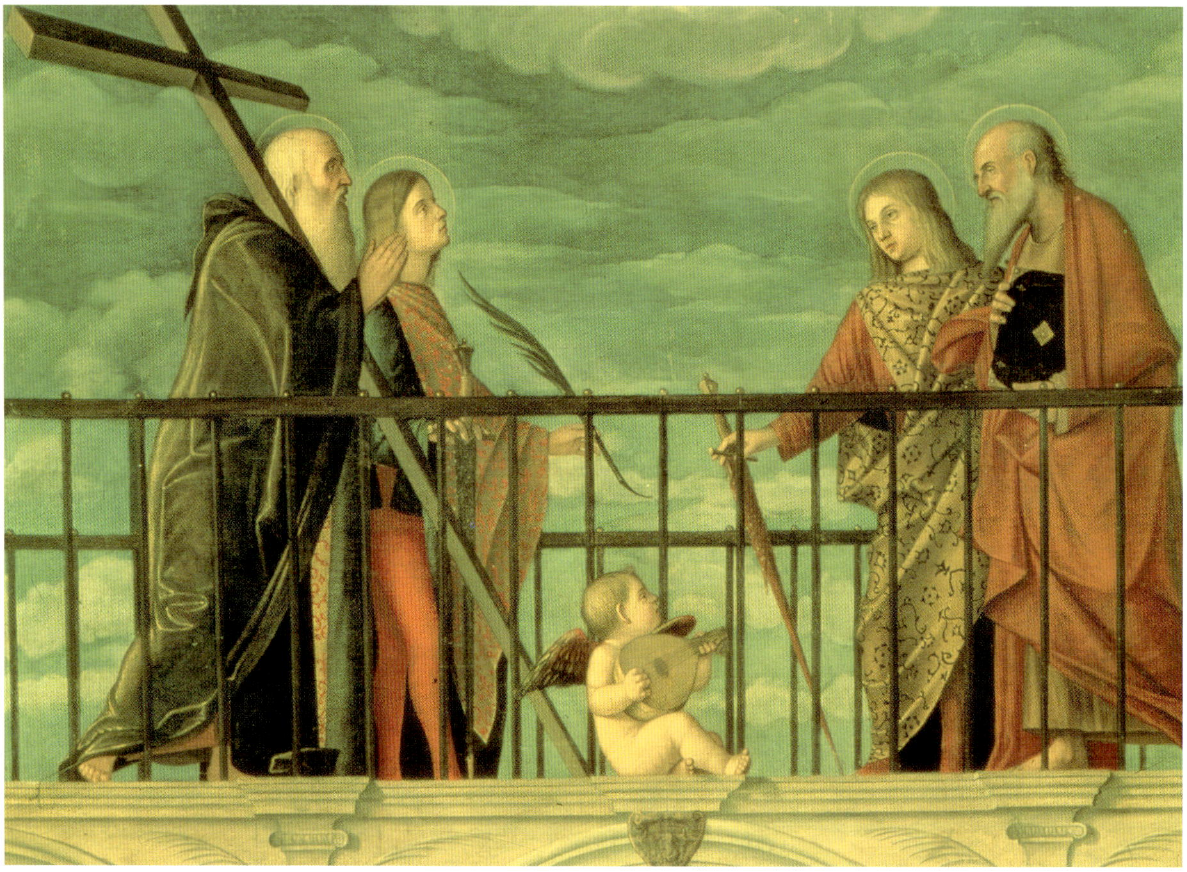

48 *ST VITALIS ON HORSEBACK*
Venice, S. Vitale.
Canvas, 445 x 214 cm. Inscribed: VICTOR CARPATHIUS/PINXIT/MDXIIII.

Still above the high altar in the now deconsecrated church of S. Vitale, Venice. St Vitalis, a soldier in the army of the Emperor Nero and titular saint of the church, is shown at the centre on horseback; beside him stand Saints James, John the Baptist and George, and a female saint who is probably identifiable as his wife, St Valeria. Gazing at an apparition of the Madonna and Child from the balcony above, are Saints Andrew and Peter, together with Saints Gervasius and Protasius, sons of Vitalis and Valeria, and titular saints of the Venétian church of S. Trovaso.

(above) Detail of pl. 48.

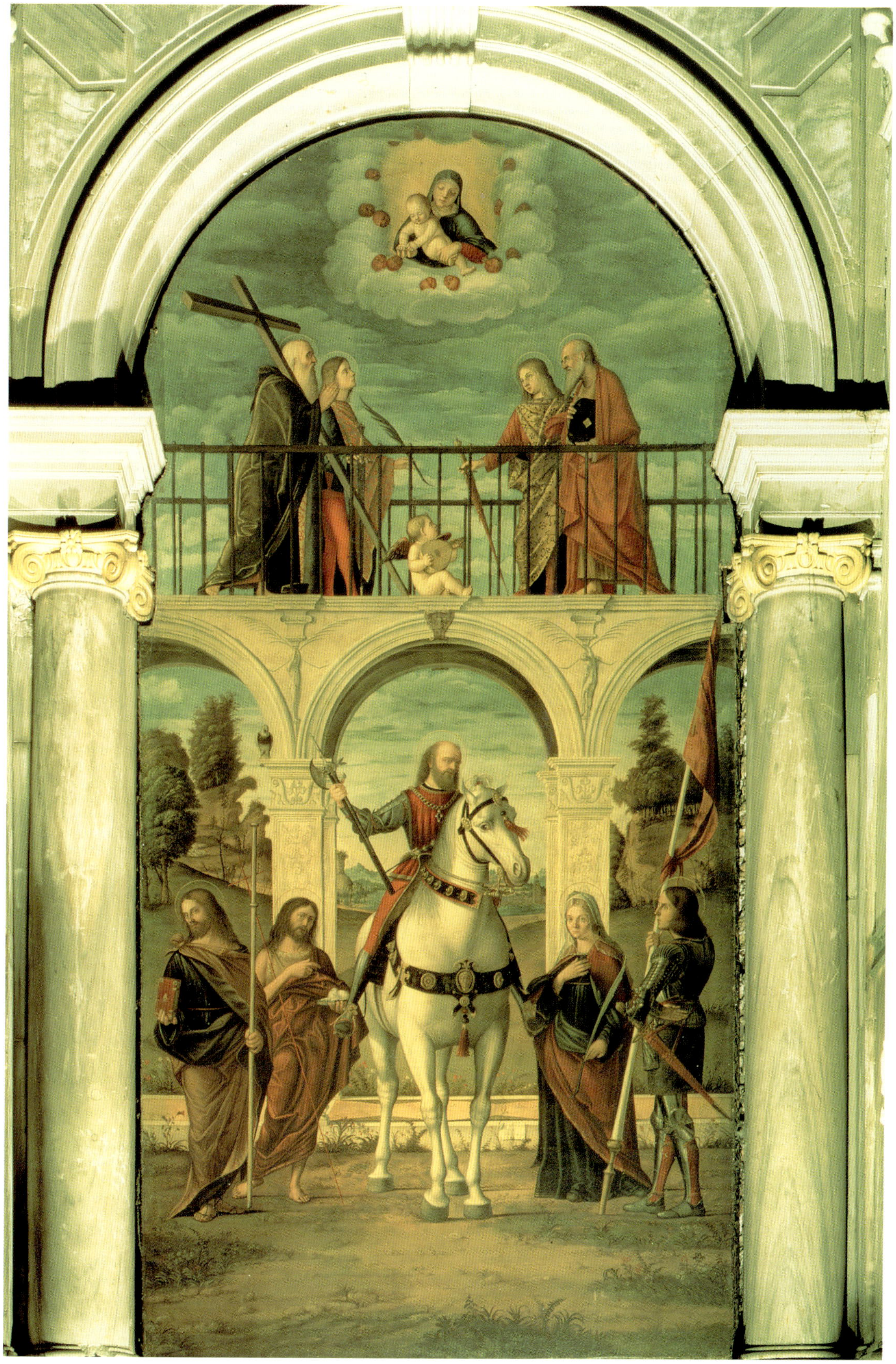

49 *THE MEETING OF JOACHIM AND ANNA*
Venice, Accademia.
Panel, 185 x 171 cm. Inscribed: VICTOR CARPATHIUS/VENETUS OP. /M.D.XV.

Formerly an altarpiece in the church of S. Francesco in Treviso. The aged couple embracing at the centre are Joachim and Anna, the parents of the Virgin, who according to the *Golden Legend*, were re-united after each had received a vision announcing that Anna would miraculously bear a child. As was common practice in altarpiece representation, Carpaccio makes no attempt at historical or geographical consistency: the figures of the Franciscan saint Louis of Toulouse and of St Ursula are anachronistic, and are meant to encourage suitably pious sentiments in the spectator; and the scene in the background refers to an earlier incident in the life of Joachim, when he was turned away from the Temple by an angry priest, upbraiding him as a man childless, and hence accursed of God.

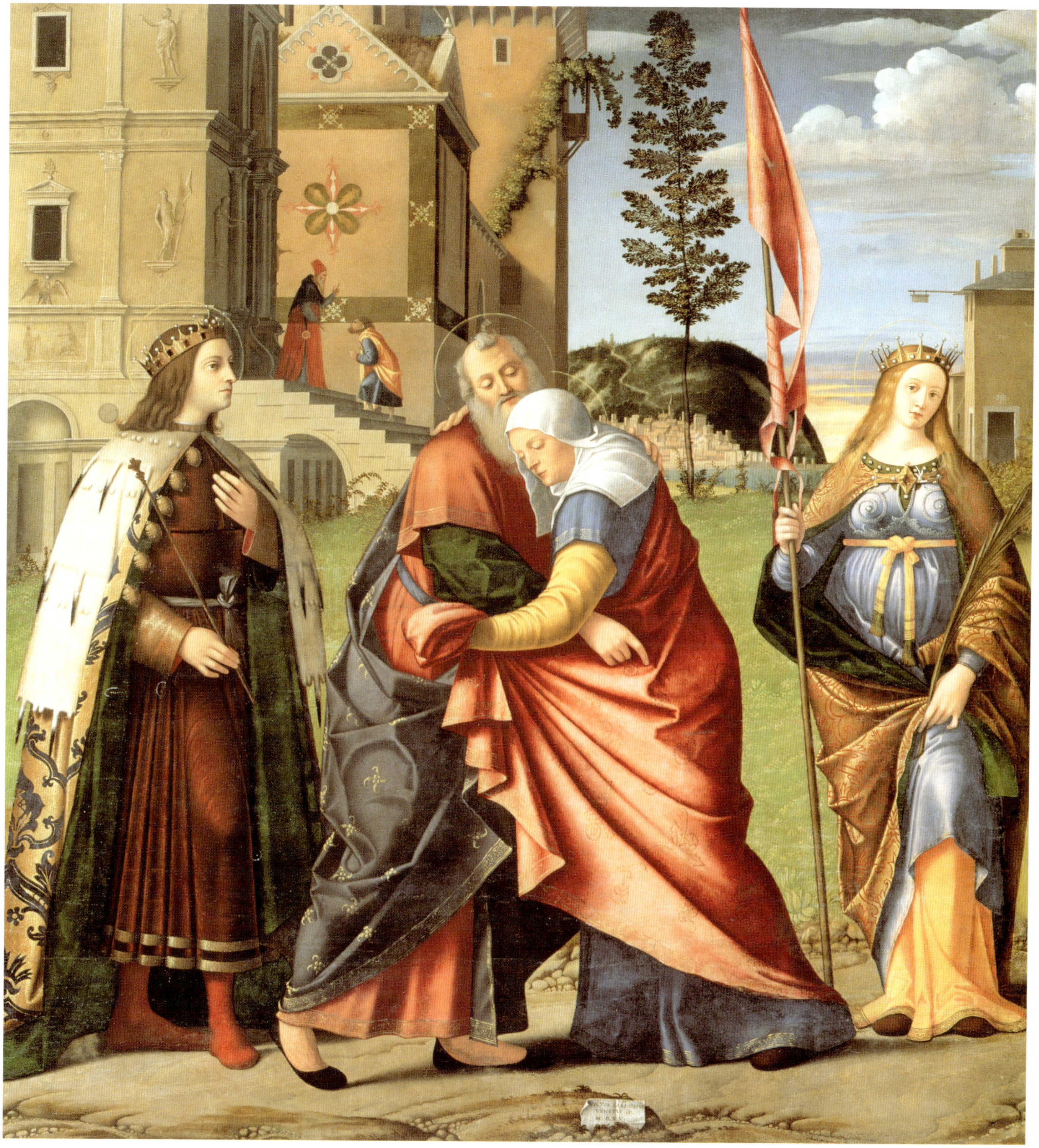

50 *THE MARTYRDOM OF THE TEN THOUSAND*
Venice, Accademia.
Panel, 307 x 205 cm. Inscribed:
V/CARPATHIUS/MDXV.

Painted for the altar of the Ottoboni family in the now-demolished church of S. Antonio di Castello in Venice. It commemorates the martyrdom of ten thousand Christians on Mount Ararat, an event that took place in the late fourth century at the hands of Shapu the Great of Persia. The king and his exotically turbaned retinue are shown in the right foreground; in the background at the top, the souls of the martyrs are received by angels into the seven circles of heaven. The subject was chosen in gratitude to the ten thousand for their prompt intercession on behalf of the plague-stricken of S. Antonio; but at a time when the Turkish infidel was becoming increasingly powerful in the eastern Mediterranean, it would have had considerable topical relevance for all Venetians. Faced with the need to represent a large number of male nudes in a variety of poses, Carpaccio has borrowed freely from a wide range of sources, including the prints of Dürer, antique sculpture, and Michelangelo's cartoon for the Battle of Cascina, then at Ferrara. The chief source of inspiration for the composition as a whole seems to have been Dürer's woodcut of the same subject, printed in the late 1490s (Kurth 98).

(overleaf) Details of pl. 50.

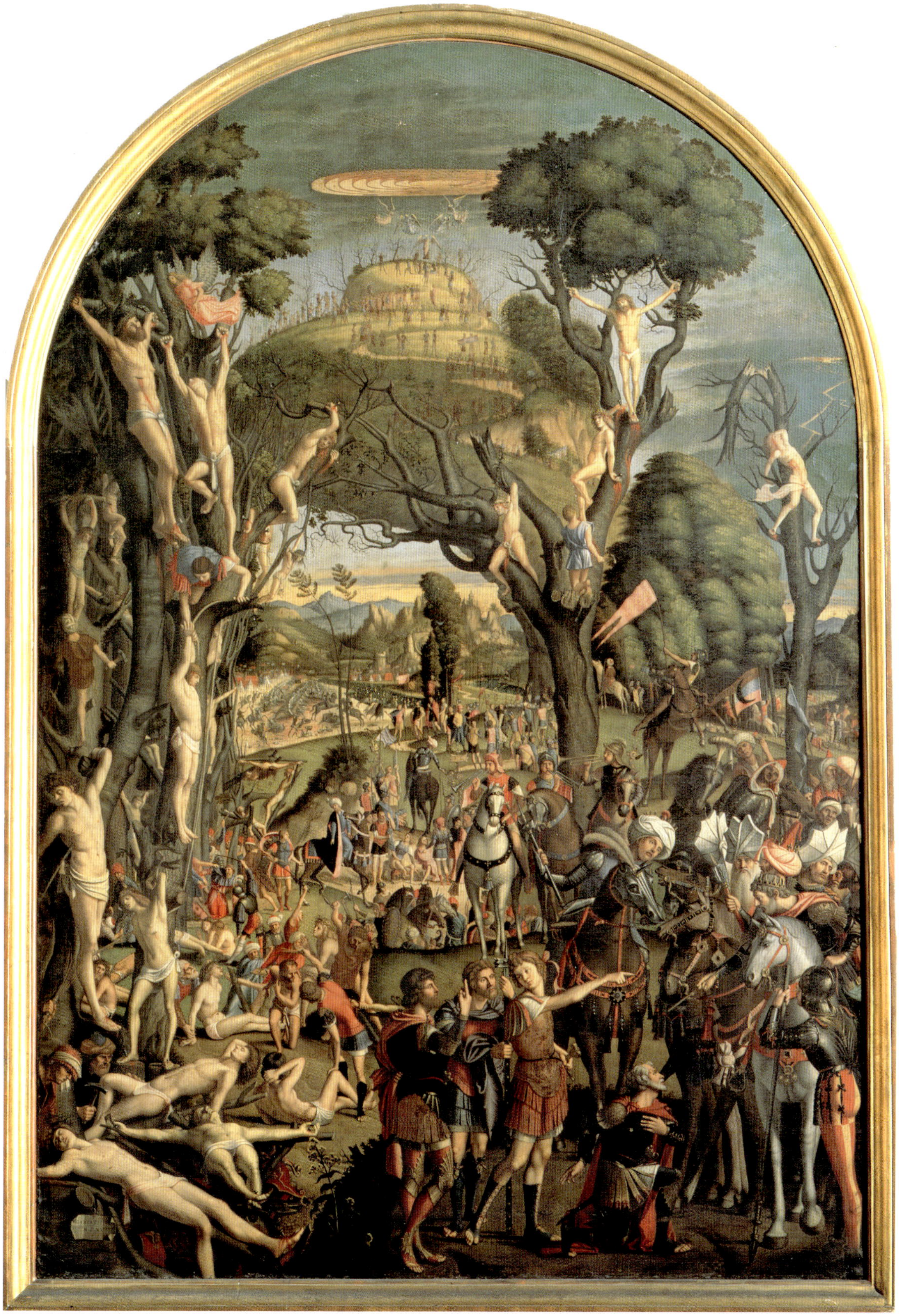

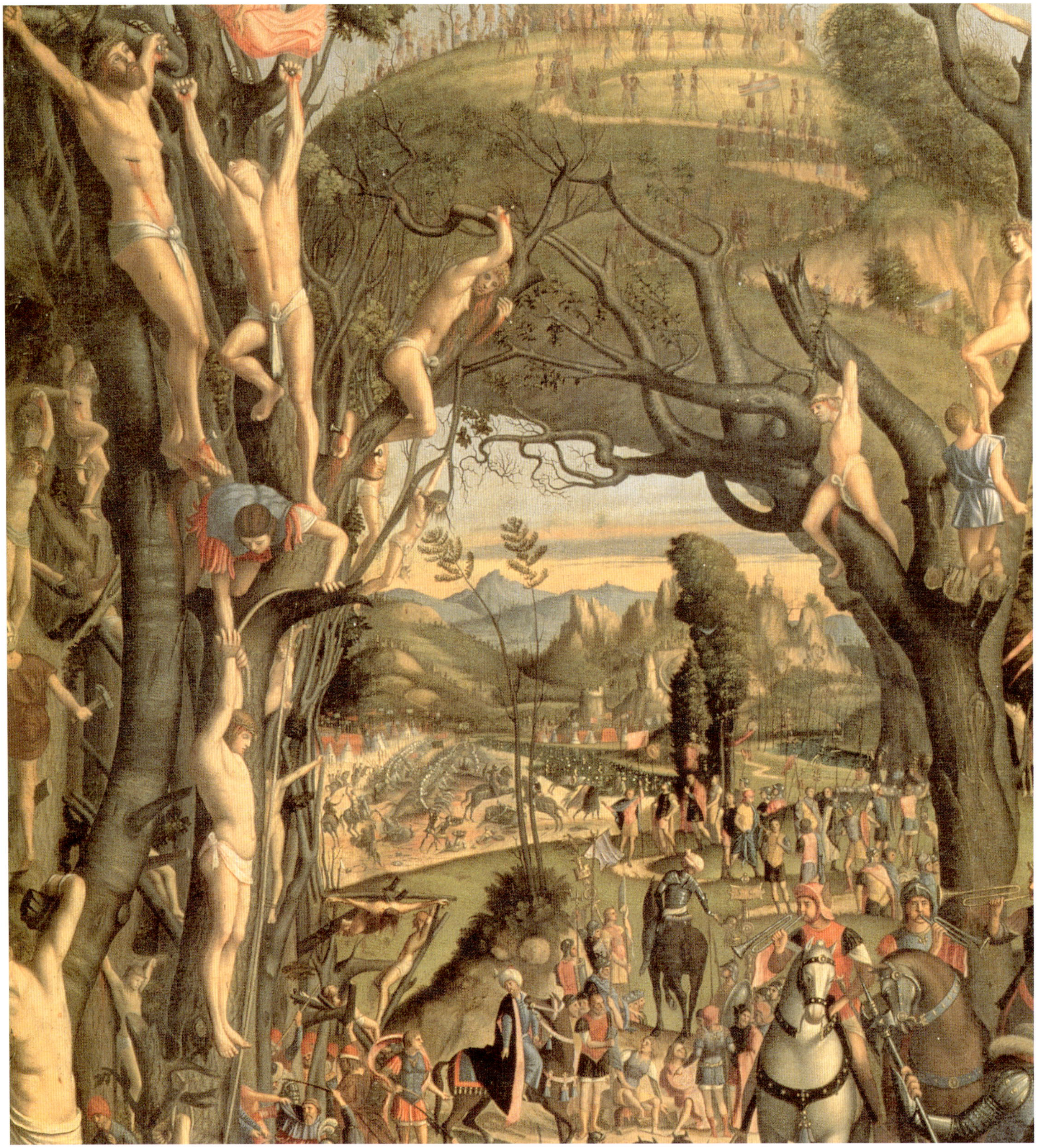

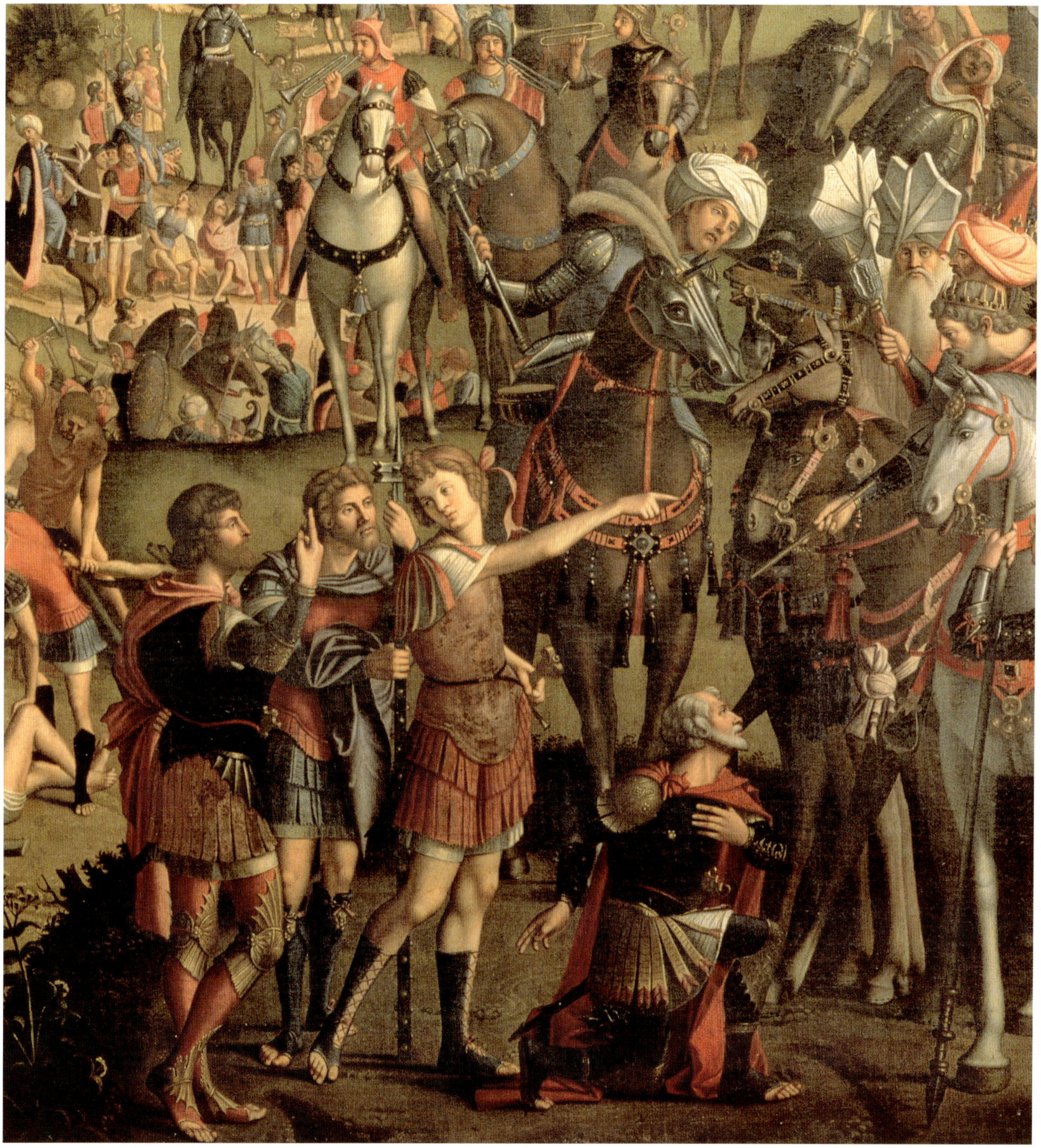

51 *THE VISION OF PRIOR OTTOBONI*
Venice, Accademia.
Canvas, 121 x 174 cm.

Carpaccio's personal authorship of this work has often been denied, and from a strictly artistic point of view, its quality is admittedly modest. It is of great documentary interest, however, since it provides a unique record of the appearance of a Venetian church interior of the second decade of the sixteenth century. The painting represents a vision granted to a certain Francesco Ottoboni, prior of the monastery of S. Antonio di Castello in Venice during the later fifteenth century. At the time of a terrible plague which had decimated his brethren, the prior invoked the ten thousand martyrs of Mount Ararat for deliverance; and his prayers were answered by this miraculous vision of the martyrs, processing down the nave of his church and carrying the crosses on which they were crucified. The plague ceased soon afterwards, and in token of his gratitude, the prior dedicated an altar to the martyrs, later decorated with Carpaccio's altarpiece. Despite the visionary nature of the event, the interior is rendered in a manner that is circumstantial, and presumably topographically accurate. Prominently visible just to the left of centre is an imposing Renaissance altarpiece, enclosed within a marble frame of a type currently fashionable, and contrasting vividly in size, style and materials with the two gilded polyptychs on the wall beside it. To the far left is a type of structure almost universal in the later Middle Ages, but increasingly rare after the Tridentine reforms of the mid-sixteenth century: the rood-screen, which served to divide off the lay section of the church from the choir. The model ships, apparently suspended from the roof, are probably ex-votos, offered by Venetian sailors in the hope of, or in thanks for, divine protection at sea.

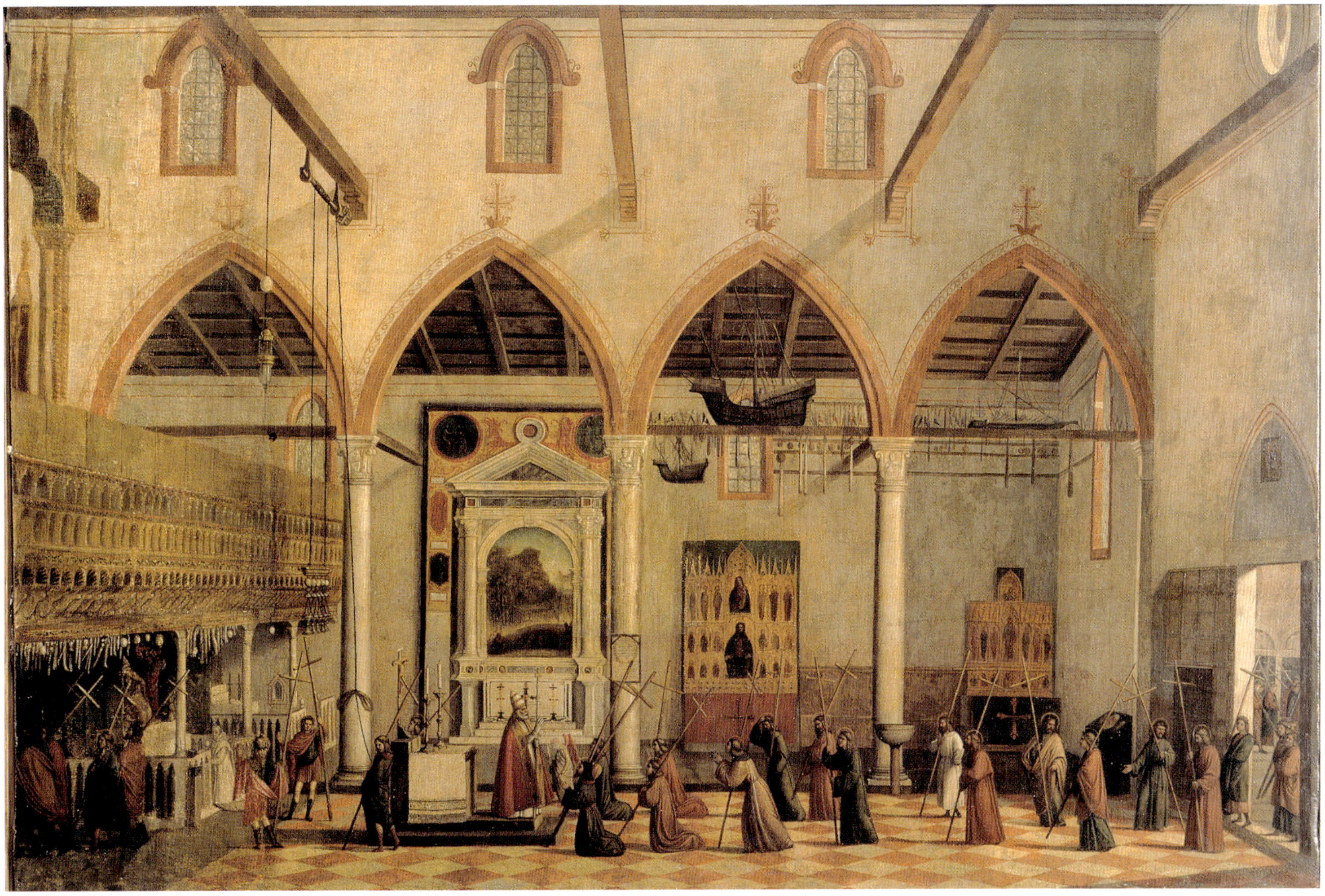

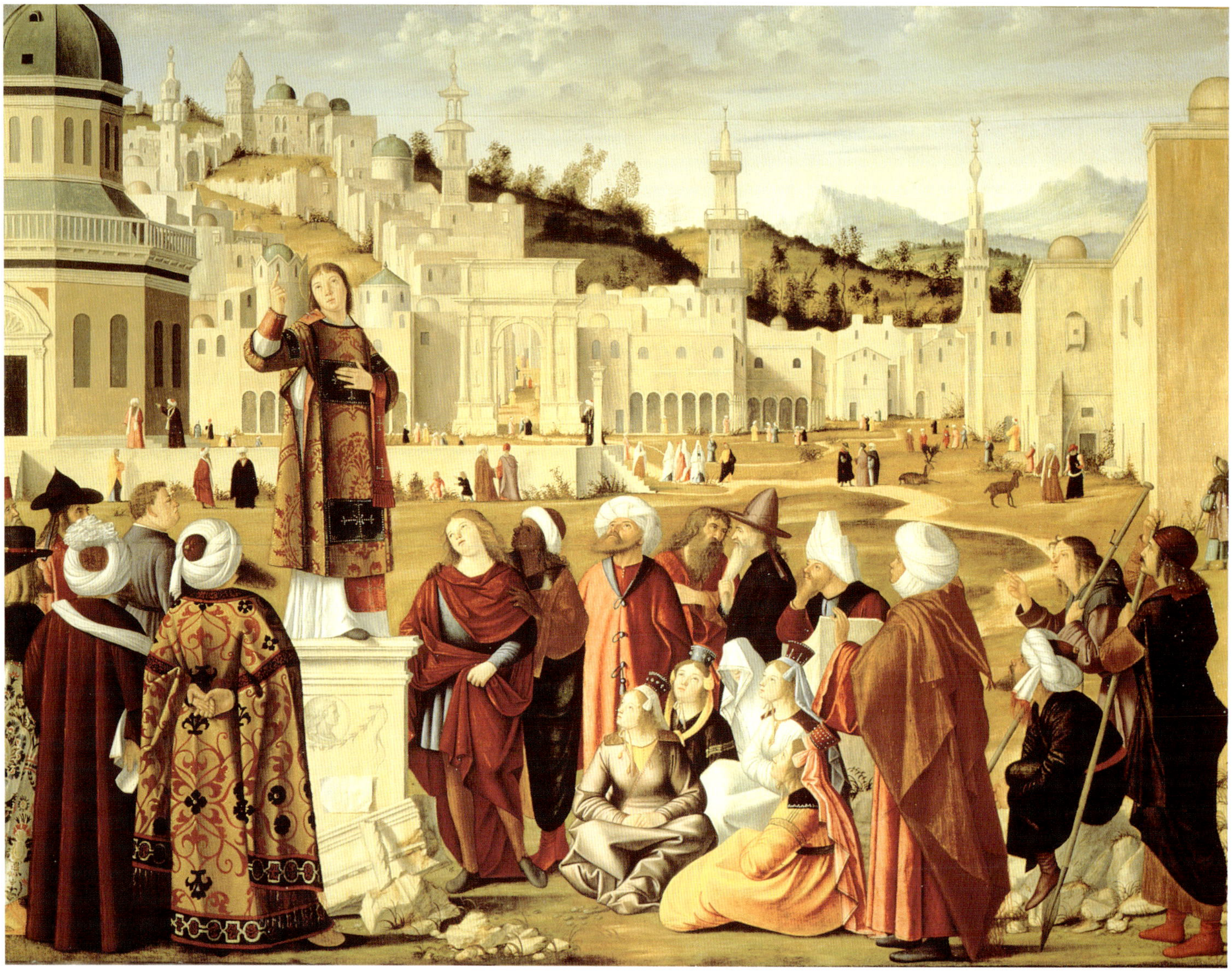

52 *THE SERMON OF ST STEPHEN*
Paris, Louvre.
Canvas, 148 x 194 cm.

Stephen preaches the word of Christ outside the gates of Jerusalem. The background cityscape may well reflect that of a very large canvas referred to as 'uno Jerusalem' presumably a biblical narrative with a view of Jerusalem in the background – which Carpaccio offered for sale to Francesco Gonzaga, Marquis of Mantua, in 1511. The crumbling fragments of classical architecture at the foot of Stephen's pedestal probably again refer to the decay of paganism with the coming of Christianity. According to Zanetti, writing in the late eighteenth century, the date of 1514 was inscribed on the original frame.

(right) Detail of pl. 52.

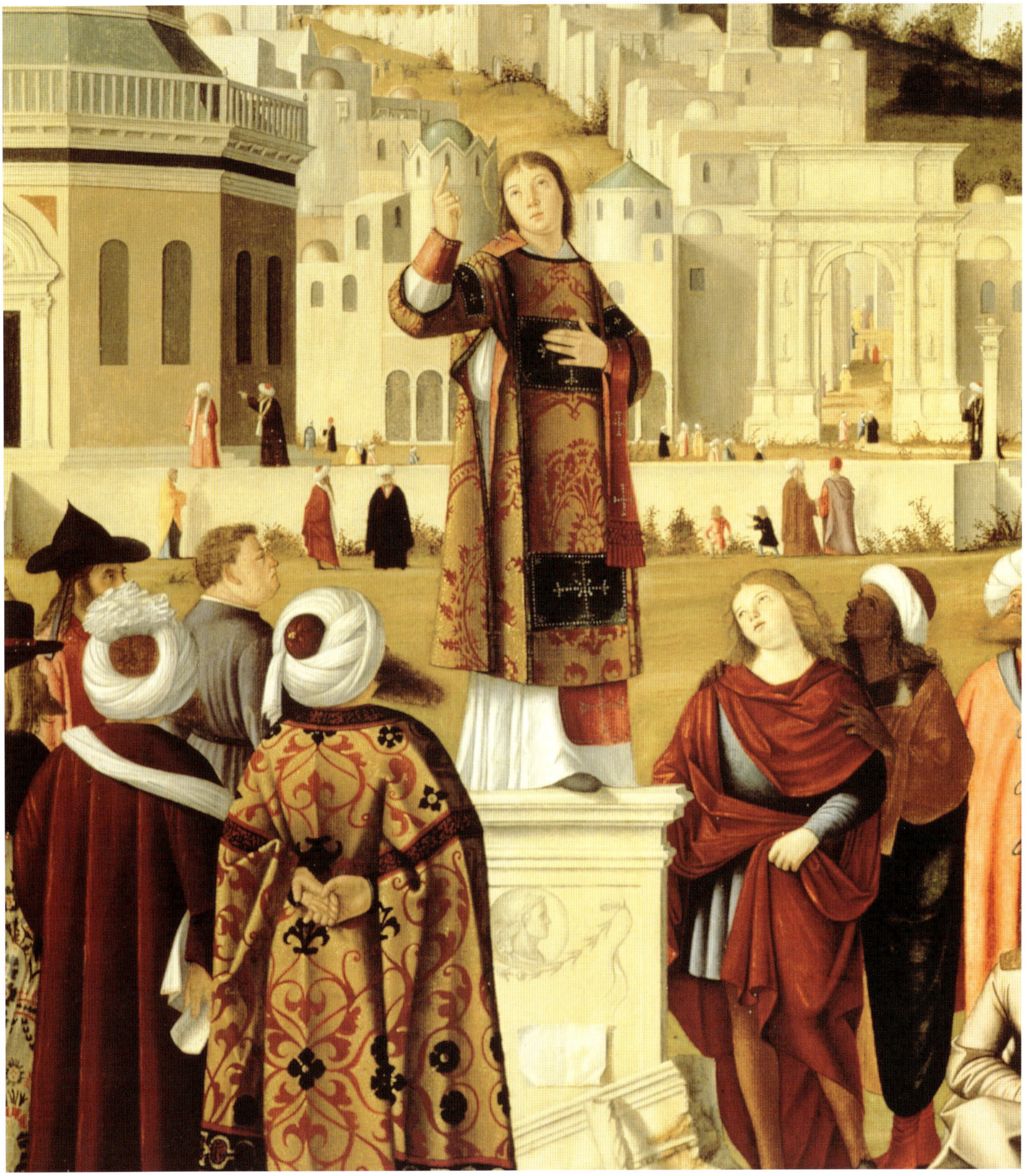

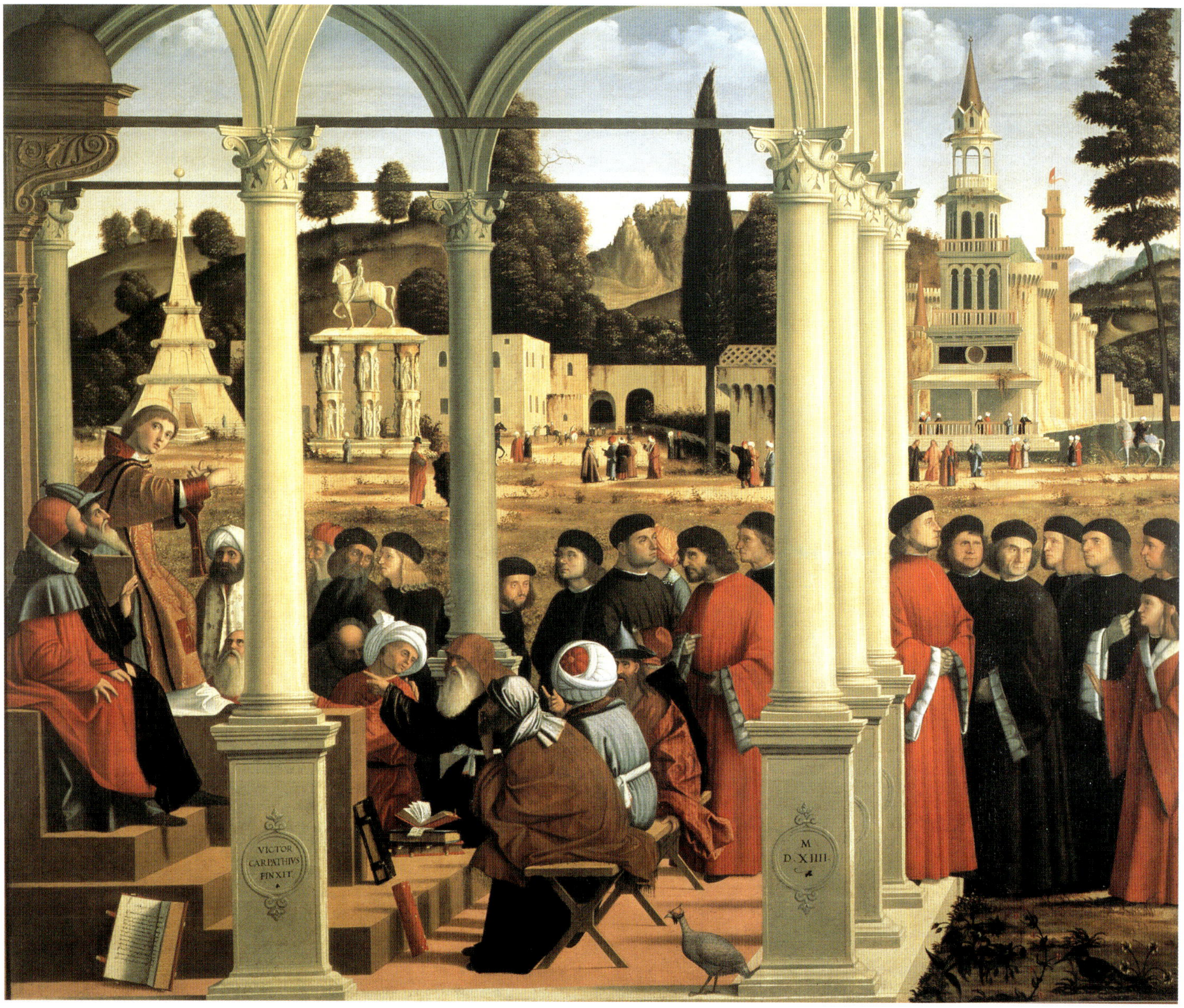

53 *THE DISPUTATION OF ST STEPHEN*
Milan, Brera.
Canvas, 147 x 172 cm. Inscribed:
VICTOR/CARPATHIUS/FINXIT e M.D. XIIII.

In the third canvas of the cycle, Stephen is seen engaged in a theological discussion with the leaders of the synagogue. Being filled with the Holy Ghost, he is easily able to confound their arguments against Christ. The gentlemen in scarlet and black who stand in a row at the back are very probably portraits of the governors of the confraternity. The equestrian monument in the background is probably intended as an indication that the event took place under the Roman Empire; but the motif would certainly also have been stimulated by Verrocchio's Colleoni monument, which had been erected some years previously in the Campo SS. Giovanni e Paolo in Venice.

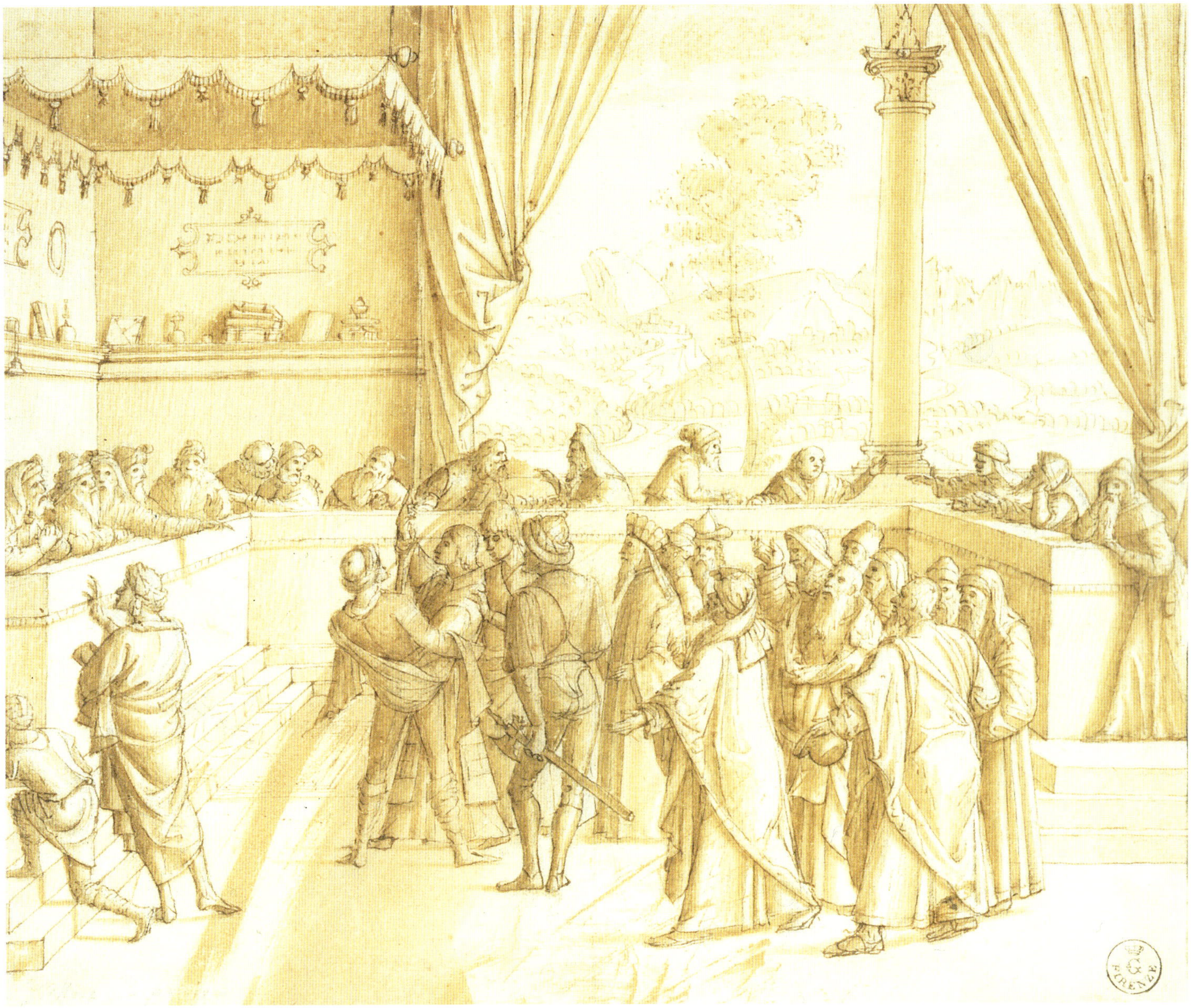

54 *THE TRIAL OF ST STEPHEN*
Florence, Uffizi.
Pen and wash, 229 x 270 mm.

Of the five canvases Carpaccio painted for the Scuola di S. Stefano, one no longer survives. Its composition is recorded in this drawing, which shows Stephen surrounded by soldiers before a panel of judges; in the right foreground is a group of the false witnesses who brought him to trial. The drawing is probably not a preliminary sketch for the painting by Carpaccio himself, but rather an early copy by another hand after the painting.

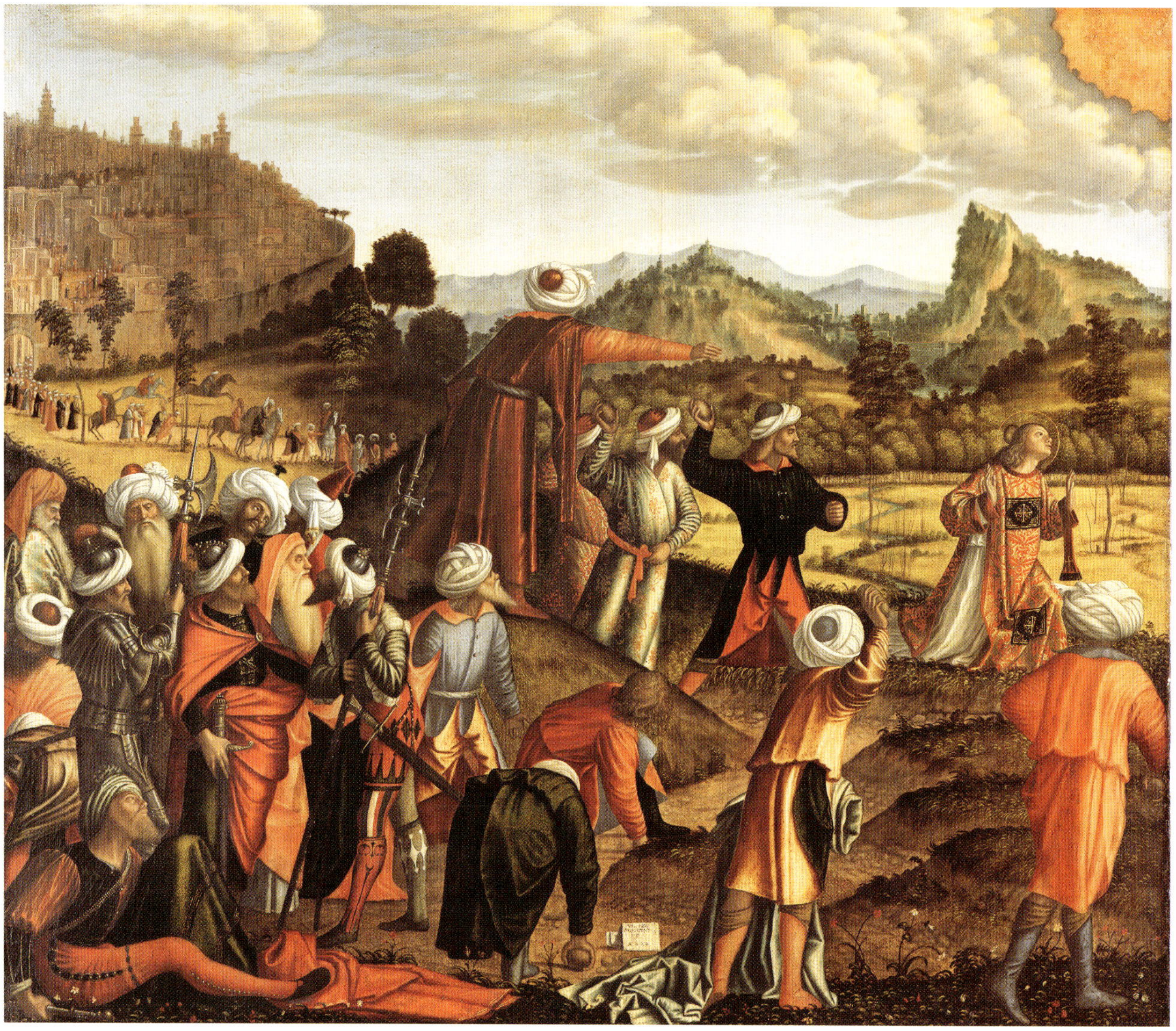

55 *THE STONING OF ST STEPHEN*
Stuttgart, Staatsgalerie.
Canvas, 149 x 170 cm. Inscribed: VICTOR / CARPA . . . / MDXX.

After he had been unjustly condemned, Stephen was taken outside the city gates and stoned to death. The figure seated in the bottom left-hand corner may be identified as Saul, the future St Paul, who witnessed the event, and shared responsibility for it insofar that he agreed to look after the outer clothes of the executioners while they performed the deed. The panoramic view of Jerusalem in the background is derived from a woodcut by Erhard Reuwich, in which the spot where Stephen is traditionally supposed to have been martyred is marked with an inscription.

(right) Detail of plate 55.

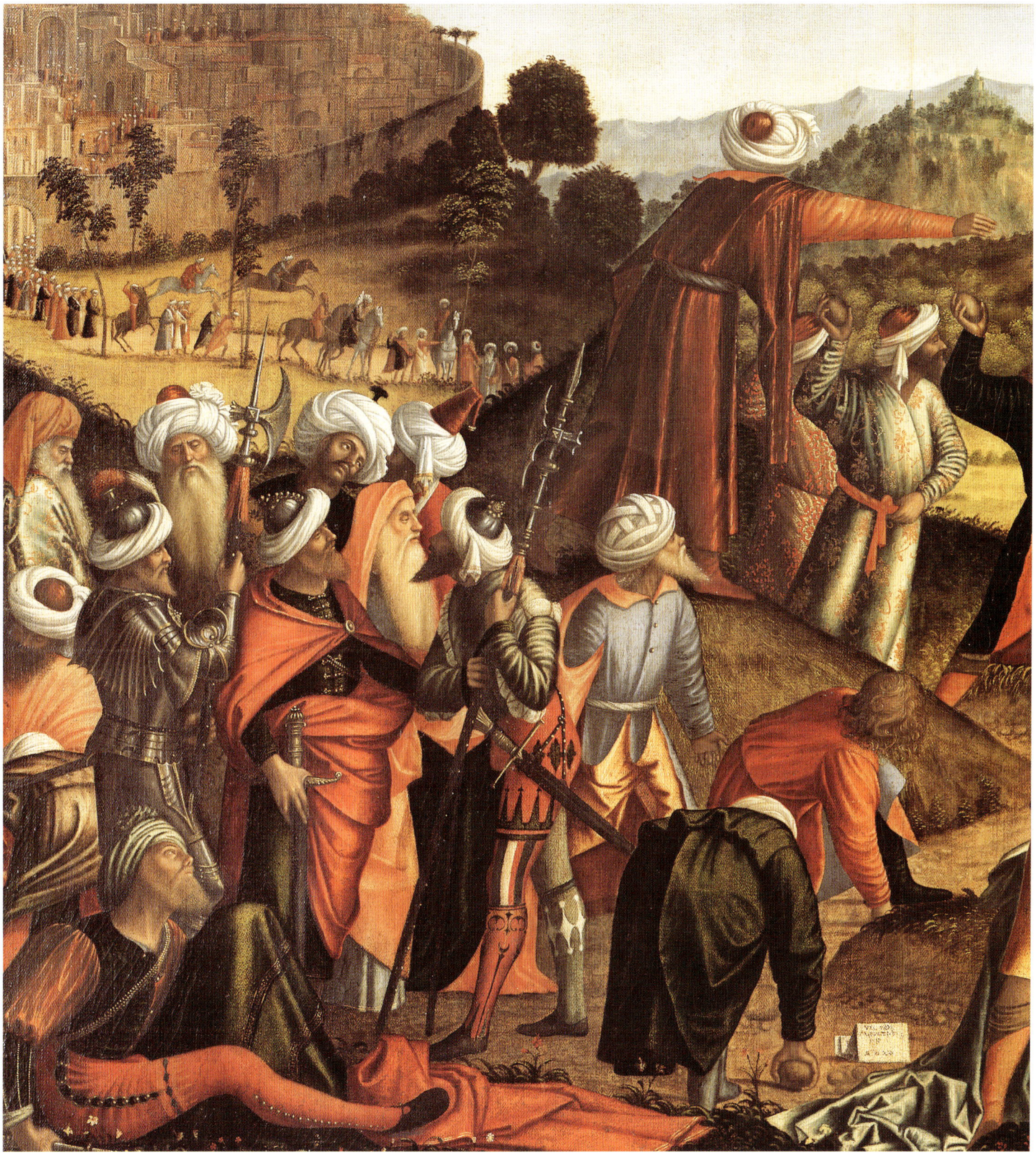

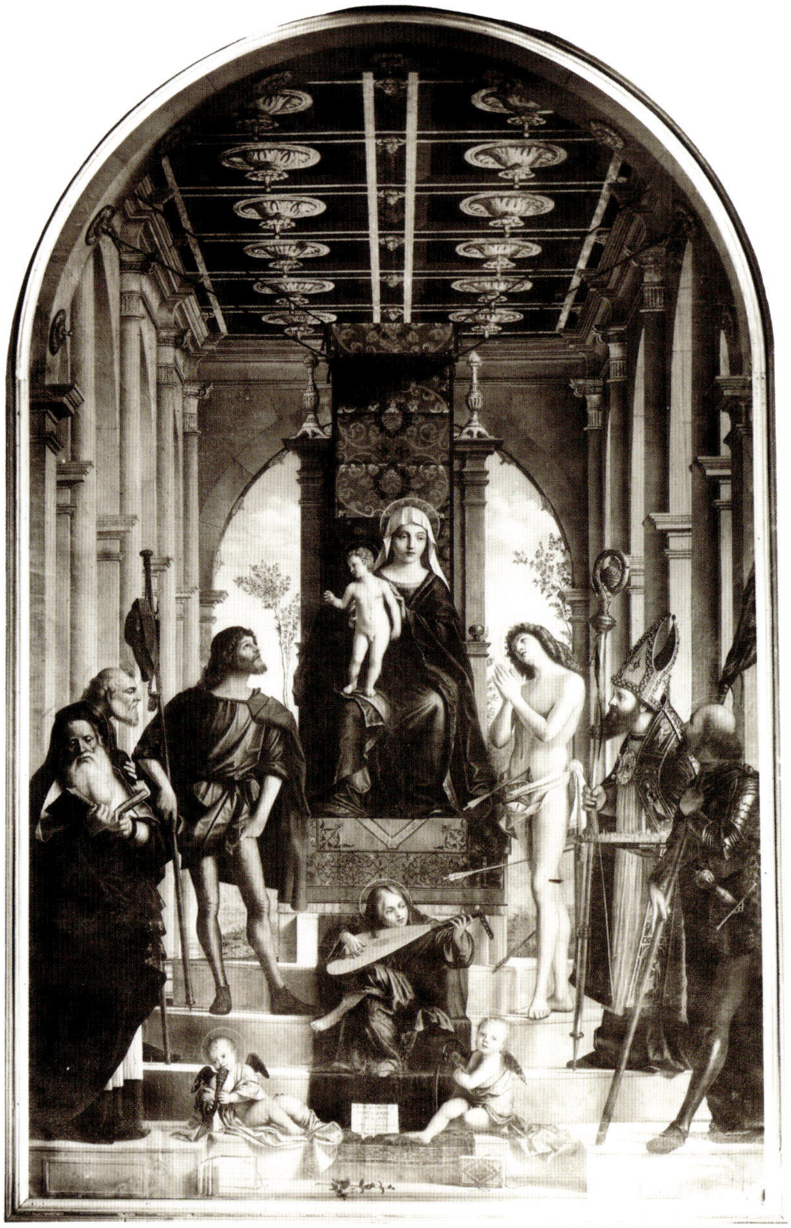

56 *MADONNA AND CHILD ENTHRONED WITH SAINTS*
Capodistria (Koper) Cathedral.
Canvas, 350 x 240 cm. Inscribed: VICTOR CARPATHIUS / VENETUS PINXIT / M.D. XVI

The Madonna and Child are shown in the company of Saints (from left to right) Jerome and not Zachariah, as formerly believed, Joseph, Roch (the titular saint of the altar in the place of honour to the Virgin's right), Sebastian, Nazaruis (patron saint of Capodistria, holding a model of the city in his hand), and Louis of Toulouse. Originally the picture had an elaborate stone frame, which would have appeared illusionistically as the extension of the architecture represented in the painting. This device, as well as the formal composition generally, derives from Venetian altarpieces of the 1480s such as Giovanni Bellini's S. Giobbe altar (Fig. C); but by 1516 the formula had become worn out, and like so many of his later works, Carpaccio's painting lacks conviction. The pupils in his workshop probably had a major share in the execution.